The
Muscular
Ideal

The
Muscular
Ideal

Psychological, Social, and Medical Perspectives

Edited by
J. Kevin Thompson and **Guy Cafri**

American Psychological Association • Washington, DC

Published by
American Psychological Association
750 First Street, NE
Washington, DC 20002
www.apa.org

To order
APA Order Department
P.O. Box 92984
Washington, DC 20090-2984
Tel: (800) 374-2721; Direct: (202) 336-5510
Fax: (202) 336-5502; TDD/TTY: (202) 336-6123
Online: www.apa.org/books/
E-mail: order@apa.org

In the U.K., Europe, Africa, and the Middle East, copies may be ordered from
American Psychological Association
3 Henrietta Street
Covent Garden, London
WC2E 8LU England

Typeset in Goudy by Stephen McDougal, Mechanicsville, MD

Printer: Maple-Vail Book Manufacturing, Binghamton, NY
Cover Designer: Naylor Design, Washington, DC
Technical/Production Editor: Tiffany L. Klaff

The opinions and statements published are the responsibility of the authors, and such opinions and statements do not necessarily represent the policies of the American Psychological Association.

Library of Congress Cataloging-in-Publication Data

The muscular ideal : psychological, social, and medical perspectives / edited by J. Kevin Thompson and Guy Cafri. — 1st ed.
    p. cm.
  ISBN-13: 978-1-59147-792-1
  ISBN-10: 1-59147-792-1
  1. Somatotypes. 2. Body image—Social aspects. 3. Muscles—Social aspects. 4. Physical fitness—Social aspects. 5. Physical-appearance-based bias. I. Thompson, J. Kevin. II. Cafri, Guy.

  GN66.5.M87 2007
  306.4—dc22
                                    2006035437

British Library Cataloguing-in-Publication Data
A CIP record is available from the British Library.

Printed in the United States of America
First Edition

CONTENTS

CONTRIBUTORS

Michael S. Bahrke, PhD, Human Kinetics, Champaign, IL

Guy Cafri, MA, University of South Florida, Tampa

Thomas F. Cash, PhD, Old Dominion University, Norfolk, VA

Joan C. Chrisler, PhD, Connecticut College, New London

Sam V. Cochran, PhD, University of Iowa, Iowa City

Canice E. Crerand, PhD, University of Pennsylvania School of Medicine, Philadelphia

Diane L. Elliot, MD, Oregon Health and Science University, Portland

Lauren M. Gibbons, BA, University of Florida, Gainesville

Rebecca L. Ginsberg, MA, American University, Washington, DC

Linn Goldberg, MD, Oregon Health and Science University, Portland

James J. Gray, PhD, American University, Washington, DC

Amanda J. Gruber, MD, Harvard Medical School, Belmont, MA

Alan Klein, PhD, Northeastern University, Boston, MA

Lynne Luciano, PhD, California State University, Dominguez Hills

Marita P. McCabe, PhD, Deakin University, Melbourne, Victoria, Australia

Donald R. McCreary, PhD, York University, Toronto, Ontario, Canada

Roberto Olivardia, PhD, Harvard Medical School, Arlington, MA

Lina A. Ricciardelli, PhD, Deakin University, Melbourne, Victoria, Australia

David B. Sarwer, PhD, University of Pennsylvania School of Medicine, Philadelphia

J. Kevin Thompson, PhD, University of South Florida, Tampa

FOREWORD

THOMAS F. CASH

Psychologists who have devoted their careers to the scientific understanding of the psychology of human embodiment are well aware of significant shortcomings in the field. Perhaps because they have been on a mission to make sense of eating disorders and because cultures often physically objectify women, their theories and investigations have typically neglected boys and men. Psychologists have also focused their empirical efforts more on the personal and cultural meanings of endomorphy and ectomorphy than on matters of mesomorphy. The correction of this myopia has begun, as J. Kevin Thompson and Guy Cafri's insightful volume attests. A renowned and prolific scholar for 25 years, J. Kevin Thompson has provided knowledgeable leadership and contributed to the credibility of this important work. At the beginning of his research career, Guy Cafri has already made notable scientific contributions to further the understanding of body image and muscularity.

Around the world, the media regularly report controversies about elite athletes' use of performance-enhancing drugs and nutritional supplements. The Internet offers the public a plethora of such potions for power, performance, and physical attractiveness. Through children's action figure toys, product-promoting bodybuilding ads, and box office icons, cultural messages about muscularity and masculinity are widely disseminated. Among other scientific journals, *Body Image: An International Journal of Research* is publishing an increasing number of empirical studies on the salience of muscularity, especially among boys and men. Using a variety of methodologies, promising assessments are becoming available to permit the measurement of persons' investments in and evaluations of the body vis-à-vis its degree of muscular definition or tone. The topic of this volume is truly timely.

The editors and chapter authors have built a book with muscle, strong in its integrative breadth and depth of coverage. It is far more than a psychology book. It educates readers about history, culture, evolution, sports, physiology, pharmacology, medicine, and surgery. Although boys and men are at the center of this volume's content, the relevance of the muscular ideal for girls and women is not ignored. The authors properly recognize and elucidate the importance of critical physical and social developmental processes during adolescence in the pursuit of muscularity as an aesthetic ideal. Because this pursuit can sometimes become pathological, the chapter authors describe body image disorders and chemical addictions as well as potential avenues for prevention and treatment. Science is not science without precise and valid measurement, and this work teaches readers what to measure and how to do it well.

Readers from diverse disciplines will benefit from this fascinating book. It is my hope, and surely that of each editor and contributor, that the wisdom shared and the questions posed in this volume become catalysts for a better discernment of the muscular ideal and the ways its internalization and embodiment influence human lives.

The
Muscular
Ideal

THE MUSCULAR IDEAL: AN INTRODUCTION

J. KEVIN THOMPSON AND GUY CAFRI

In the past decade, societal and interpersonal pressures to attain a heightened level of muscular development have increased exponentially. Body image concerns in this particular domain of appearance are enormous for men, but they also appear to be on the rise for women. Whereas the field of body image was once preoccupied with a focus on the "thin ideal," today researchers are as often interested in the area of muscularity. New developments in theory, measurement, and intervention are transforming the field. This book is an attempt to coalesce recent developments into an organized framework to help guide theory, research, and practice in this intriguing area of investigation.

The rapid rise in interest in the muscularity dimension of body image signifies a rather remarkable paradigm shift away from the dominant theme of fat, size, and weight dissatisfaction that dominated the field until the mid-1990s (Cash & Pruzinsky, 1990; Thompson, 1990, 1996; Thompson, Heinberg, Altabe, & Tantleff-Dunn, 1999). Articles with a focus on the muscular ideal increased a phenomenal 731% in the period of 2000 through 2006 in comparison with the previous 7-year period (on the basis of a PsycInfo search of the terms *muscularity* or *muscular body image* or *muscle dysmorphia*). Assessment strategies designed to measure the muscularity dimension of body image were almost nonexistent before 2000; only one of the measures we review in chapter 5 of this volume was published before 2000. Such a dramatic increase in scientific inquiry into an area deserves explanation and analysis, in particular because the extreme pursuit of muscularity is associated with dangerous behaviors (e.g., steroid use) and possible clinical disorders (e.g., body dysmorphic disorder; see, e.g., Cafri, Thompson, Ricciardelli, McCabe, Smolak, & Yesalis, 2005).

What explains the current preoccupation with the muscular ideal? A quick analysis of research findings and culturally significant moments and trends in the past decade suggests that there are at least three answers to this question. First, appearance pressures provided by societal (media) and interpersonal forces have produced an environment in which meeting an ideal of attractiveness is a highly desired and almost necessary aspect of daily life (Cash & Pruzinsky, 2002). Such pressures have driven the increase in the number of elective cosmetic procedures performed each year (Sarwer et al., 2006). The mandate to meet a goal of physical perfection, once focused primarily on women, is increasingly applied to new populations, including men.

Second, over the past 15 years or so, professional and amateur sports for both men and women have continued to increase in popularity, media coverage, and competitiveness. The desire for fame and money drove the desire for greater dominance, and the advent of strategies to enhance muscularity and additional strength followed. A group of drugs emerged for the purposes of enhancing appearance and performance, with steroids emerging as the most controversial method for directly altering appearance and strength. The issue of steroid abuse has clouded performance records, particularly in baseball, in which the integrity of home run records established by Mark McGwire and Barry Bonds will likely be in limbo for generations. Concern about not only the legality of such drug use but also negative physical and psychological side effects continues to occupy the scientific and legal community. For instance, during the final editing of this book, New Jersey became the first state to mandate testing of steroids for all high school athletes.

A third dominant influence that seems to have focused the attention of clinicians and researchers is the emergence of a particular type of body dysmorphic disorder focused on an excessive dissatisfaction with level of muscularity, termed *muscle dysmorphia*. Pope, Katz, and Hudson (1993) reported on the first cases of muscle dysmorphia in the early 1990s, documenting the phenomenon primarily in bodybuilders and weight lifters who, although objectively highly muscular, nonetheless were very dissatisfied with their physical development, often to the point of delusionally underestimating the degree of muscularity. Pope, Phillips, and Olivardia (2000) described individuals with this type of body dysmorphic disorder who excessively used steroids and experienced severe depression, low self-esteem, and social avoidance. The realization that a desire for the muscular ideal could have such dramatic clinical implications was an important driving force for greater research into this area.

In the past 5 years, our own work in the field of body image has focused sharply on the muscular ideal, investigating issues related to measurement and its associated physical and psychological features (Cafri et al., 2005; Cafri, Roehrig, & Thompson, 2004; Cafri, Strauss, & Thompson, 2002; Cafri & Thompson, 2004a, 2004b; Cafri, van den Berg, & Thompson, 2006; Smolak, Murnen, & Thompson, 2005). Our work, along with emerging work detailed in this book by other leaders in the field (Pope, Olivardia, McCreary; see also Pope et al., 2000; McCreary, Sasse, Saucier, & Dorsch, 2004), has indicated that muscle dissatisfaction is a dimension of body image disturbance that has important social, medical, and psychological implications. For instance, research suggests that a large number of individuals, primarily men, but also including women and boys, desire greater muscular development and use drugs to accomplish this goal. The press for a muscular appearance is also apparent in adolescent boys. Cafri et al. (2005) reviewed studies in this area, finding that 3% to 12% of adolescent boys used steroids; the higher percentages were found among smaller but higher-risk samples. In our cross-sectional study of adolescent boys, we found that muscle dysmorphia and sports participation significantly predicted substance use; that body dissatisfaction and body mass index were significant predictors of dieting to gain weight; and that negative affect, media influence, and sports participation predicted symptoms of muscle dysmorphia (Cafri et al., 2006).

In our review of physical and psychological factors associated with the pursuit of the muscular ideal (Cafri et al., 2005), we also provided a model (see Figure 1) of influences, many of which are examined in detail in different chapters in this book. In our model, pursuit of the muscular ideal is influenced by a variety of factors (e.g., biological, societal, psychological, sports participation). Additionally, this pursuit may drive the individual to engage in risky behaviors, such as the use of appearance- and performance-enhancing drugs or radical dieting strategies (e.g., carbohydrate depletion), to enhance muscularity. In this model, psychological factors such as negative affect and low-self esteem are also seen as contributing factors for risky health behaviors. The chapters of this book examine in detail the themes and interrelationships outlined in this heuristic model, and we hope that future research will inform and expand on this initial framework.

In sum, we think that the time is right for a distillation of recent findings to help guide future work in the area of the muscular body image ideal. This book offers a very broad range of chapters by individuals with widely divergent backgrounds who bring a variety of viewpoints and analytical strategies to the examination of a single concept: the muscular ideal. The interdisciplinary backgrounds of the chapter authors ensure a broad view of the construct under investigation. Within the broad chapter categories of cover-

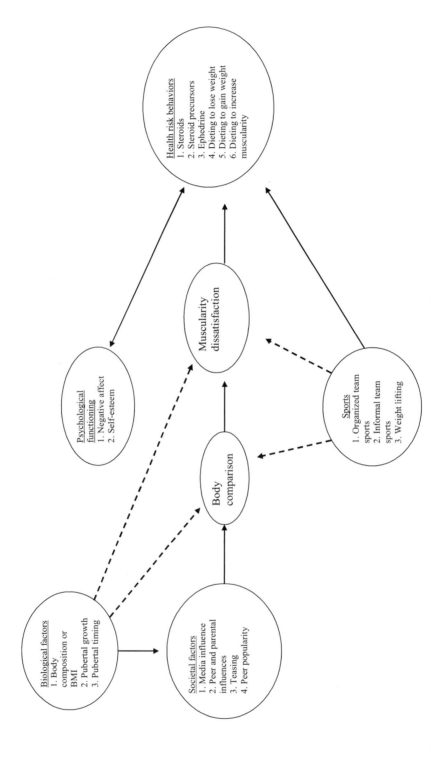

Figure 1. A model explaining factors involved in the pursuit of the muscular ideal. Solid lines illustrate strongly supported relations; dotted lines illustrate somewhat weaker directional influences. BMI = body mass index.

age, however, it is possible to discern some central themes that this book examines, including

- the complexity of appearance ideals (in general) and the muscular ideal (in particular);
- the role of history and social influences;
- the need to rethink conventional measures of body image;
- the importance of understanding biological and side effects of current (and potential) appearance- and performance-enhancing drugs;
- the critical need for prevention and treatment methods for clinical disturbance (e.g., body dysmorphia, steroid abuse); and
- the multiple influences (social, biological, psychological) that drive the pursuit of the muscular ideal.

This book is for professionals and nonprofessionals who have an interest in body image disturbance or who work with individuals who may pursue the muscular ideal to the point of impairment (e.g., who seek drugs to augment the appearance or muscularity or show signs of muscle dysmorphia). The chapters are empirically based, and the authors include clear discussions of current research findings and future research avenues. Clinicians will find state-of-the-art guidelines for diagnosis of clinically relevant symptoms and treatment and intervention strategies for adolescents and adults. In addition, we have sought to provide a volume that is engaging, informative, and accessible.

A ROADMAP FOR THIS BOOK

There are five parts to this book, and the first is entitled Cultural, Social, and Psychological Perspectives. In chapter 1, James J. Gray and Rebecca L. Ginsberg provide a broad overview of the muscular ideal, demonstrating that it has resonance for a broad range of men and women of various ages and ethnicities. They first describe the data indicating an increasing historical prevalence of muscularity concerns and review theories that might explain this increase, including evolutionary and cultural models. For instance, according to the "crisis in masculinity" approach, men in Western societies no longer need physical strength for survival, yet they desire enhanced muscularity to assert their masculinity. Cultural and social influences include media, peers, and parents.

Gray and Ginsberg provide a wealth of empirical evidence attesting to the importance of muscularity for both men and women. They explore the recent trend of increased muscularity in images contained in the media (print, TV, movie) and in toy and action figures, the presence of muscular participants in pornography and the advent of male strippers, soaring membership in gyms and fitness clubs, and the explosion in cosmetic surgery and steroid use. Finally, they provide an examination of the muscular ideal as it exists across a variety of subgroups of individuals (e.g., gay vs. straight) and in different countries, including Western and non-Western countries. Many of the topics examined in this overview chapter are explored in more detail in the rest of the book, and cross-references are provided to direct the reader to specific chapters on related content.

In chapter 2, Lynne Luciano provides a far-ranging historical overview of the tight connection between muscularity and masculinity in the United States over the past 100 years. She covers the role of increasing modernization and urbanization in limiting outlets for men to express masculinity, leading to the focus on sports, in particular bodybuilding, as a way for men to exhibit strength and muscularity (important signs of masculinity). Luciano reviews the influence of the women's movement in the 1960s and 1970s and the gay movement, as well as the fitness revolution beginning in the 1970s. The advent of the Me Generation in the 1980s and the increasing focus on body appearance (a part of pathological narcissism) also propelled many men and women to desire enhanced muscularity as a component of bodily perfection. The availability and wider use and acceptance of body change strategies via drugs and surgery also fueled the achievement of the muscular ideal. A strength of Luciano's chapter is its adept analysis of the central role of masculinity concerns as a motive for the desire of a more muscular appearance for boys and men.

Building on the initial connections among bodybuilding and the muscular ideal provided in the first two chapters, in chapter 3 Alan Klein provides a more narrowly focused treatise on the topic of bodybuilding, an avocation that is perhaps the most connected in the popular mind with the muscular ideal. His chapter offers a unique and firsthand collection of his findings from almost 20 years of fieldwork with bodybuilders. It is interesting that his chapter opens with a vignette about body depilation (i.e., hair removal, often used to enhance muscular appearance), which is an interest of ours (Boroughs, Cafri, & Thompson, 2005). He goes on to provide a very specific description of the daily routines and experiences of the serious bodybuilder, including workouts, strategies to modify appearance (e.g., tanning, shaving, poses), drug use, and food practices (including severe caloric restriction). He also reveals some of the social and interpersonal themes he identified from his interviews over the years, such as low self-esteem and parental issues, contributing to the decision to seek heightened muscularity. Throughout, he examines how the proponents of the subculture of bodybuilding and the emphasis of U.S. culture on appearance issues have led to a greater acceptance of bodybuilding. As he notes, although bodybuilding is problematic as a sport, it has become convincing as a subculture.

Part II, Definitions and Measurement, provides a sharply focused examination of the different dimensions of the muscularity ideal and the different assessment approaches. The "drive for muscularity" component of the muscularity ideal has received the most research attention, and Donald R. McCreary thoroughly examines this component in chapter 4. McCreary, who initially offered a description of the construct and a measure of its assessment (McCreary et al., 2004), provides a history of the construct, along with a wealth of data on its reliability and validity and how it relates to other measures of muscularity and psychological well-being. In chapter 5, we review the various measures, in addition to the drive for muscularity concept, that have recently been offered to allow researchers and clinicians to document the level of disturbance of various components of the muscular ideal. Our review includes Likert-based measures, silhouette scales, self-report measures, and measures of body dysmorphic disorder (which would provide a diagnosis of the muscle dysmorphia type of body dysmorphic disorder), as well as specific measures of muscle dysmorphia. We also offer indications for the use of specific measures.

Part III covers medical issues, treatment, and prevention. In chapter 6, Roberto Olivardia offers an up-close and focused look at the disorder that emerges from an excessive pursuit of muscularity: muscle dysmorphia. Reviewing a wealth of research (much of it conducted by Olivardia and his colleagues), the chapter describes the essential characteristics and defining features of the disorder, comorbidity (e.g., depression), clinical guidelines to assessment, and specific procedures for clinical management of the condition. Chapter 7 turns to the evaluation of muscle enhancement substances and strategies. Michael S. Bahrke provides an in-depth presentation of the current and emerging drugs that people use to approach the muscular ideal. He covers not only the usual suspects, such as anabolic–androgenic steroids and their precursors but also beta-2 agonists, human growth hormone, gamma-hydroxybutyric acid, insulin, testosterone precursors, human chorionic gonadotropin, a variety of stimulants, blood doping, and recreational drugs and dietary supplements. The material offered in his chapter is essential for a full understanding of the many complex strategies some individuals use in their pursuit of the ideal muscular appearance.

In chapter 8, Linn Goldberg and Diane L. Elliot outline their pioneering work in the prevention of steroid use among adolescents. Initially, their chapter builds on the previous one by exploring the specific use and abuse of drugs to enhance muscularity, but with a specific focus on adolescents. Next, they detail their prevention work with two programs: Athletes Training and Learning to Avoid Steroids (ATLAS) and Athletes Targeting Healthy Exercise and Nutrition Alternatives (ATHENA). To date, their work with these two programs has involved more than 4,000 participants. Their chapter clearly outlines the components of the two programs and presents results attesting to their effectiveness. They are at the leading edge of preventive work in this field.

In Part IV, three chapters zero in on special topics: cosmetic procedures, adolescents, and women. These topics are mentioned and analyzed in some of the previous chapters, but we felt that each merited a closer focus. In chapter 9, David B. Sarwer, Canice E. Crerand, and Lauren M. Gibbons describe the prevalence and use of a variety of cosmetic procedures, including liposuction, body contouring procedures, and abdominoplasty. They also review the research on the relation between cosmetic surgery seeking and body dysmorphic disorder, eating disorders, and other psychiatric disorders. Their comprehensive examination of the topic also includes coverage of the social forces behind the phenomenal growth in cosmetic procedures performed.

In chapter 10, Lina A. Ricciardelli and Marita P. McCabe focus on the presence of muscularity concerns and ideals in adolescent boys, examining the factors that drive or moderate such concerns such as media, peer, and family pressures, sexual orientation, and sports involvement. They also delve into the increasing pressure on young girls to enhance their muscularity level. Expanding on this topic in chapter 11, Amanda J. Gruber provides a comprehensive review of muscularity issues for women and girls. This far-ranging chapter provides not only a historical and social analysis of factors over the past several decades that have led to the current focus on fitness (and muscularity) for some women and girls, but also examines the particularities of muscle presentation in this population, which often involve definition and tone rather than bulk and size. In addition, Gruber outlines the limits of existing knowledge in this newly emerging area and provides suggestions for future work.

Finally, in Part V, Joan C. Chrisler and Sam V. Cochran offer some guidelines for future work in the area. Each author views the topic from a unique perspective. Chrisler was editor of *Sex Roles* for 5 years (she stepped down at the end of 2006), and Cochran is editor of the journal *Psychology of Men and Masculinity*. Their analysis and guidelines provide a framework for a variety of future investigations, and they offer an appropriate coda to the wide-ranging material provided by contributors in the previous chapters.

We hope that this book will serve not only as a summary of current knowledge but also as a call to action for future research. We also emphasize that although much of this book is focused on the potential negative aspects of the relentless pursuit of the muscular ideal (e.g., drug abuse, clinical disturbances); it is important not to lose sight of the potential benefits of physical activity and sports for physical and mental health. In fact, one of our earliest studies in this area (Pasman & Thompson, 1988) demonstrated that bodybuilders had a more positive body image than runners and control participants. Our primary concern in this book—the deleterious effects of an extreme focus on physical perfection and its recognition, analysis, and management—should in no way be interpreted as an indictment or judgment of the millions of individuals who benefit from sports and physical activity.

This is a new era in the way body image is conceptualized. Fortunately, it is also clear from the chapters in this book that psychologists are marshaling their energies and expertise in the search for a greater understanding of the pursuit of the muscular ideal.

REFERENCES

Boroughs, M., Cafri, G., & Thompson, J. K. (2005). Male body depilation: Prevalence and associated features of body hair removal. *Sex Roles, 52,* 637–644.

Cafri, G., Roehrig, M., & Thompson, J. K. (2004). Reliability assessment of the Somatomorphic Matrix. *International Journal of Eating Disorders, 35,* 597–600.

Cafri, G., Strauss, J., & Thompson, J. K. (2002). Male body image: Satisfaction and its relationship to well-being using the Somatomorphic Matrix. *International Journal of Men's Health, 1,* 215–231.

Cafri, G., & Thompson, J. K. (2004a). Evaluating the convergence of muscle appearance attitude measures. *Assessment, 11,* 224–229.

Cafri, G., & Thompson, J. K. (2004b). Measuring male body image: A review of the current methodology. *Psychology of Men and Masculinity, 5,* 18–29.

Cafri, G., Thompson, J. K., Ricciardelli, L., McCabe, M., Smolak, L., & Yesalis, C. (2005). Pursuit of the muscular ideal: Physical and psychological consequences and putative risk factors. *Clinical Psychology Review, 25,* 215–239.

Cafri, G., van den Berg, P., & Thompson, J. K. (2006). Pursuit of muscularity in adolescent boys: Relations among biopsychosocial variables and clinical outcomes. *Journal of Clinical Child and Adolescent Psychology, 35,* 283–291.

Cash, T. F., & Pruzinsky, T. (1990). (Eds.). *Body images: Development, deviance and change.* New York: Guilford Press.

Cash, T. F., & Pruzinsky, T. (2002). *Body image: A handbook of theory, research and practice.* New York: Guilford Press.

McCreary, D. R., Sasse, D. K., Saucier, D. M., & Dorsch, K. D. (2004). Measuring the drive for muscularity: Factorial validity of the drive for muscularity scale in men and women. *Psychology of Men and Masculinity, 5,* 49–58.

Pasman, L., & Thompson, J. K. (1988). Body image and eating disturbance in obligatory weightlifters, obligatory runners, and sedentary individuals. *International Journal of Eating Disorders, 7,* 759–768.

Pope, H. G., Katz, D. L., & Hudson, J. I. (1993). Anorexia nervosa and "reverse anorexia" among 108 male bodybuilders. *Comprehensive Psychiatry, 34,* 406–409.

Pope, H. G., Phillips, K. A., & Olivardia, R. (2000). *The Adonis complex: The secret crisis of male body obsession.* New York: Free Press.

Sarwer, D. B., Pruzinsky, T., Cash, T. F., Goldwyn, R. M., Persing, A., & Whitaker, L. A. (2006). *Psychological aspects of reconstructive and cosmetic plastic surgery: Clinical, empirical, and ethical perspectives.* Philadelphia: Lippincott, Williams & Wilkins.

Smolak, L., Murnen, S., & Thompson, J. K. (2005). Sociocultural influences and muscle building in adolescent boys. *Psychology of Men and Masculinity, 6*, 227–239.

Thompson, J. K. (1990). *Body image disturbance: Assessment and treatment.* Elmsford, NY: Pergamon Press.

Thompson, J. K. (Ed.). (1996). *Body image, eating disorders, and obesity: An integrative guide for assessment and treatment.* Washington, DC: American Psychological Association.

Thompson, J. K., Heinberg, L. J., Altabe, M. N., & Tantleff-Dunn, S. (1999). *Exacting beauty: Theory, assessment and treatment of body image disturbance.* Washington, DC: American Psychological Association.

I

CULTURAL, SOCIAL, AND PSYCHOLOGICAL PERSPECTIVES

1

MUSCLE DISSATISFACTION: AN OVERVIEW OF PSYCHOLOGICAL AND CULTURAL RESEARCH AND THEORY

JAMES J. GRAY AND REBECCA L. GINSBERG

Body dissatisfaction among men and women in U.S. culture is widespread. It has been well documented that body dissatisfaction in women generally centers on issues of thinness; however, both men and women also experience dissatisfaction in regard to muscularity. The desire for muscularity varies from culture to culture, suggesting that culture plays a significant role in the desire for muscularity.

In this chapter, we explore the role of culture in the pursuit of muscularity. Different theories of muscularity, including biological and cultural theories, are discussed. We review multiple lines of evidence regarding the drive for muscularity, whether the drive for muscularity appears to be increasing, and how the impact of the emphasis varies among different groups within U.S. culture. We then explore the presence of the drive for muscularity in some cultures and its relative absence in others. We also explore how the muscular ideal, much like the thin ideal for women, may have started to spread from Western cultures to more traditional cultures. Finally, we suggest ways to examine the area of culture and muscularity in future research.

CURRENT LEVELS OF BODY DISSATISFACTION

High levels of body dissatisfaction are found in both men and women (Vartanian, Giant, & Passino, 2001) in the United States, and this dissatisfaction appears to be on the rise. Numerous studies have demonstrated the trend toward greater body dissatisfaction. Chief among these studies are a series of *Psychology Today* articles, conducted about a decade apart, which demonstrated increasing body dissatisfaction among both men and women. In 1972, 25% of women and 15% of men were dissatisfied with their bodies (Berscheid, Walster, & Bohrnstedt, 1973). By 1985, 38% of women and 34% of men were dissatisfied with their bodies (Cash, Winstead, & Janda, 1986). By 1997, the numbers of dissatisfied individuals had risen to 56% of women and 43% of men (Garner, 1997). These three studies, although not totally comparable in methodology, had large sample sizes and are in line with other studies showing similar rates of body dissatisfaction. In a more carefully controlled study, researchers still found a high level of body dissatisfaction among men and women (Cash & Henry, 1994). Another study found that as many as 95% of men experienced some dissatisfaction with their bodies (Mishkind, Rodin, Silberstein, & Striegel-Moore, 1986).

Appearance Schemata

There are two important gender-based appearance schemata related to body image satisfaction. The first schema, relating to the absence of muscle, is primarily of concern to men. The second schema primarily concerns women and relates to thinness (Fisher, Dunn, & Thompson, 2002; McCreary & Sasse, 2000; Smolak, Levine, & Thompson, 2001; Vartanian et al., 2001). As evidence of this distinction, normal-weight women are more likely to view themselves as overweight, and normal-weight men are more likely to perceive themselves as underweight (Betz, Mintz, & Speakmon, 1994). Researchers have consistently found that men want to be more muscular (Ricciardelli, McCabe, & Banfield, 2000; see also chaps. 4 and 10, this volume). One study found that up to 91% of college men desired a more muscular frame, whereas none wanted to be less muscular (Jacobi & Cash, 1994).

Muscle Dissatisfaction

Numerous studies have documented that men choose an ideal body that is more muscular than their own (Frederick & Hazelton, 2003; Lynch & Zellner, 1999; Olivardia, Pope, Borowiecki, & Cohane, 2004; Pope, Phillips, & Olivardia, 2000). A muscular appearance is determined by the degree of muscularity but also by the absence of fat that hides the muscularity (Cafri & Thompson, 2004; Tylka, Bergeron, & Schwartz, 2005). According to the series of studies conducted for *Psychology Today* in 1972, 18% of men disliked their chest, and 25% disliked their muscle tone (Berscheid et al., 1973). By 1997, 38% of men were dissatisfied with their chest, and 45% were unhappy with their muscle size (Garner, 1997). Other researchers found that 39% of college men were "frequently" or "all the time" trying to increase their size (McCaulay, Mintz, & Glenn, 1988) and that 85% of men and 56% of women wanted to be more muscular, the women presumably more toned. It is interesting to note that Pope, Phillips, et al. (2000) reported that 17% of their male sample would give up 3 years of their lives and 11% would give up 5 years of their lives to achieve their higher muscularity goal.

Men believe that women want more muscle in men than women actually want (Frederick, Fessler, & Hazelton, 2005; Jacobi & Cash, 1994). Indeed, women prefer a male body that has 15 to 20 fewer pounds of muscle than men seek for themselves. Even more striking is that fact that 94% of women ranked the photos of bodybuilders as repulsive (Pope, Phillips, et al., 2000). Women also believe that men want more muscle in women than men actually do (Jacobi & Cash, 1994).

In addition to steroid use and overexercise, men who experience a pathological drive for muscularity may develop muscle dysmorphia, a form of body dysmorphic disorder in which individuals maintain a pathological belief that they are of small musculature even when they are muscular (Phillips, 1996; Pope, Gruber, Choi, Olivardia, & Phillips, 1997; see also chap. 6, this volume).

THEORIES OF MUSCULARITY

Society's focus on muscularity is not new and has been found in many cultures, both present and past. For example, sculptures depicting and idealizing the muscular male body have survived from the Roman and Renaissance eras. The majority of the great heroes of antiquity, such as David, Achilles, Odysseus, Alexander the Great, and Julius Caesar were described as both muscular and powerful. However, over the past few decades, in Western culture, there appears to be increased emphasis on a muscular ideal, particularly for men (see chap. 2, this volume). Several types of theory have been advanced to explain the muscular ideal, including evolutionary theory, various cultural theories, and theories of individual vulnerability.

Evolutionary Theory

The evolutionary theory of muscularity suggests that biological and evolutionary factors underlie the drive for muscularity (Jackson, 2002). According to this theory, muscularity has genetically programmed appeal. In particular, a broad chest in men and a general muscular appearance in both men and women indicate robustness and durability. Men with larger chests and smaller waists are indeed seen as more attractive by women (Maisey, Vale, Cornelissen, & Tovee, 1999; Dixon, Halliwell, East, Wigivarajah, & Anderson, 2003). Although muscularity may have a survival use for women as well as for men, cultures generally attach more meaning to muscle in men, perhaps because men are generally larger and more muscular to start with (Jackson, 2002; Klein, 1993). Indeed, although Western societies have alternately promoted extra weight and thinness as a marker of female attractiveness, a lack of muscularity in men has never been valued as a symbol of male attractiveness.

Muscularity, however, is not correlated with health and longevity in men. Thin men are healthier and live longer (Weeden & Sabini, 2005). Increased mesomorphy as well as increased endomorphy are risk factors for cardiovascular disease (Williams et al., 2000). In evolutionary terms, then, muscularity may be tied to associations with protection and food production, with long-term health and longevity less relevant. In ancestral environments, there existed a division of labor between the sexes. Women were primarily responsible for the hearth and raising children, and men protected the family and hunted for food. This division continues to the present in much of the world. It follows, then, that men needed to be strong both to work and to fight off enemies and predators. During ancestral times, muscles were likely an external indicator of these abilities. Greater muscular development in men, along with height and certain facial features, served as a marker for strength and the ability to protect and produce goods. Among early human ancestors, the more powerfully built man may have been seen as having greater reproductive value.

Cultural Theories

It is likely that the evolutionary theory of muscularity contributes to the muscular ideal found in Western society. However, if biology and the evolutionary theory fully explained the muscular ideal, we would expect to find this ideal emphasized around the globe and in all cultures and to about the same extent. However, the desire for muscularity appears to vary greatly from culture to culture and among subcultures within a single culture (see chaps. 2 and 3, this volume). Although some cultures exaggerate the value of muscularity in men and women, other cultures place only minimal emphasis on body shape in men and less than minimal emphasis on body shape in women (Jackson, 2002; Pope, Phillips, et al., 2000). Because of the pronounced cultural variations in the drive for muscularity, one must look to cultural factors to fully understand the current rise in the drive for muscularity found in Western cultures. Even more than biology, it is culture that defines what constitutes an attractive body. It is clear that the value of muscularity, and beauty in general, is both seen and constructed through a cultural lens (McKnight, 1999).

Crisis in Masculinity

Even though the physical need for muscular strength in men is decreasing, the cultural emphasis on muscularity has paradoxically increased in many societies, often in the very cultures in which muscles are no longer needed. Some researchers have posited that in cultures currently emphasizing male muscularity as ideal, women have entered male domains and have started to approach parity with men in many respects, although men continue to make higher salaries and generally have greater economic power than women (see chaps. 2 and 11, this volume). This hypothesis states that women's rise in power has created a crisis in masculinity (Faludi, 1999; Pope, Phillips, et al., 2000). In particular, in cultures in which the traditional male role as breadwinner and protector has declined and in which machine has replaced muscle, the pursuit of muscularity has become one of the few ways left for men to exhibit their masculine selves (Yang, Gray, & Pope, 2005). Ironically, then, as the actual advantage of muscle has diminished over time, men have come to seek muscle not for its usefulness in protection and work, but as a sign of masculinity. Although thinness has come to represent femininity, in many cultures muscles are now used as a marker of masculinity.

The biggest natural difference in strength between men and women is in fact concentrated in the arms, chest, and shoulders. Therefore, it is no surprise that a man who needs to exaggerate his difference from women would focus on these areas. Even in societies in which women prefer the body of "average" men to a more muscular build, men still value greater muscularity than that preferred by women (Pope, Gruber, et al., 2000). These men equate muscularity with masculinity and hold an exaggerated belief that muscles are important in attracting women (see chap. 2, this volume).

This theory fails to explain why women seek muscularity for themselves. However, women generally seek not bulk muscularity but rather a smaller, toned look (see chap. 11, this volume). Furthermore, the idea that the pursuit of muscularity represents a crisis in masculinity fits the data indicating that the muscular ideal occurs in cultures in which physical strength is less important in daily life. In most developing countries studied so far where the traditional male role remains largely intact, men are less likely to view and seek muscularity as ideal.

Media Theory

Media theory states that the media's focus on the muscular ideal plays a central role in the current increase in the drive for muscularity found in men (McCreary & Sasse, 2000). A specific media theory, media cultivation theory (Grubner & Gross, 1976), focuses on the powerful influence of the media, especially TV, through which interpretations of social reality and culture that are not objectively true are nonetheless convincingly portrayed to the viewer. According to media theory, the media send an unequivocal message that there is one preferred body type depending on a person's gender—thin for women, muscular for men.

In many Western societies, men are exposed to multiple media sources that depict the male body as far more muscular than that of the average man (Pope, Phillips, et al., 2000). The result of the bombardment of muscular male images is a desire among men to be as muscular as the models presented. It is important to recognize, however, that the media would have little chance to force a value on a culture if the value was not already part of the culture to some degree. The media likely takes its lead from the culture and builds on what is already present, in this case residual evolutionary value or the crisis in muscularity. Thus, the relationship between the media and the cultural ideal of bodily beauty is complex, reciprocal, and defined by many moderating variables. The media reflect the culture but also contribute to the cultural ideals of the time (Agliata & Tantleff-Dunn, 2004).

In countries where men are increasingly exposed to the muscular ideal, a simultaneous increase in the pursuit of muscularity has been found (Pope, Olivardia, Borowiecki, & Cohane, 2001). The fact that the rise in the pursuit of muscularity seems to parallel the rise in the appearance of very muscular models in the media supports the media theory (Leit, Gray, & Pope, 2002). For example, in the 1950s, about 3% of male models in women's magazines were partially undressed. However, by the 1990s, as many as 35% of male models in women's magazines were partially undressed (Pope, Phillips, et al., 2000). The male models in these magazines were muscular—evidence of what appears to be an increase in the sexually displayed man. Not surprisingly, then, in countries where the media do not promote the ideal of muscularity, men experience lower levels of body image dissatisfaction (Yang et al., 2005). For example, in a study of male models in women's magazines, only 5% of Taiwanese men portrayed in the magazines were partially undressed. Thus, the Taiwanese culture appears to be less focused on the male body than Western cultures. Furthermore, Taiwanese men appear to be less likely than U.S. men to abuse steroids or experience muscle dysmorphia (Yang et al., 2005).

Other Cultural Influences: Beauty Ideals, Makeover Movement, and Increase in Obesity

It is important to remember that the drive for muscularity developed within a larger context. The drive for muscularity is part of a widespread Western cultural trend toward a pronounced emphasis on physical beauty and youthful appearance. Muscularity is just one way to be youthful and beautiful. A second trend, particularly in U.S. culture, is the makeover business, which applies to houses, modes of dress, and bodily appearance. In U.S. culture, everything, including the human body, is seen as malleable (see chap. 9, this volume). Body dissatisfaction, and muscle dissatisfaction in particular, coexists with a third trend: the rapidly increasing prevalence of obesity. Thirty percent of the U.S. population is now classified as obese, and over

50% are overweight (Flegal, Carroll, Ogden, & Johnson, 2002); the drive for muscularity and the drive for thinness can be seen, in part, as a reaction against the rapidly increasing prevalence of obesity. Some men and women, recoiling from being overweight and out of shape, may attempt to mold their bodies into a more culturally sanctioned shape: thin for women and muscular for men, safely distinct from the obese.

Parents and Peers

Once a value is present within a culture, the members of that culture usually believe in and promote the value. The value of muscularity, then, is transmitted to the young by the people around them and through the media. The opinion of others has a profound effect on how one feels about one's body (Tantleff-Dunn & Gokee, 2002). The drive for muscularity found in young boys is often, in part, a product of parental pressure to achieve the muscular ideal (McCabe & Ricciardelli, 2003; Muris, Meesters, Van de Blom, & Mayer, 2005; Ricciardelli & McCabe, 2001, 2003b, 2004; see also chap. 10, this volume). Although both the mother and the father have been found to exert influence regarding ideal muscle size (Ricciardelli & McCabe, 2001), some research suggests that fathers, in particular, strongly influence body image and strategies to increase muscles in adolescent boys (Irving, Wall, Neumark-Sztainer, & Story, 2002; McCabe & Ricciardelli, 2003; Vincent & McCabe, 1999).

Peers are another powerful force in modeling and reinforcing the value of muscularity (Cash, Cash, & Butters, 1982; Ricciardelli & McCabe, 2003a). Studies have found that boys with low body mass indexes are often pushed by their peers to increase the size of their muscles (McCabe, Ricciardelli, & Banfield, 2001). Indeed, appearance-related teasing is one of the more powerful predictors of men's concerns about muscularity (Vartanian et al., 2001). During puberty, boys become more muscular and thus move closer to the ideal male body shape (McCabe et al., 2001). Perhaps related to childhood teasing, boys who experience delayed puberty seem to engage in more extreme body change strategies (Alasker, 1992; McCabe & Ricciardelli, 2003; Siegel, Yancey, Aneshensel, & Schuler, 1999).

In addition to direct peer influences, peer popularity seems to be another reason why adolescent boys try to gain muscle size (McCabe, Ricciardelli, & Finemore, 2002). For example, research has shown that boys with low to average levels of peer relations were more likely to use steroids than other boys (Kindlundh, Hagekull, Isacson, & Nyberg, 2001). Furthermore, a review of the literature on the pursuit of muscularity in boys revealed that a prime reason why adolescent boys use steroids is to increase their perceived romantic appeal or increase their popularity among male peers (O'Koon, 1997). It seems, then, that in cultures that highly value muscularity in men, both parents and peers pass on this value to others in the society. Although the influence of parents and peers appears to be powerful, according to social norms theory (Perkins & Berkowitz, 1986), some of the influence of others, particularly peers, may be due to incorrect or exaggerated perceptions of their attitudes and behaviors.

Theories of Individual Vulnerability

The media and other sociocultural influences likely play an important role in the idealization of muscularity, but it remains unclear why some individuals are more susceptible to muscular media images than others. It is probable that an individual's own history and psychological state interact with muscular cultural images to affect how an individual views his or her own body. It is quite normal and healthy for a person to try to build up his or her body to be more attractive, as long as he or she does not use excessive or self-damaging strategies. One could speculate that for men, as the cultural ideal has become more muscular, those who were more psychologically vulnerable may have been more likely to use extreme measures to achieve the muscular ideal. Boys and men with low self-esteem, marked negative affect, and a tendency to compare themselves with others were found to be more susceptible to the sociocultural imperative to be muscular (Bordo, 1999; McCabe & Ricciardelli, 2003; Ricciardelli & McCabe, 2001, 2003a).

EVIDENCE OF THE CURRENT IMPORTANCE OF MUSCULARITY IN THE UNITED STATES

In the United States, evidence from many sources points to a powerful, well-established cultural emphasis on the desirability of muscularity for men and a message to women to be not only thin but also toned. These sources include print media, movies and television, pornography and male strippers, gyms and bodybuilding, toys and comic books, male cosmetic surgery, steroid use, and muscle dysmorphia. Any available evidence of increasing emphasis on muscularity is noted in each section.

Print Media

In the United States, the media have promoted a muscular male body through advertisements, television, and specific muscle-related magazines for several decades. Furthermore, the message of the muscular as ideal has increased in the recent past. For example, *Playgirl* centerfolds have become considerably more muscular over a 20-year period to a point that they could hardly get bigger (Leit et al., 2002). Currently, magazines specifically promoting fitness and muscularity can be found in any grocery store, pharmacy, or gas station throughout the country. Perhaps one of the most widely known muscle magazines, *Muscle and Fitness*, has been in circulation since 1939 and currently has a circulation of almost 500,000 per month in the United States alone (Ulrich, 2005) and a readership of millions each month (Etcoff, 1999). Newer periodicals such as *Men's Fitness* and *Men's Health*, which both started in 1987, have even higher circulation rates (600,000 and 1,665,038, respectively). These two magazines, which do not promote the muscular ideal to the same degree as do some other muscle magazines, nevertheless focus repeatedly on appearance and often on muscular appearance under the guise of fitness and health.

The high circulation rates of these and many other muscle magazines indicate that muscular media images are far-reaching and likely to affect many men. For example, *Muscle and Fitness* magazine features page after page of enormously muscular men interspersed with scores of advertisements for liquid or solid supplements with names that include the words *stack, tight, extreme, mass,* and *megawhey*. Researchers found that over a 32-year period, the number of articles devoted to building strength and toning muscles increased significantly in two popular men's fashion magazines (Petrie et al., 1996). Furthermore, the male body marketed toward men (as found in these magazines) is more muscular than the male body marketed toward women in women's magazines such as *Cosmopolitan* (Frederick et al., 2005). Finally, more exercise and weight lifting advertisements are found in male-oriented magazines than in female-oriented magazines (Andersen & DiDomenico, 1992).

Unfortunately, many individuals who read magazines promoting the muscular ideal feel inferior and also feel that their bodies do not match those they see depicted in the magazines. Research shows that in both gay and straight men, the purchasing of fitness magazines correlates with body dissatisfaction (Duggan & McCreary, 2004) and with concerns about muscularity and general fitness, with the ingestion of dietary supplements to build muscle (Hatoum & Belle, 2004). The reading of health and fitness magazines is also related to the increased contemplation of steroid use in those who are not using steroids (Morry & Staska, 2001). Even boys as young as 6 to 12 years old admired muscular male models in both fashion catalogs and sports magazines as ideals (Spitzer, Henderson, & Zivian, 1999). At this point these connections can be considered correlational and not necessarily causal.

Although muscle magazines are geared primarily toward men, women are also affected by muscular media images (see chap. 11, this volume). Whereas some women in muscle magazines are depicted as thin and firm, others have extremely muscular bodies. Furthermore, in the United States, muscle magazines that target women seem to be gaining in popularity. For example, *Ms. Fitness Magazine*, a magazine geared toward female weight lifters, has a circulation of 150,000 (Ulrich, 2005).

Even individuals who do not read muscle and fitness magazines are likely to be exposed to the muscular ideal through the print media. In particular, advertisements found in the print media are increasingly exposing readers to the muscular ideal to sell products. Although the bare male body appears less often than the bare female body, advertisements featuring partially unclothed men are increasingly frequent. The partially undressed male body is used now even to sell products unrelated to the body, such as cars and watches (Pope, Phillips, et al., 2000).

Movies and Television

Like the print media, both television and movies also promote the muscular ideal (Dotson, 1999; Spitzer et al., 1999). Television characters fitting the hypermuscular stereotype can be found on daytime and nighttime soap operas, MTV, and shows ranging from *Baywatch* to professional wrestling (Dotson, 1999). Professional wrestlers have enormous bulk and are watched by millions of people each week. Current and recent movie stars also reflect the muscular ideal (Pingitore, Spring, & Garfield, 1997; Spitzer et al., 1999). This increased muscularity of movie stars can be seen in the extreme in examples such as Arnold Schwarzenegger, Sylvester Stallone, and Jean-Claude Van Damme. The most masculine male stars from the 1940s and 1950s, such as Humphrey Bogart and Clark Gable, were less muscular than the stars of today. Compare Marlon Brando in his prime with Brad Pitt; Pitt has considerably greater upper body definition. This increase in muscularity seen in male TV and movie stars seems to parallel the increase in the muscular ideal seen in other aspects of culture.

Pornography and Male Strippers

The same muscular stereotype is portrayed in both straight and gay pornography. Men who view pornography are essentially being told that to be an object of desire, they must look like the men they see on the screen (Dotson, 1999). The men portrayed in pornographic films are very powerfully built and have large genitals. Exposure to pornography in gay men was positively correlated with social physique anxiety, and it is likely that gay men are more affected by muscular images because they view more pornography than straight men do (Duggan & McCreary, 2004).

Although male strippers were unheard of several decades ago, the male stripper business is now a well-known and expanding industry (Pope, Phillips, et al., 2000). Muscular male strippers can be found at private parties or at specific clubs such as Chippendales. Male strippers, like men in the pornographic media, promote the idea that a man must be very muscular to be considered desirable.

Gyms and Bodybuilding

Another manifestation of the cultural focus on muscularity is the increased popularity of health and fitness clubs. People join these clubs for various reasons, but high on the list of reasons is to add tone or bulk through weight lifting. Studies have found that in the United States, 5 to 10 million people hold gym memberships and spend $2.8 billion per year in commercial gym memberships and exercise equipment (Kalb, 1999).

Bodybuilding as an activity has increased in popularity over time (see chap. 3, this volume). In 1998, an estimated 5 million people in the United States (mostly men) participated in bodybuilding (Goldfried, Harper, & Blouin, 1998). These same researchers found that male bodybuilders had more severe body image disturbances and eating problems than a matched athletic group. These investigators speculated that men with low self-esteem may gravitate toward bodybuilding to achieve personal or societal standards of attractiveness. Additionally, studies suggest that up to 10% of male bodybuilders may experience muscle dysmorphia and that a large number of female bodybuilders show features of the disorder (Pope et al., 1997; see also chap. 6, this volume).

Findings regarding the negative effects of bodybuilding are mixed, however, with some studies showing that weight lifters are not at increased risk for muscle dysmorphia. For example, one study found that competitive bodybuilders as a group were not more muscle dysmorphic than either noncompetitive weight trainers or physically active men who did not train with weights (Picket, Lewis, & Cash, 2005). Furthermore, investigators found that a mixed group of female and male weight lifters were actually more satisfied with their bodies than runners or sedentary control participants (Pasman & Thompson, 1988).

Toys and Comic Books

The changing shape of toy action figures over time reveals what may be the greatest exaggeration of muscularity in Western culture and a muscular ideal that targets the most vulnerable segment of the population—children. Action figures that have existed for over 30 years, such as G. I. Joe, have grown much more muscular over time. For example, in 1964, if G. I. Joe was projected to be a 5-foot, 10-inch tall man, he would have a chest size of 44 inches and a 12-inch bicep. By 1998, however, G. I. Joe matched a man with a 55-inch chest and a 27-inch bicep. The chest size, biceps, and rippled abdominals of many contemporary action figures now exceed the muscularity of world-class bodybuilders (Pope, Olivardia, Gruber, & Borowiecki, 1999). The bodily proportions of these action figures are now just as unrealistic as the proportions of Barbie. Like action figures, comic books also promote the muscular ideal. Although there have always been muscular superheroes like Superman and the Incredible Hulk, these heroes have become even more muscular, with sharply defined chests and chiseled abdominal muscles (Pope et al., 1999).

Male Cosmetic Surgery

Although women obtain cosmetic surgery in much higher numbers than men, the proportion of men seeking cosmetic surgery is growing (Pope, Phillips, et al., 2000; see also chap. 9, this volume). In 2001, just over 1 million men in the United States underwent cosmetic surgery not only for hair transplants and penis enlargement, but also to enhance muscularity via pectoral implants, calf muscle implants, and a liposuction procedure that removes the fat around the abdominal muscles to give those muscles greater definition (American Society for Aesthetic Plastic Surgery, 2002).

Steroid Use

Some men who feel deficient in muscularity view steroid use as a solution to their discontent (see chaps. 7 and 8, this volume). Etcoff (1999) reported that 7% of high school boys were using or had used steroids. As mentioned in the Introduction to this volume, Cafri, Thompson, Ricciardelli, McCabe, Smolak, and Yesalis (2005), in their review of studies, found a prevalence range of 3% to 12%. These findings translate to hundreds of thousands of boys and men who are using steroids to increase the size of their muscles (Pope, Phillips, et al., 2000). Cafri et al. (2005) further reported a huge underground black market that makes illegal steroids readily available to adult and teenage men.

Muscle Dysmorphia

Mental health professionals have noted the appearance of a new psychological disorder, muscle dysmorphia. This disorder was first called *reverse anorexia* and, at present, is seen as a subtype of body dysmorphic disorder (Olivardia, 2001; Pope et al., 1997; see also, chap. 6, this volume). Muscle dysmorphia, which almost exclusively affects men, involves the pathological drive for muscularity in which the person feels puny despite pronounced bodily development. Some research suggests that the drive for muscularity may be the starting point for muscle dysmorphia, just as the drive for thinness is a precursor to the development of anorexia nervosa (Choi, 2000; Olivardia, Pope, & Hudson, 2000).

RESEARCH EVIDENCE OF THE MUSCULAR IDEAL

Social trends in muscularity, described in the preceding section, provide informal evidence of the rise in the value of muscularity in U.S. culture. Studies also support the hypothesis that U.S. culture places great value on the muscular ideal (Pope, Gruber, et al., 2000).

Positive Associations With Muscularity

Research has demonstrated that attractive people are perceived as possessing a variety of positive traits, such as confidence and better adjustment. Furthermore, attractive people are treated more favorably by others (Jackson, 2002). Research also indicates that people in Western societies believe that muscularity can be equated with positive personality traits. For example, subjects assigned positive personality traits to photographs of muscular men and mostly negative traits to photographs of thin and overweight men (Kirpatrick & Sanders, 1978). Both sexes evaluated male figures with muscular chests as more assertive, athletic, sexually active, confident, and popular (J. K. Thompson & Tantleff, 1992).

Exposure to Muscular Models

Experimental studies suggest that exposure to media images of muscular men directly and immediately influences body esteem in men (Agliata & Tantleff-Dunn, 2004). Men exposed to muscular images through muscle magazines, men's magazines, and music videos have been shown to experience both a loss of body satisfaction and an increase in muscle-building activities (Hatoum & Belle, 2004; Vartanian et al., 2001).

As has been found repeatedly for women who view thin models (Groesz, Levine, & Murnen, 2002), men who look at muscular models on TV or in magazines are less satisfied with their appearance insofar as they internalize the muscular ideal (Agliata & Tantleff-Dunn, 2004; Frederick et al., 2005; Grogan, Williams, & Connor, 1996; Jacobi & Cash, 1994; Leit et al., 2002; Lorenzen, Grieve, & Thomas, 2004). However, it is important to keep in mind that evidence addresses the immediate impact, and it is unclear whether exposed subjects experience any lasting effects.

MUSCULARITY AND SPECIFIC GROUPS WITHIN U.S. CULTURE

The drive for muscularity has a differential impact on different groups within a culture. In this section we explore the impact of the muscular ideal on different U.S. subcultures.

Heterosexual Caucasian Men

It is clear that men experience the drive for muscularity more strongly than women. For men, the clear ideal is greater bulk in the form of muscles. From the preteen years through adulthood, boys and men admire and aspire to greater muscle size (Fisher et al., 2002). Whereas girls tend to feel overweight, boys are more likely to feel underweight (Page & Allen, 1995). Indeed, research indicates that being underdeveloped is the most common body concern among boys (Moore, 1990).

Women

Women and girls who say that they "want more muscle" usually mean something different than men who say the same. Women seek a lean, feminine, toned look with elongated muscles (Vartanian et al., 2001; see also chap. 11, this volume). Fashion and fitness magazines often feature female models with lean muscle in athletic poses or contexts. Thus, in addition to slenderness, today's ideal female body is firm and toned, without extra bulk (Brumberg, 1997; Choi, 2003). Even female athletes seek a muscular look that does not include bulk. Female athletes confront a dilemma, because the athletic body is not the body idealized by a culture in which the thinness ideal prevails (Krane, Choi, Baird, Aimar, & Kauer, 2004).

Some women have begun to move into serious bodybuilding. Although many female bodybuilders do not bulk up like men, they do work toward a lean but very firm appearance. Some female bodybuilders, however, defy the lean, toned ideal and choose to bulk up like male bodybuilders. Even though these bulked-up female bodybuilders have become more acceptable in the bodybuilding subculture, they still represent only a small number of women.

Gay Men

The ideal body for homosexual men is the same muscular build presented for heterosexual men (Yelland & Tiggemann, 2003). However, a considerable amount of research, summarized in an extensive literature review, suggests that gay men are more concerned about body shape than heterosexual men (Ricciardelli & McCabe, 2004). Gay men have reported a greater gap between their actual and ideal body shape and were more likely to express dissatisfaction with their body build, waist, biceps, arms, and stomach (Mishkind et al., 1986). *Playgirl* magazine, often bought by gay men, may be evidence of the emphasis on muscularity for gay men. The centerfold male models in this magazine have grown considerably in bulk muscularity over the past few decades (Leit et al., 2002). Investigators have suggested that gay men seek muscularity with more intensity than heterosexual men because they must prove that they are "real" men and disprove the stereotype that they are soft and effeminate (Bordo, 1999; Pope, Phillips, et al., 2000).

African American Men

Few researchers have investigated the role of race in the drive for muscularity. Preliminary data, however, suggest that African American boys have a higher drive for muscularity than Caucasian boys (S. Thompson, Corwin,

& Sargent, 1997; S. Thompson, Sargent, & Kemper, 1996). Furthermore, African American boys have been found to have a larger ideal self than Caucasian boys (S. Thompson et al., 1997). African American boys also have estimated girls' ideal male body as larger than Caucasian boys' estimates (S. Thompson et al., 1996).

Socioeconomic Status and Age

Research on bodybuilders suggests that before 1980, bodybuilders came overwhelmingly from working-class backgrounds. However, since 1980, more men who hold white-collar jobs have become involved in bodybuilding (Klein, 1993; see also chap. 3, this volume). According to Klein (1993), middle-class women joined gyms before middle-class men began to join in large numbers. It may be that working-class and middle-class men build up their bodies for different psychological reasons. In particular, working-class men may build muscles to compensate for their relative lack of financial resources, whereas middle-class men may do so because of the realization that having financial resources is no longer enough to attract women, who increasingly have their own financial resources.

Muscular dissatisfaction starts early and increases until adulthood. Many boys demonstrate high levels of body dissatisfaction at a young age (McCabe & Ricciardelli, 2004). The preference for a large and muscular body in boys starts to develop between the ages of 6 and 7 (Spitzer et al., 1999), and middle school boys have already internalized the importance of a muscular ideal and are likely to start adopting strategies to increase their muscle (McCabe & Ricciardelli, 2003; McCabe et al., 2002; Smolak et al., 2001; see also chap. 10, this volume).

MUSCULARITY IN DIFFERENT CULTURES

Both the theory of a crisis in masculinity in the West and the media theory predict that there would be a sharp difference in the drive for muscularity when Western and non-Western cultures are compared; this appears to be the case. Wide differences in the muscular ideal are found between Western and non-Western cultures, although there are exceptions (see Table 1.1 for a summary of findings).

Western Cultures

Men's dissatisfaction with their degree of muscularity is usually found to be greater in Western than in third world or traditional cultures (Yang et al., 2005). Nonetheless, there are exceptions to this rule, so the case should not be overstated (see Table 1.1). Pope, Gruber, et al. (2000) found that men

TABLE 1.1
Men's Muscle Dissatisfaction in Selected Cultures

Culture	Degree of dissatisfaction with muscularity	Reference
Western		
United States	Highest	Pope, Gruber, et al. (2000)
France	High	Pope, Gruber, et al. (2000)
Austria	High	Pope, Gruber, et al. (2000)
Anglo-Australians in Australia	Moderate	Mellor, McCabe, Ricciardelli, & Ball (2004)
Norway	Low	Storvoll, Strandbu, & Wichstrom (2005)
Non-Western		
Taiwan	Low	Yang, Gray, & Pope (2005)
Nigeria	Low	Balogun, Okonofua, & Balogun (1992)
Kenya	Very low	Campbell, Pope, & Filiault (2005)
Indigenous adolescents in Australia	Moderate	Mellor et al. (2004)
Samoa	High	Lipinski & Pope (2002)

from three different Western countries (Austria, France, and the United States) desired an additional 27 to 29 pounds of muscle added to their current physique, and these same men believed that women would prefer them to have about 30 pounds of added muscle. However, studies examining women's preferences for the male body suggest that women actually prefer a more "average" male body (Lynch & Zellner, 1999). Austrian women preferred a man who had 21 pounds less muscle than Austrian men's estimate of what the women would choose (Pope, Gruber, et al., 2000).

Men and women in the United States experience substantial dissatisfaction with their bodies. In particular, men are dissatisfied with the size of their muscles (Jacobi & Cash, 1994; Mishkind et al., 1986; Muris et al., 2005; Olivardia et al., 2004). Even when compared with another Western culture, Austria, U.S. male college students reported greater dissatisfaction with their bodies (Mangweth et al., 1997).

In two identical studies conducted 10 years apart, male adolescents in Norway were found to be quite polarized in their body image satisfaction ratings (Storvoll et al., 2005). In 1992, 2.65% of the young Norwegian men were extremely dissatisfied with their muscle tone, and 3.15% were extremely dissatisfied with their upper torso. Ten years later, in a comparable sample, the numbers had increased to 5.8% dissatisfied with their muscle tone and 5.8% with their upper torso. Perhaps even more remarkable were the figures from the other end of the continuum: In 1992, 13.2% of the boys were extremely satisfied with their muscle tone and 10.9% were extremely satisfied with their upper torso. By 2002, 18.6% of the subjects were extremely satisfied with their muscle tone and 17.5% were extremely satisfied with their upper torso. These findings are in sharp contrast to studies conducted in other Western cultures. In particular, muscle tone did not stand out in this study as a focus of dissatisfaction compared with height and facial features. The authors suggested that an increase in body mass index (BMI) over the 10-year period may be involved in the change (Storvoll et al., 2005). Such a change in BMI has taken place in other Western countries, however, without an increase in body satisfaction.

Non-Western Cultures

Although findings are somewhat mixed, research suggests that the presence of muscularity plays a limited role in mating or sexual attraction in non-Western cultures (Dotson, 1999).

Taiwanese men have a considerably smaller discrepancy than Western men between their own perceived muscularity and their estimate of women's preferred muscularity. Taiwanese men estimate a 5-pound difference between the average man and a woman's ideal man, whereas U.S. men estimate a 20-pound difference (Yang et al., 2005). Unlike men in Western societies, men from non-Western nations like Taiwan seem less prone to muscle dysmorphia and anabolic steroid use (Yang et al., 2005). For example, researchers have reported only a single case of muscle dysmorphia in Asia (Ung, Fones, & Ang, 2000; Yang et al., 2005). One example of the lack of emphasis on muscularity is that men in magazine advertisements in Taiwan are less likely to be partially undressed than men in U.S. magazines (Yang et al., 2005).

Kenyan male members of the Ariaal group, who have minimal exposure to Western culture, showed much less body dissatisfaction than men from the West (Campbell et al., 2005). In particular, these men showed very little discrepancy between what they perceived as the degree of muscularity preferred by women and that of the average Ariaal man. These Kenyan men, unlike many Western men, believed that women preferred a male body that represents the "average" man (Campbell et al., 2005). It should be noted that these men present a distinct physical type; they are tall and have an average BMI of 19 and a body fat percentage of 13. These findings are, however, compatible with the media exposure hypothesis and with the crisis in masculinity theory in that the continuing division of labor by gender and limited media influence coincide with a lack of emphasis on muscularity.

One study found that Nigerian women were more satisfied with their general muscle development than Nigerian men. However, both men and women evidenced more satisfaction than generally found in the West (Balogun et al., 1992).

Men in Samoa are strikingly similar to those in the United States and Europe in desiring much more muscular bodies (16–22 more pounds of muscle) than they in fact possess (Lipinski & Pope, 2002). Although they live in a nonindustrialized area, Samoans have been subject to political rule by Western nations, whose culture has been reflected in their media and ideals. This group stands out as an exception to the cultural theories presented in this chapter.

Australia is a developed country with both a White population and a non-White indigenous population. Although it would be expected that the White population would be more influenced by the drive for muscularity, the results are mixed. In one study, researchers found that indigenous adolescents were, as expected, less prone to body dissatisfaction than nonindigenous adolescents, even though indigenous Australians were more likely to be either overweight or underweight than nonindigenous Australian adolescents (Mellor et al., 2004). However, in a second study, indigenous adolescents were found to engage in more strategies to increase muscles than nonindigenous adolescents, despite being exposed to fewer media messages. The authors reported evidence that although the indigenous population may be less exposed to the media, the images they see may have a greater impact on them (McCabe, Ricciardelli, Mellor, & Ball, 2005).

The drive for thinness appears to have started in Western cultures and expanded to the less developed areas of the world, where rates of eating disorders are rising. Will the drive for muscularity for men now prominent in the West be exported in a similar way? The limited research in this area so far has provided very little evidence that such exportation has happened.

CONCLUSION

Over the past few decades, body dissatisfaction has been growing among U.S. women and men. For women, body dissatisfaction focuses primarily on thinness with less emphasis on muscularity, whereas male body dissatisfaction focuses primarily on muscularity. Most men hope to achieve muscle bulk, and most women prefer a thin, toned appearance.

Although there may be lingering evolutionary value placed on muscularity, the major reasons for the current drive for muscularity appear to be cultural. The drive for muscularity was once associated with the division of labor, but the muscular ideal may now be driven by a crisis in masculinity, prompting men who no longer rely on their muscular strength to turn to muscularity as a sign of their masculine appeal.

The increase in body dissatisfaction seen in men and women has developed in a complex cultural context involving a growing emphasis on physical beauty and youthful appearance, a belief that the body is malleable, an increase in the number of overweight and obese individuals, and changing roles for men and women. Whatever the cause of the increased interest in muscularity, this focus is clearly present in the media, which then magnify the value of muscles to attract consumers through multiple avenues. Unfortunately, men become more dissatisfied with their bodies when confronted with these muscular images, which are reinforced by parents and peers. Within this cultural context, the most psychologically vulnerable persons resort to extreme and dangerous measures to gain muscularity. The drive for muscularity appears to be culture bound and confined to Western culture, but there is some evidence that it may spread to the less industrialized world.

The study of culture and muscularity would benefit from future research in the following areas:

- *Studies of U.S. culture.* A strong muscular appearance in men and a toned appearance in women are valued in U.S. culture, but questions arise as to the relative value of muscularity compared with the value of other characteristics such as clear skin, thinness, height, and symmetrical features. Although muscularity is important, researchers must investigate how important it is compared with other physical attributes. An interesting subgroup within the culture is the female bodybuilding group; it would be interesting to explore how and why female bodybuilders value a body ideal that is so distinct from the mainstream U.S. cultural ideal.
- *Studies of subcultures in the United States.* How great is the drive for muscularity among U.S. subcultures? For example, are the Amish, who continue to have a gender-based division of labor and are isolated from the impact of the media and other aspects of the dominant culture, influenced by the drive for muscularity? Can a subculture be found in which the traditional roles of men and women have changed but the media have very little influence or, conversely, in which the media are influential but traditional roles have not changed?
- *Studies of other cultures.* Researchers know very little about the place of muscularity in other cultures. Currently, few research studies are available, some of which contradict the hypothesis that muscularity is valued only in the West and not in the less developed parts of the world. There is an opportunity for wideranging research, especially to explore the hypothesis that the ideal of muscularity will be exported to the underdeveloped world. For example, the muscular ideal seems to have taken hold in Samoa, but not in the rest of the developing world.

REFERENCES

Agliata, D., & Tantleff-Dunn, S. (2004). The impact of media exposure on males' body image. *Journal of Social and Clinical Psychology, 23,* 7–22.

Alasker, F. D. (1992). Pubertal timing, overweight, and psychological adjustment. *Journal of Early Adolescence, 12*, 396–419.

American Society for Aesthetic Plastic Surgery. (2002). *Cosmetic surgery national data bank—2001 statistics*. New York: Author.

Andersen, A. E., & DiDomenico, L. (1992). Diet vs. shape content of popular male and female magazines: A dose–response relationship to the incidence of eating disorders? *International Journal of Eating Disorders, 11*, 283–287.

Balogun, J. A., Okonofua, F. A., & Balogun, A. O. (1992). An appraisal of body image among Nigerian university students. *Perceptual and Motor Skills, 75*, 832–834.

Berscheid, E., Walster, E., & Bohrnstedt, G. (1973). The happy American body: A survey report. *Psychology Today, 7*, 119–131.

Betz, N. E., Mintz, L., & Speakmon, G. (1994). Gender differences in the accuracy of self-reported weight. *Sex Roles, 30*, 543–552.

Bordo, S. (1999). *The male body*. New York: Farrar, Straus & Giroux.

Brumberg, J. J. (1997). *The body project*. New York: Random House.

Cafri, G., & Thompson, J. K. (2004). Measuring male body image: A review of the current methodology. *Psychology of Men and Masculinity, 5*, 18–29.

Cafri, G., Thompson, J. K., Ricciardelli, L., McCabe, M., Smolak, L., & Yesalis, C. (2005). Pursuit of the muscular ideal: Physical and psychological consequences and putative risk factors. *Clinical Psychology Review, 25*, 215–239.

Campbell, B. C., Pope, H. G., & Filiault, S. (2005). Body image among Ariaal men from Northern Kenya. *Journal of Cross-Cultural Psychology, 26*, 371–379.

Cash, T. F., Cash, D. W., & Butters, J. W. (1982). "Mirror, mirror, on the wall . . . ?": Contrast effects and self-evaluations of physical attractiveness. *Personality and Social Psychology Bulletin, 9*, 351–358.

Cash, T. F., & Henry, P. E. (1994). Women's body images: The results of a national survey in the U.S.A. *Sex Roles, 33*, 19–28.

Cash, T. F., Winstead, B., & Janda, L. H. (1986). The great American shape-up. *Psychology Today, 24*, 30–37.

Choi, P. Y. L. (2000). *Femininity and the physically active woman*. London: Routledge.

Choi, P. Y. L. (2003). Muscle matters: Maintaining visible differences between women and men. *Sexualities, Evolution and Gender, 5*(2), 71–81.

Dixon, A. F., Halliwell, G., East, R., Wigivarajah, P., & Anderson, M. J. (2003). Masculine somatotype and hirsuteness as determinants of sexual attractiveness to women. *Archives of Sexual Behavior, 32*, 29–39.

Dotson, E. W. (1999). *Behold the man*. Binghamton, NY: Haworth Press.

Duggan, S. J., & McCreary, D. R. (2004). Body image, eating disorders and the drive for muscularity in gay and heterosexual men: The influence of media images. *Journal of Homosexuality, 47*(3–4), 45–58.

Etcoff, N. (1999). *Survival of the prettiest*. New York: Doubleday.

Faludi, S. (1999). *Stiffed*. New York: William Morrow.

Fisher, E., Dunn, M., & Thompson, J. K. (2002). Social comparison and body image: An investigation of body comparison processes using multidimensional scaling. *Journal of Social and Clinical Psychology, 21*, 566–579.

Flegal, K. M., Carroll, M. D., Ogden, C. L., & Johnson, C. L. (2002). Prevalence and trends in obesity among U.S. adults 1999–2000. *Journal of the American Medical Association, 288*, 1723–1727.

Frederick, D. A., Fessler, D. M. T., & Hazelton, M. G. (2005). Do representations of male muscularity differ in men's and women's magazines? *Body Image, 2*, 81–86.

Frederick, D. A., & Hazelton, M. G. (2003, May). *Muscularity as a communication signal.* Paper presented at the International Communications Association Conference, San Diego, CA.

Garner, D. M. (1997, January/February). The 1997 body image survey results. *Psychology Today, 30*, 30–44, 75–80, 84.

Goldfried, G. S., Harper, D., & Blouin, A. G. (1998). Are body builders at risk for an eating disorder? *Eating Disorders, 6*, 133–158.

Groesz, L. M., Levine, M. P., & Murnen, S. K. (2002). The effect of experimental presentations of thin media images on body satisfaction: A meta-analysis. *International Journal of Eating Disorders, 21*, 1–16.

Grogan, S., Williams, C., & Connor, M. (1996). The effects of viewing same-gender photographic models on body esteem. *Psychology of Women Quarterly, 20*, 569–575.

Grubner, G., & Gross, L. (1976). The scary world of the TV's heavy viewer. *Psychology Today, 10*, 41–45.

Hatoum, I. J., & Belle, D. (2004). Mags and abs: Media consumption and bodily concerns in men. *Sex Roles, 51*, 397–407.

Irving, L. M., Wall, M., Neumark-Sztainer, D., & Story, M. (2002). Steroid use among adolescents: Findings from Project EAT. *Journal of Adolescent Health, 30*, 243–252.

Jackson, L. A. (2002). Physical attractiveness: A socio-cultural perspective. In T. F. Cash & T. Pruzinsky (Ed.), *Body image: A handbook of theory, research and clinical practice* (pp. 13–21). New York: Guilford Press.

Jacobi, L., & Cash, T. F. (1994). In pursuit of the perfect appearance: Discrepancies among self-ideal percepts of multiple physical attributes. *Journal of Applied Social Psychology, 24*, 379–396.

Kalb, C. (1999, August 9). Our quest to be perfect. *Newsweek*, pp. 52–59.

Kindlundh, A. M. S., Hagekull, B., Isacson, D. G. L., & Nyberg, F. (2001). Adolescent use of anabolic-androgenic steroids and relations to self-reports of social, personality and health aspects. *European Journal of Public Health, 11*, 322–328.

Kirpatrick, S. W., & Sanders, D. M. (1978). Body image stereotypes: A developmental comparison. *Journal of Genetic Psychology, 132*, 87–95.

Klein, A. (1993). *Little big men.* Albany: State University of New York Press.

Krane, V., Choi, P. Y. L., Baird, S. M., Aimar, C. M., & Kauer, K. J. (2004). Living the paradox: Female athletes negotiate femininity and muscularity. *Sex Roles, 50*, 315–329.

Leit, R. A., Gray, J. J., & Pope, H. G. (2002). The media's representation of the ideal male body: A cause for muscle dysmorphia. *International Journal of Eating Disorders, 31,* 334–338.

Lipinski, J. P., & Pope, H. G. (2002). Body ideals in young Samoan men. *International Journal of Men's Health, 1,* 163–171.

Lorenzen, L. A., Grieve, F. G., & Thomas, A. (2004). Exposure to muscular male models decreases men's body satisfaction. *Sex Roles, 51,* 743–748.

Lynch, S. M., & Zellner, D. A. (1999). Figure preferences in two generations of men: The use of figure drawings illustrating differences in muscle mass. *Sex Roles, 40,* 833–843.

Maisey, D. S., Vale, E. L. E., Cornelissen, P. L., & Tovee, M. J. (1999). Characteristics of male attractiveness for women. *Lancet, 351,* 1500.

Mangweth, B., Pope, H. G., Hudson, J. I., Olivardia, R., Kinzl, J., & Biebl, W. (1997). Eating disorders in Austrian men: An intracultural and crosscultural comparison study. *Psychotherapy and Psychosomatics, 66,* 214–221.

McCabe, M. P., & Ricciardelli, L. A. (2003). Sociocultural influences on body image and body changes among adolescent boys and girls. *Journal of Social Psychology, 143,* 5–26.

McCabe, M. P., & Ricciardelli, L. A. (2004). Body image dissatisfaction among males across the lifespan: A review of past literature. *Journal of Psychosomatic Research, 56,* 675–685.

McCabe, M. P., Ricciardelli, L. A., & Banfield, S. (2001). Body image, strategies to change muscles and weight, and puberty: Do they impact on positive and negative affect among adolescent boys and girls? *Eating Behaviors, 2,* 129–149.

McCabe, M. P., Ricciardelli, L. A., & Finemore, J. (2002). The role of puberty, media and popularity with peers on strategies to increase weight, decrease weight, and increase muscle tone among adolescent boys and girls. *Journal of Psychosomatic Research, 52,* 145–153.

McCabe, M. P., Ricciardelli, L. A., Mellor, D., & Ball, K. (2005). Media influences on body image and disordered eating among indigenous adolescent Australians. *Adolescence, 40,* 115–127.

McCaulay, M., Mintz, L., & Glenn, A. A. (1988). Body image, self-esteem and depression proneness. *Sex Roles, 18,* 381–390.

McCreary, D. R., & Sasse, D. K. (2000). An exploration of the drive for muscularity in adolescent boys and girls. *Journal of American College Health, 48,* 297–304.

McKnight, J. (1999). Special feature on the uses and purposes of beauty. *Psychology, Evolution and Gender, 1,* 205–212.

Mellor, D., McCabe, M. P., Ricciardelli, L. A., & Ball, K. (2004). Body image importance and body dissatisfaction among indigenous Australian adolescents. *Body Image, 1,* 289–297.

Mishkind, M. E., Rodin, J., Silberstein, L. R., & Striegel-Moore, R. H. (1986). The embodiment of masculinity. *American Behavioral Scientist, 29,* 545–562.

Moore, D. C. (1990). Body image and eating behavior in adolescent boys. *American Journal of Diseases of the Child, 144*, 475–479.

Morry, M. M., & Staska, S. L. (2001). Magazine exposure: Internalization, self objectification, eating attitudes and body satisfaction in male and female university students. *Canadian Journal of Behavioral Science, 33*, 269–279.

Muris, P., Meesters, C., Van de Blom, W., & Mayer, B. (2005). Biological, psychological, and sociological correlates of body change strategies and eating problems in adolescent boys and girls. *Eating Behaviors, 6*, 11–22.

O'Koon, J. (1997). Attachment to parents and peers in late adolescence and their relationship with self-image. *Adolescence, 32*, 471–482.

Olivardia, R. (2001). Mirror, mirror on the wall, who's the largest of them all? The features and phenomenon of muscle dysmorphia. *Harvard Review of Psychiatry, 9*, 254–258.

Olivardia, R., Pope, H. G., Borowiecki, J. J., & Cohane, G. (2004). Biceps and body image: The relationship between muscularity and self-esteem, depression and eating disorder symptoms. *Men and Masculinity, 5*, 112–120.

Olivardia, R., Pope, H. G., & Hudson, J. I. (2000). Muscle dysmorphia in male weightlifters: A case–control study. *American Journal of Psychiatry, 157*, 1291–1296.

Page, R. M., & Allen, O. (1995). Adolescent perceptions of body weight and weight satisfaction. *Perceptual and Motor Skills, 81*, 81–82.

Pasman, L. T., & Thompson, J. K. (1988). Body image and eating disturbance in obligatory runners, obligatory weight lifters and sedentary individuals. *International Journal of Eating Disorders, 7*, 759–765.

Perkins, H. W., & Berkowitz, A. D. (1986). Perceiving the community norms of alcohol use among students: Some research implications for campus alcohol education programs. *International Journal of the Addictions, 21*, 961–976.

Petrie, T. A., Austin, L. J., Crowley, B. J., Helmcamp, A., Johnson, C. E., Lester, R., et al. (1996). Sociocultural explanations of attractiveness for males. *Sex Roles, 35*, 581–602.

Phillips, K. A. (1996). *The broken mirror: Understanding and treating body dysmorphic disorder.* New York: Oxford University Press.

Picket, T. C., Lewis, R. J., & Cash, T. F. (2005). Men, muscles and body image: Comparisons of competitive body builders, weight trainers and athletically active controls. *Journal of Sports Medicine, 39*, 217–222.

Pingitore, R., Spring, B., & Garfield, D. (1997). Gender differences in body satisfaction. *Obesity Research, 5*, 402–409.

Pope, H. G., Gruber, A. J., Choi, P., Olivardia, R., & Phillips, K. A. (1997). Muscle dysmorphia, an underrecognized form of body dysmorphic disorder. *Psychosomatics, 38*, 548–557.

Pope, H. G., Gruber, A. J., Mangweth, B., Bureau, B., deCol, C., Jouvent, R., et al. (2000). Body image perception among men in three countries. *American Journal of Psychiatry, 157*, 1297–1301.

Pope, H. G., Olivardia, R., Borowiecki, J. B., & Cohane, G. H. (2001). The growing commercial value of the male body: A longitudinal survey of advertising in women's magazines. *Psychotherapy and Psychosomatics, 70,* 189–192.

Pope, H. G., Olivardia, R., Gruber, A., & Borowiecki, J. (1999). Evolving ideals of male body image as seen through action toys. *International Journal of Eating Disorders, 26,* 65–72.

Pope, H. G., Phillips, K. A., & Olivardia, R. (2000). *The Adonis complex: The secret crisis of male body obsession.* New York: Free Press.

Ricciardelli, L. A., & McCabe, M. P. (2001). Self-esteem and negative affect as moderators of sociocultural influences on body dissatisfaction, strategies to decrease weight, and strategies to increase muscles among adolescent boys and girls. *Sex Roles, 44,* 189–207.

Ricciardelli, L. A., & McCabe, M. P. (2003a). A longitudinal analysis of the role of biopsychosocial factors in predicting body change strategies among adolescent boys. *Sex Roles, 48,* 349–359.

Ricciardelli, L. A., & McCabe, M. P. (2003b). Sociocultural and individual influences on muscle gain and weight loss strategies among adolescent boys and girls. *Psychology in the Schools, 40,* 209–224.

Ricciardelli, L. A., & McCabe, M. P. (2004). A biopsychosocial model of disordered eating and the pursuit of muscularity in adolescent boys. *Psychological Bulletin, 130,* 179–205.

Ricciardelli, L. A., McCabe, M. P., & Banfield, S. (2000). Body image and body change methods in adolescent boys: Role of parents, friends, and the media. *Journal of Psychosomatic Research, 49,* 189–197.

Siegel, J. M., Yancey, A. K., Aneshensel, C. S., & Schuler, R. (1999). Body image, perceived pubertal timing, and adolescent mental health. *Journal of Adolescent Health, 25,* 155–165.

Smolak, L., Levine, M. P., & Thompson, J. K. (2001). The use of the Sociocultural Attitudes Towards Appearance Questionnaire with middle school boys and girls. *International Journal of Eating Disorders, 29,* 216–223.

Spitzer, B. L., Henderson, K. A., & Zivian, M. T. (1999). Gender differences in population versus media body sizes: A comparison over four decades. *Sex Roles, 40,* 545–565.

Storvoll, E. E., Strandbu, A., & Wichstrom, L. (2005). A cross-sectional study of changes in Norwegian adolescents' body image from 1992 to 2002. *Body Image, 2,* 5–18.

Tantleff-Dunn, S., & Gokee, J. L. (2002). Interpersonal influences on body image development. In T. F. Cash & T. Pruzinsky (Eds.), *Body image: A handbook of theory, research and clinical practice* (pp. 108–116). New York: Guilford Press.

Thompson, J. K., & Tantleff, S. (1992). Female and male ratings of upper torso: Actual, ideal, and stereotypical conceptions. *Journal of Social Behavior and Personality, 7,* 345–354.

Thompson, S., Corwin, S., & Sargent, R. (1997). Ideal body size beliefs and weight concerns of fourth grade children. *International Journal of Eating Disorders, 21,* 279–284.

Thompson, S., Sargent, R., & Kemper, K. (1996). Black and white adolescent male perceptions of ideal body size. *Sex Roles, 34*, 391–406.

Tylka, T. L., Bergeron, D., & Schwartz, J. P. (2005). Development and psychometric evaluation of the Male Body Attitudes Scale (MBAS). *Body Image, 2*, 161–175.

Ulrich, C. F. (2005). *Ulrich's periodicals directory: A classified guide to a selected list of current periodicals foreign and domestic* (5th ed.). Oxford, England: Bowker.

Ung, E. K., Fones, C. S., & Ang, A. W. (2000). Muscle dysmorphia in a young Chinese man. *Annual Academy of Medicine, 29*, 135–137.

Vartanian, L., Giant, C. L., & Passino, M. (2001). Ally McBeal vs. Arnold Schwarzenegger? Comparing mass media, interpersonal feedback and gender as predictors of satisfaction with body thinness and muscularity. *Social Behavior and Personality, 27*, 711–724.

Vincent, M. A., & McCabe, M. P. (2000). Gender differences among adolescents in family, and peer influences on body dissatisfaction, weight loss, and binge eating behaviors. *Journal of Youth and Adolescence, 29*, 205–221.

Weeden, J., & Sabini, J. (2005). Physical attractiveness and health in Western societies: A review. *Psychological Bulletin, 131*, 654–657.

Williams, S. R. P., Goodfellow, J., Davies, B., Bell, W., McDowell, I., & Jaones, E. (2000). Somatotypes and angiographically determined atherosclerotic coronary artery disease in men. *American Journal of Human Biology, 12*, 128–138.

Yang, C.-F. J., Gray, P., & Pope, H. G. (2005). Male body image in Taiwan versus the west: Yanggang Zhiqi meets the Adonis complex. *American Journal of Psychiatry, 162*, 263–269.

Yelland, C., & Tiggemanm, M. (2003). Muscularity and the gay ideal: Body dissatisfaction and disordered eating in homosexual men. *Eating Behaviors: An International Journal, 4*, 107–116.

2

MUSCULARITY AND MASCULINITY IN THE UNITED STATES: A HISTORICAL OVERVIEW

LYNNE LUCIANO

In February 2005, publication of former American League baseball star Jose Canseco's tell-all memoir *Juiced* exposed not only Canseco's use of performance-enhancing drugs since the age of 20 but also the fact that steroids were "as prevalent in the late 1980s and 1990s as a cup of coffee" (Sheinin, 2005, p. A1) among his fellow players, including some of the most admired icons of America's national sport. Canseco's book propelled him to the top of the best-seller list and made him the darling of the Fox-and-ESPN media circuit. It also confirmed widespread suspicions that the sport's top stars had been enhancing performance, as well as body image, by using illegal drugs (Brown & Cohn, 2006).

Anabolic steroids work by stimulating cellular activities that build muscle and are used to boost athletic performance, endurance, and power. Steroids and other performance-enhancing substances like human growth hormone also increase lean body mass, leading to greater muscle definition. Thus, they are used not only to increase strength but also to produce the appearance of power by transforming athletes' physiques. These substances also carry significant health risks, including elevated estrogen levels; increased risk of cardiovascular disease, stroke, and prostate and pancreatic cancer; and unpredictable surges of aggressive behavior, known as "roid rage" (Dawson, 2001; Parssinen & Seppala, 2002). In extreme cases, withdrawal from steroid use has led to severe depression and even suicide (Kanayama, Cohane, Weiss, & Pope, 2003; Pope & Katz, 1990; Wilson, 2005). In spite of these widely publicized dangers, nearly 17 million adults, according to a national survey, use steroids and other performance-enhancing drugs. Of particular concern is their growing popularity among adolescents: 1.1 million young people between the ages of 12 and 17 have used potentially dangerous performance-enhancing supplements; so, too have 390,000 children between 10 and 14 years of age (Shaffer, 2002). Two-thirds of steroid abusers began using the drugs at age 16 or younger (Buckley et al., 1988).

Steroids are far from the only dangers men face in their quest for muscularity. As many as 1 million boys and men struggle with eating disorders, which have been shown to be strongly driven by body image concerns and are expected to increase as cultural and media pressures for "ideal" male bodies intensify (Labre, 2002; Scott, Wagner, & Barlow, 1996; Wertheim, 1992). By the early 1990s, doctors were describing a dysmorphic disorder, initially called *reverse anorexia nervosa* and later referred to as *muscle dysmorphia*, which was characterized by a pervasive belief that no matter how huge they became, these men continued to see themselves as small and puny. To counteract this image, many engaged in obsessive behaviors like excessive weight lifting and rigid preoccupation with diet; a few even gave up lucrative professions to take jobs at gymnasiums, where they had full-time access to weight lifting facilities (Olivardia, Pope, & Hudson, 2000). Men who fail to achieve body image ideals through exercise, diet, or chemicals may turn to cosmetic surgery, using silicone implants to create the illusion, if not the reality, of muscular perfection.

Why are potentially damaging body-enhancing behaviors on the increase among U.S. men? On its face, the answer is fairly straightforward: There has always been a strong link between muscularity and masculinity in U.S. culture. Yet muscularity has had different meanings at different times in history, reflecting larger cultural, social, and economic trends. It has served as an allegory for national strength in troubled times; as a class indicator, distinguishing middle-class men from those in the working class; as a means of definitively setting men apart from women and alleviating fears of feminization; as an indicator of self-discipline; and as a form of self-commodification in a culture defined by consumerism. In postwar America, the most important factors in the pursuit of male muscularity have been the shift in the gender balance of power brought about by the women's movement; pressures arising from structural changes in the U.S. job market, especially after the 1960s; and the imperative for projecting a youthful, fit, and attractive image in a profoundly image-conscious society shaped by an unprecedented proliferation of consumerism. This chapter examines the effects of each factor on male self-image and the changing ideals regarding the muscular male body.

MAKING MUSCLES RESPECTABLE: 19TH-CENTURY ORIGINS

Strength has always been prized in the United States, whose untamed frontier and wilderness validated the strong and rugged man. Immediately after the Civil War, strongmen were popular attractions throughout the country. However, they were largely regarded as spectacles that few ordinary men would seek to emulate. Yet in 1893, when the historian Frederick Jackson Turner declared the U.S. frontier officially closed, he was proclaiming the end of a historical era and also the end of a psychological one, in which Americans had the opportunity to test themselves against an unforgiving wilderness (Turner, 1996). Turner's proclamation paralleled growing concerns about the stifling effects of urbanization on manliness and a concomitant need to find substitutes for the more strenuous outdoor pursuits of earlier times. Crowded into teeming cities, removed from fresh air and regular exercise, Americans became obsessed with fitness and athleticism as antidotes to the debilitating effects of overcivilization. Competitive sports and exercise were expected to cultivate not only healthy bodies but strong character and discipline—to shape citizens for the modern nation (Green, 1984; White, 1992).

The search for suitable outlets for suppressed masculinity conflicted with entrenched attitudes about athletic activities based on sheer strength, like boxing and weight lifting. For most middle-class men, self-esteem and personal identity were derived primarily from nonphysical sources, most notably their roles as breadwinners. It was working-class men who were most likely to feel that they needed to prove themselves through more rudimentary expressions of manhood linked to displays of toughness and raw power—images based on "bulging muscles and naked virility" (Gorn, 1986, p. 187).

These concerns were overridden by anxiety about the enervating effects of modern life, which were most likely to affect the middle class: Workers, after all, sweated enough on their jobs. Sports not only offered a healthy outlet for physical exercise but were credited with channeling energy away from less uplifting pursuits, like crime (Green, 1984). Healthy fatigue from exercising the body was also expected to help men avoid the vices of masturbation and homosexuality, and served as a weapon against the greatest disorder of the newly urbanized society: nervous exhaustion (Green, 1984). Athletics were linked to the middle-class goal of success in the business community. Playing football helped young men "learn to be aggressive while controlling their tempers," a trait that would presumably transfer to the business arena; learning to lose gracefully would likewise teach them to "accept life's setbacks" (Gorn & Goldstein, 1993, p. 107). Sports also offered the clearest possible validation of masculinity by presenting an arena in which men could "prove . . . they were men, and not women or homosexuals" (Kimmel, 1994, p. 28).

Fears about feminization were related to the sedentary urban workplace, where men sat in offices performing dull, "feminine" paper-pushing tasks that sapped male vigor and virility (Kimmel, 1994). Feminization was also blamed on the predominance of female influence in the upbringing of young boys, a result of the increased presence of women as classroom teachers and boys' separation from paternal influence as men's jobs moved out of the home and into factories and offices. By the end of the 19th century, the model for male bodies was muscular bulk, replacing earlier ideals of self-disciplined inner strength represented in lean, ascetic bodies, as well as the short-lived Gilded Age model of prosperous male corpulence (Rotundo, 1993).

Physical strength was not only a virtue but a duty, necessary to preserve the integrity and overall health of the nation. In a tough new imperialistic world, the United States confronted a dangerous international arena in which only the strongest could survive. Dangers lurked both abroad and at home: Waves of poor immigrants from eastern and southern Europe flocking into U.S. cities between 1880 and 1910 to provide labor for the industrial revolution raised concerns about preserving "native"—that is, Anglo-Saxon—racial superiority. In 1916, Madison Grant, author of *The Passing of the Great Race*, argued that superior blonde northern European stock was being bred out by "lower" elements, a calamity that could spell the end of democracy if not stopped (Grant, 1916/1970). Theodore Roosevelt incorporated similar thinking in his exhortations in favor of the strenuous life, arguing that the United States needed to reconstruct "a thoroughly manly race—a race of strong, virile character" to defend and develop democracy (Testi, 1995, p. 1520). Muscles were placed in the service of ensuring supremacy of superior "native" American stock over "virile but inferior" European races (Testi, 1995).

The timing was right, in this hypermasculinized milieu, for the arrival of Prussian strongman Eugen Sandow, who came to the United States in the 1890s via a vaudeville act. At first, Sandow was considered too muscular by a U.S. public enamored with well-proportioned classical ideals. Undismayed by his initially cool reception, this irrepressible showman flaunted his image instead of toning it down, selling nearly nude photos of himself wearing only a fig leaf. Sandow's success came not only from self-promotion but from canny marketing of products and ideas in tune with the times. Underusing muscles was blamed for a host of ills, all of which could be overcome by gaining control over one's body. To help men reach this goal, Sandow marketed food supplements, the first to do so. By capitalizing on the link between health and exercise, Sandow transformed fitness into a curative measure able to effect actual healing (Chapman, 1994).

Sandow was soon joined in his aggressive promotion of bodybuilding by Bernarr MacFadden, who launched *Physical Culture* magazine in 1899. *Physi-*

cal Culture became the body-development bible of a generation of boys and young men, promoting "fitness, clean living, and abolition of sexual prudery"—the latter an admonition that fell on responsive ears, as turn-of-the-century America abandoned Victorian prudery and adopted more open attitudes about sexuality (Chapman, 1994, p. 76). Although, like Sandow, McFadden held out the promise of muscular magnificence, marketing himself through nude photographs well into his 60s, he gave an added benefit to physical culture by emphasizing its ability to overcome men's dreaded "lack of vigor"—an Edwardian euphemism for impotence. Proper diet and exercise promised to convey sexual benefits like long-lasting erections and "a perpetual zest for physical love," forging an enduring connection between muscularity and male sex appeal (Whorton, 1982, p. 273).

KICKING SAND IN THE FACE OF MALE WEAKNESS: INTO THE 20TH CENTURY

Middle-class interest in physical culture dwindled as mass culture offered other sources of entertainment, especially pastimes that men and women could enjoy together. Between 1890 and 1925, traditional "calling" courtship patterns were replaced by a dating culture that allowed young men and women to seek activities and avenues of companionship outside the home (Bailey, 1988). As the appeal of strictly masculine activities like bodybuilding declined, cultivation of extreme muscularity sank back to its earlier proletarian social position. Criticized for being "tawdry and self-indulgent," most likely to attract men "with short-person complexes" or "sexually suspect voyeurs," bodybuilding languished on the fringes of athleticism (Klein, 1993a, p. 38). It did, however, appeal to teenage boys, sensitive about their gawky, changing bodies and in need of self-validation and a sense of personal power: For them, bodybuilding promised better lives through better bodies. They found a mentor in the best-known bodybuilder of the early 20th century, Charles Atlas.

Born Angelo Siciliano in 1893, Atlas, although famous for his promotion of ideal manhood through strength, promoted himself more as a visual object than as a strongman. Before promoting his own courses, Atlas worked for years as a model, a career at which he excelled because he was strong enough to hold flexed poses for sustained periods. Atlas's trademark advertisements showing a spindly young man humiliated by sand kicked in his face are well-known even today and promoted not only the ideal of physical strength but self-confidence and sex appeal. By the 1950s, the Charles Atlas Course, based on a muscle-building system Atlas called Dynamic Tension, had been translated into seven languages, as well as Braille (Quindlen, 1982).

Atlas's career coincided with a reinterpretation of the term *shaping up*, which entered common speech in the 1880s and initially referred not to people but to cattle, which were "shaped up" by fattening before slaughter. By the 1920s, when Atlas was winning prizes for shaping up his body, the term had come to refer to physical fitness (Mathews, 1951). Nineteenth-century gymnasts had promoted the idea of reshaping the body to classical Greek proportions, but their goal had been to enhance athletic performance by making the body more graceful and powerful. Atlas took body reshaping a step further, into a realm of competition in which no skill was developed or enhanced; the body was shaped for purely visual ends. However, although he counted a few celebrities and businessmen among his disciples, the association of extreme muscularity with vanity and proletarian status limited Atlas's appeal to middle-class men (Chapman, 1994).

Publicized primarily through annual competitions like Mr. Universe and Mr. America contests, bodybuilding maintained a following throughout the 1930s, 1940s, and 1950s but was little more than a cult. Muscle men were viewed as strange anomalies, on the one hand grotesquely masculine with their bulging muscles and on the other hand oddly feminine with their posturing and anxious gazing into mirrors. In 1939, when the modern-day Muscle Beach cult was born in southern California, it was described as "the most strenuous, and often the funniest, beach in the world" (Sayre, 1957, p. 38); the Chamber of Commerce wasn't sure whether to be proud of Muscle Beach or embarrassed by it (Sayre, 1957). In the same year, the first Mr. America contest was held. Six years later, Joe and Ben Weider formed the International Federation of Bodybuilders to oversee all contests (and to provide a source of income for bodybuilders). In 1940, at the age of 18, Joe Weider had scraped together $7 to begin publishing a 12-page magazine called *Your Physique,* which within 1 year had 400 subscribers and earned him $10,000. Although over the next 30 years some top bodybuilding events drew thousands of spectators, winners rarely earned more than $1,000. In 1976, when Arnold Schwarzenegger took first place in the Mr. Olympia contest, he won $1,500. Before the release of Schwarzenegger's 1977 film *Pumping Iron,* surveys of sports fans showed that bodybuilding ranked a dismal 35th in national popularity—just behind tractor pulling (Bebbington, 1993; Darling, 1985; D. Davis, 1996).

Ten years later, purses of $50,000 had become common, and spectators were paying hundreds of dollars for a single ticket. An empire of fitness magazines and products had sprung up, and workout emporia like Gold's Gym had blossomed from a single shabby room into more than 400 worldwide franchises. The biggest change was that the cultivation of muscularity had moved outside the realm of bodybuilding and become a national pastime, engaging millions of ordinary men in a newly legitimized quest for muscular perfection (D. Davis, 1996; Goldberg, 1975).

Arnold Schwarzenegger's success was a result of his impressive physical attributes and rigorous self-discipline, but his personality and lifestyle were equally important in transforming the public image of bodybuilders.

Schwarzenegger was blatantly heterosexual, with women clamoring in his wake wherever he went. Recognizing the posing and flexing of bodybuilding competition as "pure theater," Schwarzenegger capitalized on it to his own benefit and that of his sport, while wisely emphasizing its health and fitness benefits (Darling, 1985; Hall & Hall, 1977). In addition, his success was shaped by a juxtaposition of several major social and cultural currents.

If Schwarzenegger had come along in the 1950s instead of the 1970s, it is doubtful that he would have had the same influence. Recalling his obsession with weight lifting as a 16-year-old in the early 1950s, a New York businessman described weight lifting in those days as "an act of male vanity" that he and his friends did because they wanted to look good, adding that "of course, none of us would admit that. Not in 1952" (B. Lieberman, personal communication, August 17, 1999). Society's views about excessive muscularity were reflected in popular culture: Films, for example, rarely featured muscle-bound male stars except in genres like pseudohistorical "spear and sandal" epics. Overwhelmingly, audiences preferred lanky, tall men with "nonostentatious" bodies (Malone, 1979).

If blatant muscularity held little appeal for most Americans, national defense concerns thrust fitness into the spotlight. In Cold War America, fears of being "soft" on communism were transposed to the soft physical condition of Americans, revealed by national fitness tests that showed U.S. school children lagging behind European and Japanese schoolchildren in flexibility, strength, and overall fitness (Kraus & Hirschland, 1953, 1954; Silver, 1962). After the humiliation of the 1957 Soviet launch of *Sputnik*, the revelation of Americans as lagging both academically and physically behind their Russian archenemies was a jolting wakeup call. Programs to bolster physical education in schools began during the Eisenhower administration and came to full fruition under the stewardship of John F. Kennedy, who declared the physical vigor of U.S. citizens a precious national resource and a necessary weapon in the Cold War (Kennedy, 1960).

Despite Kennedy's rhetoric and Cold War fears, fitness remained a low priority for Americans throughout the 1960s. One reason for this lack of interest was the cultural climate shaped by the Sixties Generation, the idealistic cohort of baby boomers who spent the decade trying to find themselves through drugs and other semimystical experiences and vocally protesting the preeminence of technology and the military—especially the Vietnam War. As television brought the war into their living rooms, millions of Americans recoiled against its destruction and bloodshed. Many middle-class young men tried to distance themselves from the war not only by protesting against it and in large measure avoiding having to serve in it but also by looking as unlike fighting Marines and soldiers as possible. Returning veterans, casting about for explanations for the ill treatment many of them felt they received at the hands of an ungrateful nation, blamed what many saw as a growing feminization of society for negating their sacrifices on the battlefield. Masculinity seemed no longer to be valued or appreciated in a society in which young men walked around with flowers in their hair. Just as long hair distinguished the antiwar college student from the macho Marine, rejection of overt muscularity distanced him from traditional male displays of strength and power and their negative association with violence.

Conditioning the body to play sports was also associated with basic training and preparation for war (Jeffords, 1994; Wheeler, 1984). The ideal 1960s male body tended toward leanness (which was in vogue for both sexes), reflecting not only a rejection of aggressive masculinity as expressed through muscularity but an asceticism that blended naturally with the popularity of vegetarianism, meditation, and macrobiotic diets; lean, slim bodies became badges of "living lightly" in an environmentally conscious society (Belasco, 1989). In this milieu, grumbled a disgruntled gym owner, "lousy bodies became a status thing" (Overend, 1981). By the latter part of the decade, however, perceptions about the desirability of muscularity were changing, impelled in part by feminism.

NO PECS, NO SEX[1]: MEN, WOMEN, AND MUSCULARITY

In 1963, publication of Betty Friedan's book *The Feminine Mystique* launched the modern women's movement, with significant social and economic consequences for U.S. men. Energized by the most important social movement of the century, civil rights, feminism challenged male hegemony and traditional notions of masculinity in both bedroom and boardroom. Workplace equality and women's access to equal pay put particular pressure on men, especially in the professions and other highly paid segments of the economy.

The movement of women into formerly male domains, especially in the workplace, was paralleled by the emergence of another marginalized group in the U.S. cultural mainstream: Within the gay community, good looks were traditionally tied to cultivating and maintaining a youthful, fit body. Gay men were also more likely to wear stylish, form-fitting clothing that, especially in the immediate postwar period of the 1940s and 1950s, set them distinctly apart from the somber wardrobes of America's corporate men. These trends were largely confined to gay neighborhoods and the gay community through the 1960s. In the wake of the 1969 Stonewall riot in Greenwich Village, gay activism brought homosexuality out of the closet and diminished the demarcation between gay and straight lifestyles. Shortly after Stonewall, and partly inspired by it, a tough, virile new look emerged in the gay community, and jeans, T-shirts, and construction boots made many gay men

---

[1]"No Pecs, No Sex" was the opening line in a 1986 flyer promoting the upscale David Barton gymnasium in Manhattan, New York.

look more macho than their straight counterparts while simultaneously revealing and eroticizing the male body (Chauncey, 1994; Edwards, 1990).

The backlash against stereotypes of homosexual effeminacy included an explosion of interest in bodybuilding, which could hardly be classified solely as a gay activity because it so clearly articulated classic masculine physical attributes of strength and muscularity. By the 1990s, Christopher Cakebread, a professor of advertising at Boston University, cited the prevalence of straight men "bulging all over the place, showing off their gym bodies" on Boston's streets, a development that led him to conclude that "the gay marketplace [had] . . .trickled down to the heteros" (quoted in Shaw, 1994, p. C6).

Paralleling the increased visibility of gays was the emergence of an even larger demographic: singles culture, fueled by rising divorce rates, later age of first marriage, and changing attitudes about sexual freedom—the so-called sexual revolution of the 1960s and 1970s. Initially, single men and women flocked to bars for their mating and dating rituals. Yet as disillusionment and AIDS undermined the appeal of such frankly predatory gathering places, singles turned to a more wholesome venue: the health club.

The health club explosion of the 1970s represented a sharp break with earlier gym and health club concepts. Gyms were typically low-rent, smoke- and sweat-saturated hangouts for boxers and bodybuilders, neither of whom represented a sizable population group, and certainly not within the middle class. Major cities had health and athletic clubs, the latter generally by invitation only and serving the upper crust. Health clubs were described as "Turkish baths with trimmings," more like vacation spas than serious exercise centers (Lefferts, 1958). Their function was primarily to help overworked executives relax; sunlamps and massage tables were more in evidence than barbells. The general view, promulgated by many proprietors, was that exercise was a necessary evil, to be made as palatable as possible by reasonably pleasant surroundings and the congenial company of fellow sufferers (Gehman, 1957). Proprietors were supported in their attitudes by physicians, who, although recommending some exercise as beneficial, especially for harried executives, warned against "excessive" overexertion. Harvard nutritionist Frederick Stare (1967), an outspoken advocate of men's fitness, recommended light gardening or fishing as desirable exercise activities. Leonard Larsen, chair of physical education at New York University, who confessed to indulging in a vigorous 10-minute daily workout, cautioned that for the less fit, average man, a "few minutes of [daily] passive exercise at his desk," followed by a sauna, were sufficient (Gilroy, 1952, p. 12). As for the pursuit of overt muscularity, cardiologist Frank Foster suggested that the most important physical needs for the average young man were "muscles sufficient for a firm handshake" (Foster, 1964, p. 15). Health clubs were havens of middle-class men—and men only—whose reasons for joining had less to do with health than with social interaction: Instead of sweating with free weights, members were likely to lounge in steam rooms and conduct business transactions.

The glitzy new health clubs that emerged as part of the fitness revolution were no longer male-only preserves and quickly became popular mating-and-dating venues. In the quick-image bar scene, potential mates were judged by facial attractiveness and the stylishness of their clothing. In the health club, judgment centered on the condition of their bodies. Working out offered compelling benefits in the form of healthier and more attractive bodies and, by extension, heightened sex appeal: Even if a prospective mate was not captivated by a man's intelligence and wit, advised one fitness advocate, she would be "less inclined to kick you out of bed if you're toned and muscular" (Geist, 1984, p. L25).

But exactly how muscular did women expect men to be? Women's preferences typically reflect a universal perception formalized by psychologist William Sheldon in his 1940 book *Varieties of Human Physique* (Sheldon, 1940/1970). Sheldon identified three basic body types: the endomorph, who tended toward fat; the more muscular middle-of-the-road mesomorph; and the thinner, more slightly built ectomorph. Sheldon did not regard these categories as merely physical: Despite lack of any empirical support, he attached personality traits to each body type. The endomorph's rounded shape suggested positive qualities like warm-heartedness and conviviality but was also associated with greed, sluggishness, and gluttony. The thin ectomorph was likely to be intelligent, sensitive, and ambitious but also tended toward nervousness and hypersensitivity (Jackson, 1992; Well & Siegel, 1982). Nearly everything about the V-shaped mesomorph, with his broad arms and upper trunk, small buttocks, and moderate muscularity, evoked positive responses, especially among women (Maida & Armstrong, 2004). However, women have not been found to respond positively to the hypermuscular Atlas-type physique: In a 1975 survey, only 1% responded positively to this type of male body, and 2 decades later, despite the gym-and-fitness revolution and the mainstreaming of bodybuilding among middle-class men, they still gave top ranking to male bodies that were "medium with moderate muscle mass" and ranked "competition bodies" only slightly above significantly overweight ones (Frederick, Fessler, & Haselton, 2005; Lavrakas, 1975; Pertschuk & Trisdorfer, 1994).

Long subjected to the objectification of the critical male gaze, women had become more openly judgmental about male physical appearance by the 1970s. Heightened female expectations about male body image were reflected in personal advertising, which proliferated in the 1980s as the singles culture expanded. I conducted an informal survey of personal advertisements that appeared in the upscale magazine *Los Angeles* between January of 1982 and December of 1989. I reviewed 3,370 personal advertisements placed by women seeking men, of whom 1,035 (31%) specified desired male physical characteristics. I reviewed 4,966 personal advertisements placed in the *Los Angeles*

Times by women between June 1995 and September 1995, and 1,679 (33 %) specified desired male physical characteristics. One-third of women's ads "in search of" men specified desired physical qualities, among the most frequently cited of which were "fit," "trim," and "muscular" My findings revealed that women, generally believed to be much more concerned with men's financial prospects than their physical attributes, did, in fact, care about appearance. Men were evidently not unaware of these female preferences: Although women were likely to describe themselves as thinner than their actual weight in personal advertisements, men tended to describe their weight as above average (A. E. Andersen, Woodward, Spalder, & Koss, 1993). Women's demands were driven not only by a sense of feminist egalitarianism resulting from the women's movement but also by women's gains in financial independence: As feminist Gloria Steinem wryly observed, attractive women are less likely to date "potbellied men . . . thirty years older than they [are] when there is no economic advantage to doing so" (quoted in Agins, 1994, p. A1). Of perhaps even greater significance was a seismic sociocultural shift that greatly increased the importance of image and self-presentation: the emergence of the Me Generation.

MUSCULARITY AND THE ME GENERATION

In 1981, psychologist and social researcher Daniel Yankelovich reflected that people in the United States were operating under a set of "new rules" in which individual desires and needs superseded those of nation, community, and even family. Two years earlier, in 1979, historian Christopher Lasch proclaimed that the United States had become characterized by a "culture of narcissism." The individualism and self-actualization ideals of the 1960s, according to Lasch, in combination with an increasingly hedonistic consumerism, had displaced traditional notions of sober self-denial, replacing them with a narcissistic focus on the self. A key component of this new self-consciousness was that individuals in the United States judged themselves not only against others but through others' eyes, a perspective that enormously elevated the importance of image as projected through possessions and physical appearance and created a sense of perpetual unease and unfulfillment (Lasch, 1979).

The term *pathological narcissism* was first used by Sigmund Freud at the turn of the century. Narcissism exists in everyone but becomes pathological when associated with unrealistic expectations and preoccupations (Lasch, 1984). Narcissism, although manifesting itself externally in behavior that appears egoistic, is actually rooted in feelings of insecurity and inferiority. The fourth edition of the *Diagnostic and Statistical Manual of Mental Disorders* (DSM–IV) identifies narcissism as a "pervasive pattern of grandiosity [and] need for admiration" that begins in early adulthood (American Psychiatric Association, 1994, p. 661). Characteristics of the narcissist include an exaggerated sense of self-importance; a need for excessive admiration; and "preoccupation with fantasies of unlimited success, power, brilliance, beauty, and ideal love" (p. 661), thereby forging a link between body image and self-esteem.

The Me Generation—so named by journalist Tom Wolfe in 1976—did not regard itself as self-centered so much as taking control in a world that had become unpredictable and complex (Wolfe, 1976). American men were especially at risk for feeling off balance and insecure as they found themselves in the unaccustomed position of competing with women for jobs just as jobs were vanishing in the face of a tidal wave of foreign competition and a shrinking U.S. economy.

In 1971, the United States experienced a negative balance of trade for the first time in the 20th century. Two years later, in 1973, the OPEC oil embargo shocked Americans into the realization that they could no longer arbitrarily order events in the world, even among smaller and weaker countries. By mid-decade, Japanese and European displacement of U.S. dominance in major industries like automobiles and electronics eliminated hundreds of thousands of well-paid blue- and white-collar jobs. The fallout from this economic meltdown continued into the 1980s, ending a virtually unbroken 30-year span of unparalleled prosperity and upward mobility and leaving Americans bewildered and fearful. Hardest hit were those most accustomed to hegemony in the workplace—White men. Taking control of one's body became a metaphor for taking control of one's life: Going to the health club transcended mere physical goals, offering moral, psychological, and spiritual rewards. It also offered economic benefits.

Studies have indicated that physical attractiveness affects hiring, salary, and career success for both men and women. Attractive employees (and attractive people in general) tend to be perceived as smarter, more socially competent, and even more trustworthy than their less-attractive counterparts (Eagly, Ashmore, Makhijani, & Longo, 1991; Mulford, Orbell, Shatto, & Stockard, 1998; Patzer, 1985). Good-looking men consistently earn more than average-looking ones, who in turn earn more than homely ones (Frieze, Olson, & Russell, 1991). In the downsizing corporate world of the turbulent 1970s, "attractive" increasingly meant "young looking": As companies ruthlessly streamlined their operations and hiring and job opportunities shriveled away, so, too, reported *The New York Times* in 1996, did "a few institutions of another type: the C.E.O. belly . . . and wizened Walter Cronkite face of experience" (Spindler, 1996, p. III-8). In the tough new U.S. workplace, it became essential not only to be qualified for the job but to look as if one were, and the applicant best able to present himself or herself as youthful and dynamic—attributes effectively signaled by a muscular, fit body—was the one most likely to get hired (Harrison & Bluestone, 1988; Maccoby, 1976; Sampson, 1995).

In 1986, *The New Republic* announced that next to jogging, weight lifting had become the second most popular U.S. recreational sport (Sullivan, 1986). On a professional level, bodybuilding was still confined to a relatively small, mostly working-class elite of devotees. However middle-class men had also become committed to developing muscularity not so much to be strong as to look strong, a goal that Edward W. L. Smith, an expert in the psychology of weight lifting, called "self-image actualization" (Smith, 1989). In an age of diminishing expectations in many conventional areas of male self-esteem, muscles conveyed a sense of power even if real power was lacking, allowing ordinary men, as one personal trainer stated, to consider themselves "part of the warrior class without ever putting [themselves] in danger" (Brubach, 1993, p. 32).

The historian Daniel Boorstin was among the first to recognize the importance of image making in U.S. culture; in his 1962 book *The Image: Or, What Happened to the American Dream*, Boorstin described image as "a studiously crafted . . . profile of an individual, institution, corporation, product or service (p. 186)" whose effectiveness lies in its appeal to the senses. In an image-driven society, good qualities, whether they belong to products or people, are insufficient in themselves: Their value lies in how vividly and effectively they are displayed. In a nation beguiled by consumerist display, the external self becomes the ultimate commodity, a symbol of its owner's worth and status (Ewen & Ewen, 1992).

Bodies have not only become more visible culturally; they are much more visible overall. Impelled in part by more open dialogue about sexuality, marketing of the nearly nude male body has been instrumental in male body objectification. The origins of this trend can be traced to the revolutionary 1980s advertising introduced by Calvin Klein men's underwear. Before the 1980s, underwear manufacturers and advertisers emphasized features like wash-and-wearability calculated to appeal to the person—most likely a woman—likely to be doing the washing and ironing. Stressing benefits like "seat room" and perspiration absorption promoted underwear on the basis not of sex appeal but of functionality. Live models were rarely used; ads relied on simple line drawings and color sketches showing men in modest briefs and undershirts, as if to separate the half-clad male body as completely as possible from the product.

Calvin Klein's revealing displays of muscle-bound young men was a radical departure from this long-standing formula, because it flatly equated underwear with sex (something European manufacturers had been doing all along). Jockey had actually preempted the sex appeal approach in 1981 with ads featuring Baltimore Oriole pitcher Jim Palmer wearing seductively tight briefs, but the photographs were discreetly airbrushed. Klein's ads showed far less restraint, beginning a trend toward much more graphic and widespread exposure of the male body.

Harvard Medical School researchers who examined advertisements in popular women's magazines like *Glamour* and *Cosmopolitan* over a 40-year period discovered that although the percentage of women portrayed by the magazines in a "state of undress" had stayed relatively constant over time, the percentage of men so portrayed rose from "virtually zero" to surpass that of women by the 1990s (Cromie, 2005; Swint, 2000).

Along with greater exposure have come more exacting standards for exposed male bodies, upping the ante for muscularity. Sports and fitness magazines, which often market themselves as primarily concerned with health, stress the rewards of attaining "perfect" bodies and provide definitive images, like the ubiquitous "six-pack" abs that adorn their covers, against which men, and especially adolescents, are likely to measure themselves (Botta, 2003). Critics of the objectification of women's bodies point out that the average weights of *Playboy* centerfolds and Miss America contestants are far below those of average U.S. women, but male bodies are now subject to similar objectification, especially with regard to muscularity. In contrast to women, whose body image issues are likely to center on shedding pounds, men tend to see themselves as smaller and less muscular than they really are and seek to add, rather than shed, bulk (C. Davis, Karvinen, & McCreary, 2005; McCreary & Sasse, 2000). Male centerfolds in *Playgirl* magazine have lost approximately 12 pounds of fat and gained 27 pounds of muscle over the past 25 years, with some of these models displaying levels of muscular development almost impossible to achieve without the use of steroids (Leit, Pope, & Gray, 2001). Even male mannequins have acquired more muscular builds since the 1990s (Olivardia, 2002).

Television is an even more influential source of image making, selecting male characters for good looks and muscular bodies, thus sending negative messages about men who don't measure up to those standards. A 2003 content analysis of 27 prime-time television situation comedies that focused on 75 main male characters showed negative portrayals of heavy or fat characters. For that matter, heavier men were less likely to even have roles on these shows (Fouts & Vaughn, 2003). The messages sent by this image-driven selection process do not go unnoticed: When shown advertisements featuring muscular men, men were more likely to express discontent with their own bodies in follow-up assessments than men who were not shown this type of advertising (Fawkner & McMurray, 2003; Leit, Gray, & Pope, 2002).

Although the media tend to focus on young men, older men also confront issues of body image and especially muscularity, which, like leanness, becomes harder to maintain with aging. For men in search of a quick fix, body parts that stubbornly resist workouts and weight routines, like pectorals and calves, can be surgically contoured with silicone implants. Originally developed to correct deformities resulting from birth defects or trauma, calf and chest implants were initially used most commonly by transsexuals in search of more feminine bodies; the muscularity revolution of the 1980s gave them heterosexual legitimacy (Novack, 1991; Schwade, 1993). Chest implants, teardrop-shaped translucent silicone wedges inserted into 2-inch incisions under the armpits, have been called "the male version of breast implants" (Personal communication, M. Rosenstein, April 12, 1995). Calf implants, muscle-shaped silicone forms that come in a variety of sizes, are laid over calf muscles. Undersized buttocks can also be augmented with disc-shaped implants (Courtiss, 1991; Farnham, 1996; Mladick, 1991).

Implants serve no functional purpose; they simply masculinize the body. They do not enhance athletic performance, only athletic appearance, and indeed are likely to hamper performance and decrease function. Implants are banned by the International Federation of Body Builders, which uses X-rays to detect them (Aiache, 1991). Dr. Melvin Bircoll of Beverly Hills, designer of the chest implant, identified the most likely candidates as aging baby boomers who "had always had a pretty good build, but as [they've] gotten older and just can't work out [they've] gotten flabby in the chest and it really looks terrible" (Sherrill, 1992, p. F2). The best candidate, concurred another surgeon, is "the guy who promises not to lift a weight. . . who just wants to strut up and down the beach and look good" (Yoffe, 1990, p. 72). It is not only men reluctantly entering middle age who are candidates for physical enhancement through the scalpel; by the 1990s, *The New York Times* reported that a "boom in teen-age plastic surgery" was luring teenage boys into "beefing themselves up with chin and buttocks implants" (Fleming, 1989, p. C10).

Looking good may come at a cost. Skin sloughing, infection, and neuromuscular problems can result from improper placement or from implants that are inappropriately large for clients' body frames. Pectoral implants can cause irritation because of the constant stress caused by working the surrounding muscles and can even erode underlying bone. Because they are held in place by the chest muscle, implants may slip, necessitating surgery for repositioning. Calf implants can exert pressure on weight-bearing calf muscles, causing debilitating damage over time. Buttock implants, because they are heavily weight bearing, are subject to rupture and formation of hard encapsulated ridges (Aiache, 1991; Mladick, 1991; Novack, 1991; Schwade, 1993).

Men's willingness to undergo these potentially risky procedures to attain the appearance of physical fitness is indicative of the strange dichotomy between looking fit and actually being fit—they project an image that may in fact be diametrically opposed to reality. When professional bodybuilder Sam Fussell, son of two upper-middle-class New York academics, expressed surprise about the physical miseries bodybuilding imposed on him, the response of his gym mates was, Do you really think this has anything to do with health? (Fussell, 1991). Nowhere is the dichotomy more glaring than in the debate over the use of steroids and supplements.

BETTER BODIES THROUGH CHEMISTRY

Using drugs to enhance athletic performance is deeply rooted in Western history. Greeks in the original Olympic games took strychnine and hallucinogenic mushrooms to "psych up" for athletic events, and long-distance runners chewed on sesame seeds, which were believed to enhance endurance. In 1886 a French cyclist died after taking a lethal combination of cocaine and heroin, the first athlete known to have died from using performance drugs. Doctors used monkey testicle injections to boost male athletic and sexual performance in the 1920s and 1930s. Adolf Hitler took testosterone derivatives for mental and physical enhancement and is alleged to have had them administered to German troops to increase aggressiveness. Because of its sexual overtones—testosterone therapy was called "sexual TNT" in the 1930s and 1940s—it was not well received in the medical community, which could see no benefit to it because it did not cure any specific disease (Taylor, 1991; Todd, 1987).

After World War II, physician John Ziegler, in affiliation with Ciba Pharmaceuticals, observed that Russian athletes were using testosterone in the 1956 World Games. Fearing that the Russians were gaining an advantage over U.S. athletes, Ziegler, when he returned to the United States, produced a testosterone synthesis, christened Dianobol, which was administered in small (5 milligram) doses to U.S. athletes. Within a few years, pleased with the drug's effects, bodybuilders were sporting T-shirts reading "Dianobol, Breakfast of Champions" (Todd, 1987). Doctors responded to the spread of Dianobol by claiming that users would experience "dramatic, toxic side effects" while simultaneously denying that it could actually enhance athletic ability (in the face of clear evidence to the contrary), a misstep that undermined legitimate criticisms in the eyes of skeptical athletes (Ambre, 1990; Yesalis, Wright, & Bahrke, 1989).

Before the 1980s, media attention to steroid use focused almost exclusively on Olympic athletes and other high-profile professionals, with little recognition of abuse among ordinary men. However use became widespread among college and professional athletes, especially in strength sports like weight lifting. As with any drug, the effects of steroids are fleeting: When usage stops, so do muscular development and feelings of masculinity, making withdrawal difficult (Fussell, 1991; Taylor, 1991). In the deceptively health-oriented ambience of the modern health club, steroids are likely to be perceived as just another training aid. "You can go to almost any gym," according to Gregory Florenz, chief executive of Salt Lake City–based First Fitness, Inc., "and find . . . people who are peddling steroids or know how to get them" (Stein, 2005, p. E1). Among those most interested in finding these drugs are high school boys (Yesalis & Bahrke, 2000); although less likely than boys to experiment with steroids or body-altering supplements, girls are also increasing their use of these substances (Salzman, 2004).

When New York narcotics police arrested three students returning from Mexico in a van filled with steroids early in 2005, they found that the target clientele included not just football players and other athletes; according to an arresting officer, "they had a lot of customers, kids who will do anything to get that buff look" (Egan, 2002, p. A1). His analysis was confirmed by a suburban New York high school senior who added 50 pounds of muscle mass to his body over a 2-year period; most boys, he claimed, were not weight lifting or using steroids for sports; it was "for girls . . . for the look" (p. A24). If you're going to test athletes for drugs, suggests a Connecticut high school coach, "you should test band members and people in plays," who are just as likely as athletes to be potential candidates for an enhanced body image (Salzman, 2004, pp.14-1, 14-4).

By the time they reach their teens, boys have been exposed to enough media images to define muscularity as an essential facet of masculinity, especially if they were teased in childhood about being too fat, too short, or poor at sports. Just as girls are raised on images of Barbie doll perfection, boys are exposed virtually from infancy to action figures like buffed-up G. I. Joes and Hulk Hogans. Even cartoon characters like Batman and figures based on *Star Wars* characters have bulked up to unrealistic proportions since their introduction in the 1960s and 1970s, their muscularity far exceeding that of "even the largest human bodybuilders" (Pope, Olivardia, Gruber, & Borowiecki, 1999, p. 65). Action toys also have acquired sharply increased muscular definition, displaying "rippled abdominals" (p. 65) and "distinct serratus muscles" (p. 67) rarely visible on male bodies other than those of bodybuilders. Boys as young as 5 years old express a desire to emulate these unrealistic action figures (Labre, 2002).

Boys also learn at an early age that sports, especially masculinized sports that emphasize power and aggression, are an important locus of masculine identity as well as a means of forging relationships with male friends and family members (Drummond, 2003). Sports and athletics are traditionally masculine spheres associated with muscularity and strength, and men and boys who exercise regularly are likely to report higher body satisfaction and lower levels of anxiety about their physiques (Hausenblas & Fallon, 2002). The irony of sports and athletics is that although they do provide a more positive body image, they may promote dangerous and extreme behaviors that undermine the body rather than enhancing it. Aside from drug abuse, overtraining leads to injuries, chronic physical pain, and lack of sleep. Athletic involvement also increases the risk of eating disorders; although extreme eating behaviors are worst among athletes in sports with weight restrictions, like wrestling, they are found throughout sports and athletics (R. E. Andersen, 1995).

Ideals of male body image have been shaped by diverse currents over the past century. Foremost among these has been the evolution of a culture defined by a profound emphasis on individual fulfillment, largely expressed through consumerism. The transformation from a culture of production to one of consumption, in which the value of making things was superseded by the importance of being able to buy them, was already well under way by the early 20th century, by which time the basic needs of most middle-class Americans—food, shelter, clothing—were being met. Businesses relied on advertising to create desire in place of need, striving (with great success) to convince consumers that their identities were dependent on ownership of the right products. In such a milieu, it was perhaps inevitable that the body would be transformed into a commodity whose desirability and perceived value, like those of any commodity, lay primarily in its visual appeal.

Men have also had to contend with a radically altered gender power balance. As long as they held tight control over the economic resources, physical appearance was of secondary importance In particular, highly paid occupations have traditionally been a locus of masculine identity and until recently were an almost exclusively male domain (Drummond, 2003). Today, women hold almost half of all executive, management, and administrative jobs. Nearly one-third of wives outearn their husbands, and the proportion of women earning more than $100,000 annually has tripled since 1990, whereas men's comparable earnings declined for the same period. Women are also better educated, holding 58% of all college degrees and 59% of master's degrees (Shellenbarger, 2005). If men no longer hold the economic cards, they must find other ways to display masculinity. Cultivating a powerful body sends a message that even though men have to share the workplace with women, they are still stronger and physically superior (Shaw, 1994). Pope, Phillips, and Olivardia (2000) agreed that muscularity remains "one of the few . . . grounds on which women can never match men" (p. 24).

As masculine as muscularity is perceived to be, the cultural importance of image has ironically pulled men into a realm once reserved almost exclusively for women. Although male body objectification has not attained the same levels as for women—men are still permitted a much wider range of "acceptable" bodies than women—the consequences are much the same for both, setting unrealistic standards that require "measuring up" to a muscular ideal. With pressure coming from such fundamental areas of male self-esteem as women and the workplace, men's commitment to the cultivation of muscularity is likely to continue.

It is also likely to spread outside the United States. Propelled by powerful media images from the world's largest consumer nation, cosmetic surgery is on the increase worldwide. Breast implants are becoming status symbols in China and other Asian countries, as are rounder, "westernized" eyes for both men and women (Rosen, 2004). A study of adolescent girls in Fiji showed striking increases in body dissatisfaction after television became widely available (Cromie, 2005). Asian countries still place far less emphasis on the appeal of muscularity than is the case in the United States; however, a study of male body image in Taiwanese men suggested that their much lower levels of body dissatisfaction may be linked to lower exposure to media images than is the case with U.S. men, particularly with regard to images of undressed men (Yang, Gray, & Pope, 2005). In Europe, where cultural ideals and media penetration more closely resemble those of the United States, a study of Austrian, French, and U.S. men indicated that men from all three countries wanted bodies on average 28 pounds more muscular than their own and believed—erroneously—that women preferred this body type (Pope, Gruber, et al., 2000). The penetration of U.S. culture into the rest of the world as other nations embrace the consumerist ideal and raise their social expectations has been amply demonstrated; exposed to the endless imagery of the Western media, it may be only a matter of time before the muscular ideal goes global—for better or for worse.

REFERENCES

Agins, T. (1994, October 25). Belly roll blues. *The Wall Street Journal*, p. A1.

Aiache, A. E. (1991). Male chest correction. *Clinics in Plastic Surgery*, 18, 823, 857–862.

Ambre, J. J. (1990). Medical and nonmedical uses of anabolic-androgenic steroids. *Journal of the American Medical Association*, 264, 2923–2927.

American Psychiatric Association. (1994). *Diagnostic and statistical manual of mental disorders* (4th ed.). Washington, DC: Author.

Andersen, A. E., Woodward, P. J., Spalder, A., & Koss, M. (1993). Body size and shape characteristics of personal ("in search of") ads. *International Journal of Eating Disorders*, 14, 112.

Andersen, R. E. (1995). Weight loss, psychological and nutritional patterns in competitive male body builders. *International Journal of Eating Disorders*, 18, 49–57.

Bailey, B. L. (1988). *From front porch to back seat: Courtship in twentieth-century America*. Baltimore: Johns Hopkins University Press.

Bebbington, J. (1993). Getting classic with Arnold. *The Saturday Evening Post*, 265, 36–37.

Belasco, W. (1989). *Appetite for change: How the counterculture took on the food industry, 1966–1988*. New York: Pantheon.

Boorstin, D. (1962). *The image: Or, what happened to the American dream*. New York: Atheneum.

Botta, R. A. (2003). For your health? The relationship between magazine reading and adolescents' body image and eating disturbances. *Sex Roles*, 48, 389.

Brown, T., & Cohn, G. (2006, June 8). Pursuit of baseball's drug users heats up. *Los Angeles Times*, p. A1.

Brubach, H. (1993, January 11). Musclebound. *The New Yorker*, p. 32.

Buckley, W., Yesalis, C., Friedl, K., Anderson, W., Streit, A., & Wright, J. (1988). Estimated prevalence of anabolic steroid use in high school seniors. *Journal of the American Medical Association*, 260, 3441–3445.

Canseco, J. (2005). *Juiced: Wild times, rampant 'roids, smash hits, and how baseball got big*. New York: ReganBooks.

Chapman, D. L. (1994). *Sandow the magnificent: Eugen Sandow and the beginnings of bodybuilding*. Urbana: University of Illinois Press.

Chauncey, G. (1994). *Gay New York: Urban culture and the making of the gay male world, 1890–1940*. New York: Basic Books.

Courtiss, E. H. (Ed.). (1991). *Male aesthetic surgery*. St. Louis, MO: Mosby.

Cromie, W. J. (2005, February 10). Male body image: East doesn't meet west [Electronic version]. *Harvard Gazette Archives*. Retrieved December 5, 2006, from http://www.hno.harvard.edu/gazette/2005/02.10/11-bodyimage.html

Darling, L. (1985). How much bigger can Arnold Schwarzenegger get? *Esquire, 103*, 130.

Davis, C., Karvinen, K., & McCreary, D. R. (2005). Personality correlates of a drive for muscularity in young men. *Personality and Individual Differences, 39*, 349–359.

Davis, D. (1996, January 26). Muscle Inc. *Los Angeles Weekly*, pp. 21, 23.

Dawson, R. T. (2001). Drugs in sport—The role of the physician. *Journal of Endocrinology, 170*, 55–61.

Drummond, M. J. (2003). Retired men, retired bodies. *International Journal of Men's Health, 2*, 183–199.

Dyreson, M. (1989). The emergence of consumer culture and the transformation of physical culture: American sport in the 1920s. *Journal of Sport History, 16*, 264.

Eagly, A. H., Ashmore, R. D., Makhijani, M. G., & Longo, L. C. (1991). What is beautiful is good, but . . . : A meta-analytic review of research on the physical attractiveness stereotype. *Psychological Bulletin, 110*, 109–128.

Edwards, T. (1990). Beyond sex and gender: Masculinity, homosexuality and social theory. In J. Hearn & D. Morgan (Eds.), *Men, masculinities and social theory* (pp. 114–115). London: Unwin Hyman.

Egan, T. (2002, November 22). Body-conscious boys adopt athletes' taste for steroids. *The New York Times*, pp. A1, A24.

Ewen, S., & Ewen, E. (1992). *Channels of desire: Mass images and the shaping of American consciousness* (pp. 189–191). Minneapolis: University of Minnesota Press.

Farnham, A. (1996, September 9). You're so vain. *Fortune*, p. 68.

Fawkner, H. J., & McMurray, N. E. (2003). Body image in men: Self-reported thoughts, feelings and behaviors in response to media images. *International Journal of Men's Health, 1*, 137–161.

Fleming, A. (1989, December 20). Youths who look for a "10" in the mirror. *The New York Times*, p. C10.

Foster, F. P. (1964, February 9). Warning against a "physical fitness mania." *The New York Times*, p. 15.

Fouts, G., & Vaughn, K. (2003). Television situation comedies: Male weight, negative references, and audience reactions. *Sex Roles, 46*, 439–442.

Frederick, D. A., Fessler, D. M. T., & Haselton, M. G. (2005). Do representations of male muscularity differ in men's and women's magazines? *Body Image, 2,* 81–86.

Frieze, I. H., Olson, J. E., & Russell, J. (1991). Attractiveness and income for men and women in management. *Journal of Applied Social Psychology, 21,* 1039–1057.

Friedan, B. (1963). *The feminine mystique.* New York: Norton.

Fussell, S. W. (1991). *Muscles: Confessions of an unlikely bodybuilder.* New York: Poseidon.

Gehman, R. (1957). Toupees, girdles and sunlamps. *Cosmopolitan, 142,* 42.

Geist, W. E. (1984, May 19). The mating game and other exercises at the vertical club. *The New York Times,* p. L25.

Gilroy, H. (1952, December 21). Beneficial exercise. *New York Times Magazine,* p. 12.

Goldberg, V. (1975, November 30). Body building. *New York Times Magazine,* p. 46.

Gorn, E. (1986). *The manly art: Bare-knuckle prize fighting in America.* Ithaca, NY: Cornell University Press.

Gorn, E., & Goldstein, W. (1993). *A brief history of American sports.* New York: Hill and Wang.

Grant, M. (1970). *Passing of the great race: Or, the racial basis of American history.* New York: Ayer. (Originally published 1916)

Green, H. (1984). *Fit for America: Health, fitness sport and American society.* Baltimore: Johns Hopkins University Press.

Hall, A. S., & Hall, D. K. (1977). *Arnold: The education of a bodybuilder.* New York: Simon & Schuster.

Harrison, B., & Bluestone, B. (1988). *The great U-turn: Corporate restructuring and the polarizing of America.* New York: Basic Books.

Hausenblas, H. A., & Fallon, E. A. (2002). Relationship among body image, exercise behavior, and exercise dependence symptoms. *International Journal of Eating Disorders, 32,* 179–185.

Jackson, L. (1992). *Physical appearance and gender: Sociobiological and sociocultural perspectives.* Albany: State University of New York Press.

Jeffords, S. (1994). *Hard bodies: Hollywood masculinity in the Reagan era.* New Brunswick, NJ: Rutgers University.

Kanayama, G., Cohane, G. H., Weiss, R. D., & Pope, H. G. (2003). Past anabolic-androgenic steroid use among men admitted for substance abuse treatment: An under-recognized problem? *Journal of Clinical Psychiatry, 64,* 156–160.

Kennedy, J. F. (1960, December 26). The soft American. *Sports Illustrated,* pp. 12–15.

Kimmel, M. (1994, Winter). Consuming manhood: The feminization of American culture and the recreation of the male body, 1832–1920. *Michigan Quarterly Review, 33,* 18–19, 28.

Klein, A. (1993a). *Little big men: Bodybuilding subculture and gender construction*. Albany: State University of New York Press.

Klein, A. (1993b). Of muscles and men. *Sciences, 33*, 37.

Kraus, H., & Hirschland, R. P. (1953). Muscular fitness and health. *Journal of Health, Physical Education and Recreation, 24*, 17–19.

Kraus, H., & Hirschland, R. P. (1954). Minimum muscular fitness tests in school children. *Research Quarterly, 25*, 178.

Labre, M. P. (2002). Adolescent boys and the muscular male body ideal. *Journal of Adolescent Health, 30*, 233–242.

Lasch, C. (1979). *The culture of narcissism: American life in an age of diminishing expectations*. New York: Norton.

Lasch, C. (1984). *The minimal self: Psychic survival in troubled times*. New York: Norton.

Lavrakas, P. J. (1975). Female preferences for male physiques. *Journal of Research in Personality, 9*, 332.

Lefferts, B. (1958, March 23). Swanky sweatshops. *The New York Times*, p. 47.

Leit, R. A., Gray, J. J., & Pope, H. G. (2002). The media's representation of the ideal male body: A cause for muscle dysmorphia? *International Journal of Eating Disorders, 31*, 334–338.

Leit, R. A., Pope, H. G., & Gray, J. J. (2001). Cultural expectations of muscularity in men: The evolution of Playgirl centerfolds. *International Journal of Eating Disorders, 29*, 90–93.

Maccoby, M. (1976). *The gamesman*. New York: Simon & Schuster.

Maida, D. M., & Armstrong, S. L. (2004). The classification of muscle dysmorphia. *International Journal of Men's Health, 4*, 73–91.

Malone, M. (1979). *Heroes of eros: Male sexuality in the movies*. New York: Dutton.

Mathews, M. (1951). *A dictionary of Americanisms on historical principles*. Chicago: Chicago University Press.

McCreary, D. R., & Sasse, D. K. (2000). An exploration of the drive for muscularity in adolescent boys and girls. *Journal of American College Health, 48*, 297–304.

Mladick, R. A. (1991). Male body contouring. *Clinics in Plastic Surgery, 18*, 797–813.

Mulford, M., Orbell, J., Shatto, C., & Stockard, J. (1998). Physical attractiveness, opportunity and success in everyday exchange. *American Journal of Sociology, 103*, 1565–1592.

Novack, B. H. (1991). Alloplastic implants for men. *Clinics in Plastic Surgery, 18*, 829–855.

Olivardia, R. (2002). Body image and muscularity. In T. F. Cash & T. Pruzinsky (Eds.), *Body image: A handbook of theory, research, and clinical practice* (pp. 210–218). New York: Guilford Press.

Olivardia, R., Pope, H. G., & Hudson, J. I. (2000). Muscle dysmorphia in male weightlifters: A case–control study. *American Journal of Psychiatry, 157*, 1291–1296.

Overend, W. (1981, May 6). Flocking to the body temples with the gym generation. *Los Angeles Times*, p. V1.

Parssinen, M., & Seppala, T. (2002). Steroid use and long-term health risks in former athletes. *Sports Medicine, 32*, 83–94.

Patzer, G. L. (1985). *The physical attractiveness phenomenon*. New York: Plenum Press.

Pertschuk, M., & Trisdorfer, A. (1994). Men's bodies: The survey. *Psychology Today, 27*, 44–50.

Pope, H. G., Gruber, A. J., Mangweth, B., Bureau, B., deCol, C., Jouvent, R., & Hudson, J. I. (2000). Body image perception among men in three countries. *American Journal of Psychiatry, 157*, 1297–1301.

Pope, H. G., & Katz, D. L. (1990). Homicide and near-homicide by anabolic steroids. *Journal of Clinical Psychiatry, 51*, 28–51.

Pope, H. G., Olivardia, R., Gruber, A., & Borowiecki, J. (1999). Evolving ideals of male body image as seen through action toys. *International Journal of Eating Disorders, 26*, 65–72.

Pope, H. G., Phillips, K. A., & Olivardia, R. (2000). *The Adonis complex: The secret crisis of male body obsession*. New York: Free Press.

Quindlen, A. (1982, June 30). Kicking sand in the face of time. *The New York Times*, p. B3.

Rosen, C. (2004, Spring). The democratization of beauty. *New Atlantis, 5*, 19–35.

Rotundo, E. A. (1993). *American manhood: Transformations in masculinity from the revolution to the modern era*. New York: Basic Books.

Salzman, A. (2004, December 19). Playing fields and the threat of steroid use. *The New York Times*, pp. 14-1, 14-4.

Sampson, A. (1995). *Company man: The rise and fall of corporate life*. New York: Random House.

Sayre, J. (1957, May 25). The body worshippers of Muscle Beach. *Saturday Evening Post*, p. 34.

Schwade, S. (1993, January). Body shop. *Muscle and Fitness*, p. 211.

Scott, D. M., Wagner, J. C., & Barlow, T. W. (1996). Anabolic steroid use among adolescents in Nebraska schools. *American Journal of Health, 53*, 2068–2072.

Shaffer, I. (2002, January). *Final report of the Conference on the Science and Policy of Performance-Enhancing Products*. Bethesda, MD: National Institutes of Health.

Shaw, D. (1994, May 29). Mirror, mirror. *The New York Times*, p. C6.

Sheinin, D. (2005, March 18). Baseball has a day of reckoning in Congress. *The Washington Post*, p. A1.

Sheldon, W. H. (1970). *The varieties of human physique: An introduction to constitutional psychology*. New York: Hafner. (Originally published 1940)

Shellenbarger, S. (2005, April 7). The female midlife crisis. *The Wall Street Journal*, p. D3.

Sherrill, M. (1992, March 8). Breast him-plants: The joy of pecs. *The Washington Post*, p. F2.

Silver, G. A. (1962, June 9). Fits over fitness. *Nation*, p. 516.

Smith, E. W. L. (1989). *Not just pumping iron: On the psychology of lifting weights*. Springfield, IL: Charles C Thompson.

Spindler, A. (1996, June 9). It's a face-lifted, tummy-tucked jungle out there. *The New York Times*, p. III-8.

Stare, F. J. (1967, December). How to live five years longer. *Nation's Business, 55*, 78–81.

Stein, J. (2005, June 6). Bulging with risks: Unsupervised steroid use is rising among young men. *Los Angeles Times*, p. E 1.

Sullivan, A. (1986, September 15–22). Muscleheads. *New Republic*, p. 24.

Swint, S. (2000, October 21). You've come a long way, bubba. *WebMD Medical News Archive*. Retrieved June 11, 2005, from http://www.webmd.com/content/article/26/1728_59692.htm

Taylor, W. N. (1991). *Macho medicine: History of the anabolic steroid epidemic*. Jefferson, NC: McFarland.

Testi, A. (1995). The gender of reform politics: Theodore Roosevelt and the culture of masculinity. *Journal of American History, 81*, 1520.

Todd, T. (1987). Anabolic steroids: The gremlins of sport. *Journal of Sports History, 14*, 90.

Turner, F. J. (1996). *The frontier in American history*. New York: Dover.

Well, W., & Siegel, B. (1982). Stereotyped somatotypes. *Psychological Reports, 8*, 77–78.

Wertheim, E. H. (1992). Psychological predictors of weight loss behaviors and binge eating in adolescent girls and boys. *International Journal of Eating Disorders, 12*, 151–160.

Wheeler, J. (1984). *Touched with fire: The future of the Vietnam generation*. New York: Avon.

White, K. (1992). *The first sexual revolution: The emergence of male heterosexuality in modern America*. New York: NYU Press.

Whorton, J. C. (1982). *Crusaders for fitness: The history of American health reformers*. Princeton, NJ: Princeton University Press.

Wilson, D. (2005, March 10). Steroids are blamed in suicide of young athlete. *The New York Times*, p. A1.

Wolfe, T. (1976, August 23). The "Me" decade and the third great awakening. *New York*, pp. 26–40.

Yang, C. F., Gray, P., & Pope, H. G. (2005). Male body image in Taiwan versus the West: Yanggang Zhiqi meets the Adonis complex. *American Journal of Psychiatry, 162*, 263–269.

Yankelovich, D. (1981). New rules. *Psychology Today, 15*, 35.

Yesalis, C. E., & Bahrke, M. S. (2000). Doping among adolescent athletes. *Ballieres Best Practice & Research: Clinical Endocrinology & Metabolism, 14,* 25–35.

Yesalis, C. E., Wright, J. E., & Bahrke, M. S. (1989). Epidemiological and policy issues in the measurement of the long term health effects of anabolic-androgenic steroids. *Sports Medicine, 8,* 129–138.

Yoffe, E. (1990, November 26). Valley of the silicone dolls. *Newsweek,* p. 72.

3

SIZE MATTERS: CONNECTING SUBCULTURE TO CULTURE IN BODYBUILDING

ALAN KLEIN

Two years ago, I shared a room with my graduate student at a conference. A former collegiate hockey player, he was not overly macho, yet he embraced athletic masculine ideals that included many bodily practices such as working out to retain "the look" and maintaining closely cropped hair which was common to collegiate hockey players of the time. An hour or so after he went out for the evening, I walked into the bathroom and was jolted by the scene: The bathtub was caked with dried shaving cream and hair; short stubbly hairs were everywhere. When I asked him about it later, the student matter-of-factly described what he was up to: "I shave, dude." "Everywhere?" I asked. "Yeah . . . chest, legs, crotch, why?" It was the "Why?" that got me. Apparently, I had missed something in recent years, something that had become ordinary enough to warrant a response amounting to "You never heard of this before? Where've you been?"

Full-body depilation is known as "man-scaping." I'd first seen it 25 years earlier in Gold's Gym in Santa Monica, California, where bodybuilders used depilatories before contests so that their musculature would be more visible. Was my roommate's blasé attitude an indication of just how mainstreamed bodybuilding practices had become? The fact that the current circulation of bodybuilding's premier magazine, *Muscle and Fitness*, exceeds 450,000 a month is another indicator (Smith, 2006), as is the election of former bodybuilding icon Arnold Schwarzenegger as governor of California.

There can be little doubt that bodybuilding has become culturally mainstreamed. In this chapter, I explore two aspects of this process. First, how and when did bodybuilding cross over to become mainstream? And second, will this mainstreaming alter bodybuilders' sense of themselves as participants in a sport and in a subculture? Answering these questions involves delving not only into cultural matters but into the social psychology of bodybuilders as well. (This article deals primarily with research on male bodybuilders, and comments about bodybuilders apply to men, unless otherwise specified.)

Bodybuilding's rise to respectability can be tracked in a variety of ways. Gym memberships have grown by 25% since 1998, to over 41 million members (Reidy, 2005). Publications on bodybuilding have proliferated. In a recent search of amazon.com, I counted 433 bodybuilding books. All but nine were either how-to books or biographies. Over the past 20 years, a small corpus of scholarly studies of bodybuilding has accumulated. Most of the social scientific articles have been of the cultural sort, but there have been several important psychological works as well (e.g., Pope, Phillips, & Olivardia, 2000). In the fields of sociology, anthropology, and history, a small but steady string of studies have emerged (Bolin, 1992, 1998; Chapman, 1994; Fair, 1999; Fussell, 1991; Heywood, 1998; Klein, 1985, 1989, 1993; Lowe, 1998; West, 2000).

Within much of the scholarly work on bodybuilding, there is a pronounced tendency to leap back and forth between subcultural and cultural categories. The work is insufficiently grounded in ethnography and relies on poorly understood cultural variables. Much of the impetus for this work comes from the current popularity of considering the body as a cultural site. By referring to the body as a cultural site, one is prepared to interpret the surfaces of the body as being inscribed by cultural norms and practices (e.g., tattooing, piercing, or a certain manner of hairstyle). Bourdieu's (2001) work and Foucault's (1995) examination of the body have pushed body interpretation to new heights (e.g., see Bordo, 1999; Fussell, 1994). Even studies that do not focus on the body err by overprivileging culture. My own research has suffered from this confusion; for instance, in one analysis I explored parallels between fascist and bodybuilding aesthetics. Rather than build my argument slowly, in stages, from micro practices in bodybuilding to macro cultural products in the Third Reich, I extrapolated between them (Klein, 1987).

This chapter proposes an ethnographic view of bodybuilding subculture that is linked at various points to ever-larger levels of culture. I submit that understanding bodybuilding's place in culture involves critically examining two key assumptions: (a) that when defining bodybuilding (or, for that matter, any sport), the sport and subculture aspects are organically linked and (b) that, unlike in sport, form is separated from function in bodybuilding. Regarding the first assumption, that sport and the subculture of sport is organically linked means that the subculture flows from the sport without any external influences such as administrative apparatus or media influence. The subculture is, in turn, dependent on the sport being played. Regarding the second assumption, form follows function insofar as the practice of a sport (e.g., major league baseball pitcher) selects for certain physical attributes and then exaggerates them (e.g., long arms, powerful legs). Pitchers are steered away from heavy weightlifting because it would harm their delivery. On the basis of my own research and other qualitative work, I examine the manner in which bodybuilding subculture works around certain core social psychosocial issues in such a way as to foster the creation of practices and a subculture that is the outcome of these issues. I show that bodybuilding as sport is fraught with difficulty, but bodybuilding as subculture has the ability to articulate with larger cultural currents thereby, in time, gaining a measure of credibility.

My fieldwork on competitive bodybuilders took place between 1979 and 1986; afterward, I continued intermittently to interview bodybuilders and track developments in their lives (Klein, 1985, 1986, 1987, 1993, 1995, 1998). Fortunately, my initial entry coincided with the first real round of popular interest in the sport. At the time, bodybuilding was presented as the grotesque that had become curious: the "marginalized world" (Yinger, 1960) of exaggerated muscle and strange practices (e.g., shaving the body, pumping iron). Beginning in the mid-1980s, there was a steady increase in images of bodybuilders in the media, including television commercials, advertisements, and rock videos. One bodybuilder, Arnold Schwarzenegger, even crossed over into movie stardom in *Conan* and later the *Terminator* series. His impact was quickly made apparent as other, equally buffed leading men (e.g., Sylvester Stallone, Jean-Claude Van Damme, and Wesley Snipes) began appearing in action films. It is tempting to state that the use of bodybuilders in pop culture formats indicated their cultural acceptance. But it is more revealing to consider how linkages between the insular world of bodybuilders and culture writ large were formed.

Despite the significant presence of women in competitive bodybuilding, the sport and subculture of bodybuilding have historically been fueled by a cultural dialogue between men and muscle. Every man engages in some sort of dialogue with muscle; it does not matter whether he embraces or repudiates it—he holds an internal dialogue concerning muscle (see Connell, 1995; Gilmore, 1990). It is an essentialist cultural principle and one that distinguishes men from women. Size matters when it comes to muscle. Indeed, because of sexual dimorphism (i.e., muscular differences between the men and women of a population as a whole), the whole question of maximum muscular development is framed in male terms. Size matters in bodybuilding, in part, because in a world in which gender divisions have shrunk, muscle still separates men from women (it also separates men from other, "lesser" men).

I studied male competitive bodybuilders (both pro and amateur) in an elite West Coast gym over a 7-year period to examine these kinds of gender-based issues. By studying an exaggerated form of masculinity, I felt I could get at some of the issues that periodically crop up in crises of masculinity. This community comprised many of the elite competitors, and thus they differed even from other bodybuilders. One key distinction was that they subordinated all other areas of their lives (e.g., social relations, employment, leisure) to competing. The pursuit of maximum muscular development within a competitive framework fosters extreme behavior (Klein, 1993).

RITUALS OF PRODUCTION

Any attempt to demonstrate the relationships between a subculture and mainstream culture should proceed from the ethnography of muscle production. The social settings, behaviors, and language that make up bodybuilding ironically reflect a cohesiveness born of both repudiation and slavish imitation of the larger society; members of this community simultaneously desire to be accepted by mainstream society and engage in behavior that distances them from it. Bodybuilders want to be considered athletes (Klein, 1993). One of the earliest promoters of bodybuilding, Joe Weider, has spent a lifetime trying to get bodybuilding recognized as an Olympic sport. There are many factors that preclude that from happening, among them that most people do not regard it as a sport and that certain practices of bodybuilders appear bizarre and unathletic to the public.

At the core of the bodybuilder's existence is "the workout," the complex of behavior associated with building the body. In calling it a *ritual of production*, I am conflating two distinct cultural areas: the act of production and ritualized behavior. The production that occurs is both cultural and physiological. Indeed, all subcultures are consumed with fashioning a cultural identity that is at once distinct yet related to the larger society of which it is a part. The core of cultural production may be a bodily practice (e.g., circumcision, scarification), a ritual practice of some sort, or a fashioning of belief. Ritual is, according to Rappaport (1999), socially encoded, more or less invariant, communicative, self-referential, and performance driven. It functions to validate social groupings and norms and enhances one's sense of psychological security. Subcultures rely on ritual in all of these ways, in addition using it to distinguish themselves from the larger society.

The bodybuilder's workout is a complex ritual built around the body. The ritual he assembles from among the many available is rigidly adhered to, is performed with impressive regularity, and is symbolically loaded with meaning. It is called a "routine," but it is actually ritualistic. A routine involves mundane activities performed repeatedly, and bodybuilders indeed work out in a repetitive way, but the behavior provides the ritualistic functions Rappaport outlined. There is also a strong element of obsessiveness in almost everything bodybuilders do with reference to their bodies. Training, eating, and resting are all planned in minute detail, and any change is liable to invoke anxiety. Hence, in training for competition, the bodybuilder wakes at a certain time to eat carefully selected food that will be digested in time for him to begin one of two marathon training sessions that day. Between sessions, he will eat and rest in a prescribed fashion. To the outsider, a breakfast may look like two slices of whole wheat bread and two poached eggs, but to a bodybuilder it represents 286 calories, 13.2 grams of fat, 18.0 grams of protein, and 24.8 grams of carbohydrates—all of which has to be in place in his body at the proper time.

The workout routine centers on the body parts "du jour" (e.g., Tuesdays may be arm and back days). The routine almost never varies, so if he is doing reverse grip pull downs (a back exercise) with four sets (of 15, 12, 8, and 6 repetitions), there can be no fewer. The first half of a bodybuilder's training for a competition involves eating and working out to gain maximum muscle mass. As the contest nears, he begins to restrict calorie intake and beefs up his exercise levels, the goal being to shed as much subcutaneous body fat as possible (*shredded* is the term used for the resulting look). Once calories have become severely restricted and energy levels follow suit, the bodybuilder shuns new exercises and increased sets. The routine, not the contest, in fact becomes the end. Training for a contest is very much akin to what an Ironman triathlon competitor endures: a personal test of physical endurance under conditions of deprivation. One fights one's own body, and the routine becomes one's daily mission. Each set is an act of will, a testimony to one's commitment and a signifier of one's worthiness (Klein, 1993). After the contest, bodybuilders engage in institutionalized binging, or "pigging out," and sometimes gain 15 to 20 pounds in just 2 days. Hence, in bodybuilding both anorexic and bulimic elements (e.g., extreme dieting, cutting calories below what is needed to function, purging in the form of diuretics) are intimately tied to competing.

To aid the quest for a win, the bodybuilder takes large doses of supplements, both legal and illegal. The types, dosage, and combinations are also carefully determined, although with little or no medical oversight. Gym lore serves to justify and direct this phase of the bodybuilder's life (Klein, 1995). Bodybuilders often cite fictional results of medical studies as a rationalization for taking certain drugs in various combinations; I have never been able to track down such studies, because anyone I queried would simply say that they got the information from another person involved in bodybuilding. Buying and taking steroids, human growth hormones, and other banned substances fosters subcultural identity by furthering separation from non-substance-taking endeavors.

Other bodybuilding practices include tanning, shaving, carefully selecting music and costumes, and practicing posing. Just as with training and eating, nearly everything a bodybuilder does is related to the goal of total mastery and garnering size; one competitor turned to me and gleefully declared, "I don't need an alarm clock to get up. I get up at 6:30 on the button to take a dump! Never fails!"

The ritualized dimension of the bodybuilder's world is filled with repetition and standardization; however, there are subtle and powerful social psychological processes at work as well. Nieber (1973) noted that in the objectification inherent in ritual, "the inner becomes the outer, and the subjective world picture becomes social reality" (p. 30), by which he meant that internal concerns are fetishized via ritual to become externalized and a bit more real. In the bodybuilder's case, however, this process can be reversed; the external-idealized world (the massive body) is a questionable form of "social reality" that is never completely real. The internal psychological state of bodybuilders reveals a pattern of flaws that fuels the need for creating the external edifice (i.e., the bodybuilder's body).

SOCIAL PSYCHOLOGY OF MALE BODYBUILDERS

What these ritualized bodily practices reveal or conceal about the bodybuilder's inner world is essential for an understanding of their subculture. I collected life histories of 39 competitive bodybuilders during my fieldwork years. They ranged in age from 20 to 43 years old. I collected them in a nonrandom fashion because it was such a small population (112). In the life histories I collected, some very clear themes emerged that point to a neurotic core in many bodybuilders. I use the term *neurotic*, as did Butt (1975), not to impugn so much as to suggest that for this sport subculture, a collective response to a set of shared psychological issues constitutes a central pillar for the construction of their community. Dorcus Butts was not the only one to characterize bodybuilding as neurotic. Other psychological texts also noted that bodybuilders were overly insecure with their sex roles (see Pleck, 1983; Thune, 1949).

One theme that came up regularly in the life histories was that of bodybuilding as an effort to compensate for lack of self-esteem:

- These guys are drawn into bodybuilding for some reason, insecurities or whatever. Myself, it was 'cuz my brother and I got beat up all the time. . . . But these guys, I think a lot of them are insecure. That's why they pump those lats out and walk around like that.

- See, we had dyslexia, so in school we didn't excel, but in physical things we excelled. So we fought a lot. . . . Bodybuilding seemed like a natural thing for us 'cuz of that.
- See, my father is tall, and I'm not. So if I can't be as tall as him, I wanna be as big as him. (From film *Pumping Iron* [Butler & Fiore, 1977].)

Another theme has to do with faulty parental relations, particularly father–son relations:

- My parents never gave me credit for anything, and that's where it [insecurity] came from. We had a minor league team in our town, and you know how fathers take their kids to the games. But mine never did. Mine never did nothin' with me.
- My dad never gave me support. I was always wrong. Hell, I'm still always wrong.
- I was small and weak, and my brother Anthony was big and graceful, and my old man made no bones about loving him and hating me. . . . The minute I walked in from school, it was, "You worthless little shit! What are you doing home so early?"

With self-esteem and parental issues so seemingly prevalent, it is no surprise that bodybuilders appear to be insular and have difficulty developing meaningful social relations (Klein, 1993). They are prone to holding others at bay by valuing bodybuilding as an individual sport (and disparaging team sports) and by characterizing themselves as loners:

- I began developing a strong sense of individuality quite early. I was always turned off by team sports. I just didn't like being part of a team and the backslapping and groping, sweating, and all that shit. I would rather spend the time by myself in the basement pumping iron.
- Friends, I don't have. I don't believe in them. I'm a loner, and you have to be in bodybuilding.

Put into a context of like-minded questers seeking to compensate for the "diminished self," they have fashioned a subculture that fetishizes power through imposing physiques. Bodybuilders share a world in which physical grandiosity is the daily currency, and no one (no man, at any rate) can be too big (Fussell, 1991; Klein, 1993). The men I interviewed also live in a world in which ingesting anything rumored to have growing properties is encouraged and in which greetings, photo shoots, and training for contests all bear the mark of secular ritual. In this regard, bodybuilding is far more successful as a subculture than as a sport, a point that is critical to an understanding of this group.

SEPARATING SPORT FROM SUBCULTURE

Separating the subculture from the sport of bodybuilding sheds light on the factors that led to mainstreaming of bodybuilding in the late 20th century. Being considered a legitimate sport has always proved difficult for bodybuilding. Coakley's (2000) criteria for sport—physical prowess of some sort, institutionalization, and competition—have been problematic for bodybuilding. Without doubt, bodybuilding is both highly organized and competitive. Meeting the criterion of physical excellence or prowess, however, poses problems on two fronts. Bodybuilders can claim only physical exertion—not "excellence"—from their weight training sessions. Sessions are designed only to build muscle, which overlaps only slightly with the sport of weight lifting or power lifting. In fact, because training with weights is now standard in most sports, most athletes are also bodybuilders. Are we to consider hockey, basketball, or football players two-sport athletes because they train with weights and build muscle? In addition, what passes for physical prowess in bodybuilding is not coterminous with the competition that occurs. Rather, working out and bodybuilding competition take place at different times and in different places. The competition consists of a visual display—posing only—not weight lifting. Perhaps because of these issues, the perception of bodybuilding by the cultural (and sport) mainstream has been somewhat clouded and acceptance limited. Reluctance to accept bodybuilding into the sports pantheon is fueled by the perception that, for bodybuilders, form is separated from function.

Form Versus Function

Bodybuilding began as crowd-pleasing displays tacked onto the end of the "strongmen exhibitions" of the late 19th and early 20th centuries. (T. Todd and J. Todd, personal communication, April 5, 2003; see also Fair, 1999). In this way the question of its legitimization as a sport was skirted. By the 1940s, when Joe Weider emerged as bodybuilding's leading promoter, the effort to separate from strength exhibitions had begun, and with it came aspersions about the emptiness of the form (Fair, 1999). York Barbell Co. owner Bob Hoffman dismissed Weider's move to establish bodybuilding as sport. In Hoffman's *Strength and Health* (as cited in Fair, 1999), he derisively referred to the emerging bodybuilding movement as "boobybuilding" (p. 168).

Sport assumes a union between form and function, but bodybuilding is a striking and perhaps novel case of a subculture striving for sport legitimacy in which function is sheared off from form. Key to understanding this separation is the social psychology of bodybuilders and the need to compensate by building imposing physiques. If these men sought success, power, and mastery, they would be better served by going into martial arts or law, but it is overwhelmingly the physical trappings of these endeavors that draw them into bodybuilding. It isn't the functioning dimension of boxing, power lifting, football, and so forth that appeals to these men; rather, it is the appearance of power. It is not what those muscles can actually do, but rather what they look like they can do:

- [Building my muscles is preferable to engaging in competitive sport because] I would never be called upon actually to use these muscles. I could remain a coward and no one would ever know. (Fussell, 1991, p. 25)

Self–Other Objectification

Form comes to mask function through a range of practices. First, the body is made partible, viewed as an assemblage of very distinct muscle groups. These parts are named and given a life of their own. One's arms, for instance, are not simply biceps and triceps, but "guns" and "canons," as in, "He's got some serious guns." An informal sociolinguistic survey of bodybuilders' language and bodybuilding publications extends the objectification. Body parts are often likened to animals or machines in action. One possesses "arms like pythons" or "zeppelin-like arms." Muscle groupings command their own times; the days of the week are divided according to body parts, as in "Tuesday is leg day" or "I'm only working back today." One has autonomous parts that both act and are acted on; hence, one "releases the beast" or "corrals bigger calves."

The objectification proceeds in two ways: (a) by viewing the body as something to be worked on and (b) by developing language and practices that bestow a dynamic quality (action) on an inherently static demonstration. The latter is dramatically illustrated in the photos of bodybuilders in contests as they pose next to each other; cultural commentator Susan Sontag (1983) referred to "static virile posing." Language lends a dynamic quality to the static form. Terms like "chiseling" and "polishing" connote the creative work of sculptors, but most descriptions of what bodybuilders do to themselves are far more violent. Hence, one does not simply chisel a muscle group, one "shocks," "rips," or "blasts" it. This language has been constant since I began my interviews 20 years ago. Building up a body part may be referred to as an act of destruction, as in "I've gotta rip that waist to shreds" or "Nuke your arms." Self is distinguished from body, and the body is beaten into the desired shape.

Once an individual sees himself as separated into self and other, he can project the other as imposing, as a powerful animal or machine. The image of a machine that works ceaselessly, precisely, and powerfully is alluring and often called up in workouts. The looks and functioning of machines—their hardness, their power—have entered the language of bodybuilding. Bodybuilders "pump iron" or "battle iron." "Hardness" is part of the everyday language of the bodybuilder, and one avoids terms denoting its opposite—"softness" or "smoothness."

The body is under constant scrutiny in bodybuilding subculture, and the mirror plays a central role. To the more serious competitor, the mirror enables him to visually check progress and readiness for competition. Others may see their reflection in the mirror as an actual person working on the set: "It's funny, but if I'm doing a set and there's only a wall, and I can't see myself, it doesn't feel the same as when I see myself in the mirror moving my arms" (Klein, 1993, p. 210). The person relies on the presence of the mirror-being to complete the set. Other forms of visual validation are found in the institutionalized requirement that bodybuilders possess and scrutinize photos and videos of themselves and others.

The Image of Power

Although bodybuilding remains problematic as a sport, it has become convincing as subculture. The subculture projects the image of power, not because it actually exudes it so much as because it seeks to deflect the question altogether. The look of power, vitality, and health is seemingly working to conceal its opposite, and this look currently seems to be playing to larger audiences than in the past. Seeking answers to questions of how and why the sport and subculture of bodybuilding is so successful just now demands a discussion of two of the great promoters of physique during the 20th century: Bob Hoffman and Joe Weider.

With Hoffman forging power lifting into a sport and solidifying his hold on it, Weider was left free to carve out a subcultural niche for the bodybuilding scene. He did so with a series of publications that were more glossy and colorful than Hoffman's, and the writing style appealed to non–strength devotees of health and fitness. Power lifting and bodybuilding were being separated on every level. By the late 1970s, Weider had altered the titles of his premier magazines to reflect lifestyle rather than sport; *Muscle Builder* and *Muscle Power* were combined and renamed *Muscle and Fitness*. The cover of the magazine departed from featuring men only to standard covers of men and women together holding some sort of bodybuilding apparatus. The overall circulation of these magazines in the 1950s and 1960s lagged behind mainstream publications, and even as late as 1979 I had difficulty finding copies of *Muscle and Fitness* in Los Angeles, which had long been a bodybuilding bastion.

This would change dramatically during the 1980s. Weider sought to develop more substantive links with the health industry through nutrition. First, *Muscle and Fitness* began to attract nutrition and fitness advertising from large companies (e.g., Twin Labs). Still, the magazine contained mostly advertisements for Weider products, books, magazines, and events. Today the magazine contains only a small number of Weider-based ads, along with ads for a bewildering array of supplements, drinks, and assorted products (e.g., U.S. Army recruitment, hair restorers). As he worked to build linkages between bodybuilding and fitness, Weider was simultaneously separating them as markets. He moved to split the bodybuilding hard core from the larger audiences he hoped to woo when he introduced *Flex* for the serious bodybuilder in 1984. During the 1980s, he created *Men's Fitness* and *Shape* to capture niche sectors of the fitness market. These efforts succeeded way beyond anything Weider and Hoffman had tried 40 years earlier.

MARKETING: THE MISSING LINK

Hoffman and Weider competed for hearts, minds, and muscles as well as for market share. Weider's *Muscle and Fitness,* one of bodybuilding's biggest publications, has a monthly circulation of 450,000 (Smith, 2006). *Men's Fitness* spun off of *Muscle and Fitness,* as did *Flex* and, for women, *Shape. Men's Fitness* and *Shape* have garnered a much larger mainstream following than *Muscle and Fitness* or *Flex* and serve as effective links to more hard-core bodybuilding. Premier bodybuilding events such as the Mr. Olympia or Arnold Classic contests are broadcast nationally on ESPN. More important, the gray area between bodybuilding and fitness has burgeoned as well. The 2000 Arnold Classic, a major bodybuilding event, also hosted a fitness and health expo with 50,000 in attendance and hundreds of exhibitors (T. Todd, personal communication, April 5, 2003). Gym memberships continue to grow as people in the U.S. commit to a lifestyle that centers on health, fitness, and the accompanying benefit of increased muscularity. Industry figures show that gym and health club memberships grew more than 25% between 1998 and 2004 (Reidy, 2005).

The separation of bodybuilding from weight lifting (and later power lifting) was rooted in the attempts of these moguls to control market share. What emerged from it all was a structural division between sport and subculture. Promoting the recognition of bodybuilding as an Olympic sport has consumed most of Weider's efforts; bodybuilding as sport may have significantly greater legitimacy than it did 40 years ago, but it is lagging behind the gains made around bodybuilding as a marketed subculture.

Contemporary anthropological and sociological research has focused on consumption as one of the means by which people define themselves. In Miller's (1997, 1999), studies of Londoners and Trinidadians, for instance, he argued that buying is also reconfirming social relations and emotions such as affection, sacrifice, and so forth. Consumer behavior has, in this anthropological sense, become a significant cultural variable to be studied for its links between consumption and existing norms, values, and aspirations. Consumption can be considered therapeutic in that people engage in personal and, ultimately, mass attempts to bolster their self-esteem by buying products and lifestyles. People believe that the dissatisfaction that emanates from their pasts contains the possibility of being worked out, or at least ameliorated, via consumption of a certain order. In this context, consumption is linked not only to identity but to enhanced psychological well-being as well.

Bodybuilding Meets Body Work

Marketers like Weider were busy connecting their sport with that of health and fitness, but it was the subculture of bodybuilding (that part of it that is synonymous with the form or look of muscle) that actually crossed the border into the larger territory of practices collectively referred to as "body work." There is no formal network or mutual recognition between the sport of bodybuilding and body work, and there is no distinction between their practitioners according to demographic characteristics, but they share one fundamental concern: bodily makeovers in response to the individual's will. *Body work* is an umbrella term covering a range of practices that involve visual physical transformation (Gimlin, 2002). The spectrum of body work practices extends from the mundane, such as hair styling and dress, to the extreme, including tattooing, piercing, bodybuilding, and cosmetic surgery.

Cosmetic surgery—enlarging or reducing, raising or lowering, breasts, waists, hips, lips, thighs, eyes, and so forth—is by far the most physically invasive of all body work. It is the fastest growing medical specialty in the country, with an annual expenditure of $15 billion (Gaines, 2001). Although 90% of these procedures are performed on women, men are turning to it in greater numbers (English, 2001). The number of men who underwent liposuction, for instance, tripled between 1994 and 2000, and the number of men having cosmetic surgery grew 50% between 1992 and 2000 (English, 2001).

Several factors are regularly mentioned in connection with the rise of cosmetic surgery, the most important being changing demographics. Baby boomers are the major group of consumers of cosmetic surgery. In 2000, they numbered 75 million, and they are at their income peaks and expect to be youthful into old age. Technology advances have made cosmetic surgery more sophisticated and precise, less invasive, and quicker to heal. The market reflects these trends; plastic surgery has proliferated as a specialty (6,125 physicians belong to the Board of Plastic Surgeons, fewer than half of all those legally practicing nationally; English, 2001), and subsequently procedures have become more affordable.

Motives for undergoing plastic surgery range from despair to the desire for a makeover to be attractive to partners (English, 2001). Many people see it as no different than getting new clothes or working out more: "I just want to maintain my fitness, and this is one small way I can do that. . . . I'm not vain, but the world does respond to how you look," explained one patient (English, 2001, p. C-1). In cosmetic surgery, well-being, fashion, and marketing meet. Consumers enhance their self-esteem and improve their psychological viability and social desirability, a consumer rendition of Goffman's (e.g., 1959) presentation of self.

Practice Makes Perfect

Bodybuilding subculture fused seamlessly with body work, which in turn is consistent with secondary (self-help) and primary (Protestant ethic, Enlightenment) U.S. value systems. Bodybuilding is but one of a wave of practices that can be viewed as attempts to enact a re-presentation of self through the body. In short, bodybuilding has entered the mainstream as subculture, not sport. Puritanical at its core, the self-help movement, including physical self-improvement, is a secondary value that flows into primary cultural values articulated by the Protestant ethic and the Enlightenment. To explain further, the Protestant ethic and the Enlightenment movement are most often seen as a primary core of values (e.g., self-reliance, self-control). Secondary values flow from these; therefore, self-help and delayed gratification are illustrations of values that flow from the aforementioned primary cores. Self-improvement transforms into self-reliance, and control of one's destiny is furthered through perseverance, reverence for science, and technology. Through bodybuilding practices (e.g., workouts, diet), the bodybuilder is anatomically lifting himself by his own bootstraps. Hence, there is linkage between bodybuilding and other bodily practices and between them both an increasingly generalized strata of cultural values. Therefore, on the basis of an informal observation, I conclude that this path has led to the dismantling of barriers to the acceptance of bodybuilding. Weider's marketing acumen and ability to link bodybuilding with key sectors of health and fitness have formed one wedge of the popular appeal of bodybuilding, but there is another wedge that has little, if anything, to do with Weider's efforts.

Weider has always had a conservative (some would say Victorian) core that is reflected in his views of the sport and his path to legitimacy (Fair, 1999; Klein, 1993). Building on 19th-century connections between physique and fitness places Weider in the tradition of Sandow and, later, Charles Atlas. Weider's preoccupation with gaining legitimacy for his sport prompted him to eschew anything that might have been construed as off color. Hence, it never occurred to him to expand his market by incorporating marginal elements (e.g., the circuslike display of bodybuilding contests). Rather, he sought to conceal these elements with lofty displays of patriotism and masculinity. Although he has pretty much determined the official direction of sport marketing in bodybuilding, the subculture has escaped his control. There is no formal link between bodybuilding and body work; there are no networks or common identity among practitioners. Youth culture, and perhaps elements of gay culture and the women's movement, has converged with the aging of baby boomers in the elaboration of a range of practices that express themselves through the body, more precisely the surface of the body. These practices have become a quasi-lifestyle and form of expression, perhaps even a form of performance. And although this convergence represents a new market, it also represents a yet-to-be-determined outline of a supersubculture focused on fashioning visual identity alterations. What is unusual in this context is the entrance of bodybuilding into the mix, because it emphasizes subculture at the expense of sport.

CONCLUSION

Better comprehension of bodybuilding's cultural position involves distinguishing sport from subculture; bodybuilding as sport continues to seek legitimization, and bodybuilding as subculture has already claimed a major share of it. Understanding why is rooted in the ability to distinguish form from function. Instead of interpreting the subcultural success in mainstreaming in purely cultural terms, this chapter has highlighted some additional factors, including the role of marketing—specifically, the ability to market the body as both a visual display of health and as a set of practices that appear to correlate with larger cultural values. Regarding the latter, I have noted the fact that bodybuilding has moved beyond the direction or control of its most powerful figures. By connecting to the pantheon of body work, bodybuilding seems to have escaped the gravity pull of marketing to conventional constituencies and bonded with other practices and populations involving the superficial look of youth, vigor, alternative expression, power, and so forth. In a similar way, bodybuilding passes back and forth into the world of fashion and therapeutic enhancement.

Where does cultural analysis sit in all of this? In regard to bodybuilding, I see the role of culture as having been initially neutral and later receptive. Mainstream cultural recognition must be distinguished from the marginal forces that feed it by constantly forging new sources, products, and fashions. Bodybuilding pioneers and marketers found success through promoting a sport organization; were they concerned only with pioneering their sport, bodybuilding would probably still be languishing in obscurity. It was by joining their zeal for the sport with marketing it that they propelled bodybuilding into one dimension of public consciousness. Yet the purely surface appeal of bodybuilding as it moved into body work culture is not something Weider or any of the others would have condoned (or even, in all likelihood, have noticed). This connection was subcultural serendipity—fortuitous, and not by conscious design. The resulting popularization of the look also helped the bodybuilding subculture become more accepted, but it is ironic that the path taken resulted in a coupling of bodybuilding with more iconoclastic elements, at odds with the path Weider took to achieve the same goal.

The increased popularity of bodybuilding should not be taken as an indication that mainstream culture has embraced bodybuilding in its entirety. The neurotic core of insecurity driving bodybuilders continues despite popular acknowledgment, but it is being brushed aside in favor of another, more valuable linkage—the marketing of the appearance of power, confidence, and control via the muscled body. The link between body practices and culture is rooted in buying into the promise of transformation prompted by insecurity (e.g., stopping time, overcoming flaws) or the fickleness of fashion. Bodybuilding is valued because of its fit into bigger cultural projects: body work and the U.S. values surrounding the Protestant ethic. The U.S. culture's long-standing veneration of self-reliance articulates nicely with the marketing of the self-help movement, of which it is a part. At bottom, it is about control: Taking control of one's body. Whether this is hubris or a common choice is open to cultural interpretation. Cultural interpretation, then, comes at the end of a string of connections that begin in concrete practice. To interpret culture otherwise is to fashion a form of analysis in which the tail wags the dog.

REFERENCES

Bolin, A. (1992). Flex appeal, food, and fat: Competitive bodybuilding, gender, and diet. *Play and Culture, 5,* 378–400.

Bolin, A. (1998). Muscularity and femininity: Women bodybuilders and women's bodies in culture–historical context. In K. Volkwein (Ed.), *Fitness as cultural phenomenon* (pp. 187–212). Münster, Germany: Waxmann.

Bordo, S. (1999). *The male body: A new look at masculinity in public and in private.* New York: Farrar, Straus & Giroux.

Bourdieu, P. (2001). *Masculine domination.* Palo Alto, CA: Stanford University Press.

Butler, G. (Director), & Fiore, R. (Director). (1977). *Pumping iron* [Motion picture]. United States: White Mountain Films.

Butt, D. (1975). *Sports psychology.* New York: Van Nostrand.

Chapman, D. (1994). *Sandow the Magnificent: Eugen Sandow and the beginnings of bodybuilding.* Champaign: University of Illinois Press.

Coakley, J. (2000). *Sport in society 2000* (7th ed.). New York: McGraw-Hill.

Connell, R. W. (1995). *Masculinities.* Berkeley: University of California Press.

English, B. (2001, April 2). He nipped, she tucked. *Boston Globe,* p. C-1.

Fair, J. (1999). *Muscletown, USA: Bob Hoffman and the manly culture of York Barbell.* University Park: Pennsylvania State University Press.

Foucault, M. (1995). *Discipline and punishment: The birth of the prison.* New York: Vintage.

Fussell, S. (1991). *Muscle: Confessions of an unlikely bodybuilder.* New York: Poseidon.

Fussell, S. (1994). Bodybuilder americanus. *Michigan Quarterly Review, 32,* 577–597.

Gaines, J. (2001, March 18). Body work. *Boston Globe Magazine,* pp. 32–35.

Gilmore, D. (1990). *Mankind in the making: Cultural concepts of masculinity.* New Haven, CT: Yale University Press.

Gimlin, D. (2002). *Body work: Beauty and self-image in American culture.* Berkeley: University of California Press.

Goffman, E. (1959). *The presentation of self in everyday life.* Garden City, NY: Doubleday.

Heywood, L. (1998). *Bodymakers: A cultural anatomy of women's bodybuilding.* New Brunswick, NJ: Rutgers University Press.

Klein, A. (1985). Women and bodybuilding. *Society, 22*(6), 68–74.

Klein, A. (1986). Pumping irony: Crisis and contradiction in bodybuilding. *Sociology of Sport Journal, 3*(2), 112–133.

Klein, A. (1987). Fear and self-loathing in Venice: Narcissism, fascism, and bodybuilding. *Journal of Psychoanalytic Anthropology, 10,* 117–138.

Klein, A. (1989). Juggling deviance: Hustling and homophobia in bodybuilding. *Deviant Behavior, 10,* 11–27.

Klein, A. (1993). *Little big men: Bodybuilding subculture and gender construction.* Albany: State University of New York Press.

Klein, A. (1995). Life's too short to die small: Health risk rationale in male bodybuilding. In D. Sabo & D. Gordon (Eds.), *Men's health and illness: Gender, power, and the body* (pp. 78–99). Newbury Park, CA: Sage.

Klein, A. (1998). Form follows function? The case of bodybuilding reconsidered. In K. Volkwein (Ed.), *Fitness as cultural phenomenon* (pp. 31–50). Münster, Germany: Waxmann.

Lowe, M. (1998). *Women of steel.* New York: New York University Press.

Miller, D. (1997). *Capitalism: An ethnographic approach.* Oxford, England: Berg.

Miller, D. (1999). *A theory of shopping.* Cambridge, England: Polity Press.

Nieber, H. (1973). *Culture storm: Politics and the ritual order.* New York: St. Martins Press.

Pleck, J. (1983). *The myth of masculinity.* Cambridge, MA: MIT Press.

Pope, H., Phillips, K., & Olivardia, R. (2000). *The Adonis complex: The secret crisis of male body obsession.* New York: Free Press.

Rappaport, R. (1999). *Ritual and religion in the making of humanity.* Cambridge, England: Cambridge University Press.

Reidy, C. (2005, December 30.). Fitness clubs resolve to bulk up in New Year. *Boston Globe,* p. C-1.

Smith, S. D. (2006, June 16). AMI to focus on core titles. *Adweek.* Retrieved January 23, 2007, from http://www.adweek.com/aw/search/article_display.jsp?schema= vnul&vnu_content_id=1002689966&WebLogicSession

=RXNypYYyNTFYC2Grb1HEE28iXn1s4a3XTAvXx6m2X5xE85oEJthh%
C2257698591720039093/16885487/6/7005/7005/7002/7002/7005-1

Sontag, S. (1983). Fascinating fascism. In *Against interpretation* (pp. 98–113). New York: Farrar, Straus & Giroux.

Thune, J. B. (1949). Personality of weightlifters. *Research Quarterly, 20,* 296–306.

West, P. (2000, August). *From Tarzan to the Terminator: Boys, men, and body image.* Paper presented at the Institute of Family Studies Conference, Sydney, Australia.

Yinger, M. (1960). Contraculture and subculture. *American Sociological Review, 25,* 625–635.

II

DEFINITIONS AND MEASUREMENT

4

THE DRIVE FOR MUSCULARITY SCALE: DESCRIPTION, PSYCHOMETRICS, AND RESEARCH FINDINGS

DONALD R. McCREARY

Until recently, body image researchers have tended to focus exclusively on the associations among adiposity, body dissatisfaction, and the pursuit of the thin ideal. These researchers have shown that compared with girls and women, boys and men are less concerned about or dissatisfied with their degree of body fat, have a lower drive for thinness, are less likely to be dieting to lose weight (even though they are more likely to be overweight; Must et al., 1999), and experience clinical eating disorders (e.g., anorexia and bulimia nervosa) at a fraction of the rate that women experience them (e.g., Feingold & Mazzella, 1998; Garner, Olmstead, & Polivy, 1983; Muth & Cash, 1997; Olivardia, Pope, Mangweth, & Hudson, 1995). These types of gender

Many individuals contributed to the development of the Drive for Muscularity Scale. The initial research was supported by a Brock University General Research Grant awarded to the author. My colleague Doris Sasse has moved on to other challenges but was an important contributor to the scale's development and validation. Kim Dorsch, Deb Saucier, and Caroline Davis have been valued collaborators in recent years and, I hope, will continue to be in the future. Finally, I wish to thank all those who have found room for the Drive for Muscularity Scale in their research.

differences have been relatively robust and consistent, leading many to assume that boys and men are happy with their bodies and do not have body image concerns (e.g., Feingold & Mazzella, 1998). However, this is an incorrect assumption stemming from a general failure to understand that the social standard of bodily attractiveness for boys and men is different than that for girls and women and that this standard has different consequences than those typically observed among girls and women.

But what are the social standards of bodily attractiveness for the two sexes? The current social standard for girls and women is to be small and thin. The thin ideal is reflected throughout Western culture in the many images of the ideal woman that are projected both to girls and women and to boys and men on a minute-by-minute basis, as well as through the social pressures put on girls and women to be thin (Harrison, 2003; Silverstein, Purdue, Peterson, & Kelly, 1986; Stice, 2002). This social pressure can lead to what many refer to as the *drive for thinness* (e.g., Garner et al., 1983). Given the nature of this thin ideal, it is not surprising that many girls and women, but hardly any men, overestimate their weight. For example, McCreary (2002) showed that almost one third of women age 20 to 64 years perceived themselves to be heavier than they really were. Other researchers have shown that between 30% and 67% of percent of normal weight young women believed they were overweight and were on diets to lose weight (e.g., Huon & Brown, 1986; Kelly & Patten, 1985; Rosen & Gross, 1987).

However, whereas girls and women are pressured to be thin, society's socially prescribed body size and shape for boys and men is big and muscular, what Mishkind, Rodin, Silberstein, and Striegel-Moore (1986) referred to as the *muscular mesomorphic* shape. This is the shape that men pick as their ideal (Jacobi & Cash, 1994; Jones, 2001; O'Dea & Abraham, 1999), that heterosexual men feel make them most attractive to women (Pope et al., 2000), and that the various media promote as the ideal male body (e.g., Frederick, Fessler, & Haselton, 2005; Leit, Gray, & Pope, 2002; Leit, Pope, & Gray, 2001; Pope, Olivardia, Gruber, & Borowiecki, 1999). Because of these findings, researchers have suggested that men are pressured by society to be big and muscular in the same way that women are pressured to be small and thin, leading to a *drive for muscularity* (McCreary & Sasse, 2000) among boys and men.

This chapter explores the drive for muscularity construct in detail. In the next section, I describe the drive for muscularity construct by outlining the research that has explored boys' and men's desire to be more muscular. To date, this research has been fairly descriptive and, for the most part, has not been linked explicitly to a formal drive for muscularity construct, mostly because there was no direct way to measure that construct until recently. I then explore the options for measuring the drive for muscularity construct, focusing on the development of the Drive for Muscularity Scale (DMS; McCreary & Sasse, 2000) and its reliability and validity.

WHAT IS THE DRIVE FOR MUSCULARITY?

In general, the drive for muscularity (McCreary & Sasse, 2000) represents people's motivation to become more muscular. However, for boys and men, it also is an expression of the extent to which they have internalized society's expectation that the muscular mesomorphic shape is the social standard of bodily attractiveness for their gender. This focus on muscularity has a marked effect on boys' and men's attitudes about, and behaviors toward, their bodies, an effect resulting in marked differences from the way girls and women view and treat their bodies.

For example, whereas girls and women tend to see themselves as heavier than they really are, the muscular focus means that boys and men are more likely to perceive themselves as smaller and lighter than they actually are, making them more likely to want to gain weight and muscle mass to become bigger. Perhaps in an attempt to overcome this sense of feeling small, between 28% and 68% of normal weight boys and men either are on diets to gain weight (McCreary & Sasse, 2002; O'Dea & Rawstorne, 2001) or want to gain weight even though there is no health-related or physical need to do so (e.g., Drewnowski & Yee, 1987; Raudenbush & Zellner, 1997; Rosen & Gross, 1987). Between 40% and 50% of overweight adult men think they are normal weight (McCreary, 2002), and approximately 19% of normal weight men think they are underweight (McCreary & Sadava, 2001). Although some men do want to lose weight (e.g., Cafri, Strauss, & Thompson, 2002; Rosen & Gross, 1987), weight loss desire among men tends not to affect their sense of well-being the way it does among women (Stice, 2002).

However, a desire to gain weight is only tangential to the drive for muscularity (McCreary & Sasse, 2002). Many boys and men who are trying to gain weight also are trying to gain muscle mass (McCabe & Ricciardelli, 2003; O'Dea & Rawstorne, 2001). Men are more motivated than women to weight train (Leslie, Owen, & Sallis, 1999) and tend to choose an ideal body that has between 8 and 13 kilograms more muscle than they feel they already have (Cafri et al., 2002; Pope et al., 2000). If men are asked where they want that extra muscle to go, most say they want larger pectorals, biceps, wrists, shoulders, or forearms and flatter abdominal muscles (Huenemann, Shapiro, Hampton, & Mitchell, 1966; Moore, 1990).

Perceiving one's body as muscular has been shown to be important to men's psychological health. The more involved men are in weight training activities, the more satisfied they are with their bodies, irrespective of their actual muscle mass (Tucker, 1983, 1987). Other research has shown that a perceived lack of muscularity has been associated with increased risk for body dysmorphic disorder (Phillips & Diaz, 1997) and muscle dysmorphia (Maida & Armstrong, 2005), greater levels of depression, poorer self-esteem, and lower levels of life satisfaction (Cafri et al., 2002; McCreary & Sasse, 2000; Olivardia, Pope, Borowiecki, & Cohane, 2004). A smaller body size also has been linked to increased suicide ideation and attempted suicide among men (Carpenter, Hasin, Allison, & Faith, 2000). Some men want or need muscle mass so badly that they ingest or inject anabolic–androgenic steroids (AAS), which are illegal and have several negative side effects (e.g., Cafri, Thompson, et al., 2005; see also chap. 7, this volume).

Although the drive for muscularity construct is directed mostly toward men, the role of gender is important to consider. Just as some men pursue the thin ideal (Olivardia et al., 1995), some women desire to become highly muscular (see, e.g., chap. 11, this volume). However, the overall percentage of women who have a high drive for muscularity or who display maladaptive consequences of the muscularity drive (e.g., AAS abuse) should be low, perhaps similar to the rates of men who become anorexic or bulimic. Thus, when studying the drive for muscularity construct, it may be important for the research questions being considered to include women as comparison or control groups. It may even be important to study the drive for muscularity among groups of only women (e.g., female athletes vs. nonathletes). In other words, the drive for muscularity is not a male-only construct.

MEASURING THE DRIVE FOR MUSCULARITY

Until recently, most body image researchers have tended to use three types of assessment tools: adiposity-based silhouette measures (e.g., Stunkard, Sorenson, & Schulsinger, 1983; Thompson, Heinberg, Altabe, & Tantleff-Dunn, 1999), general measures of body dissatisfaction (e.g., Body Dissatisfaction subscale of the Eating Disorder Inventory; Garner et al., 1983), and clinically based self-report scales that measure disordered eating attitudes and behaviors such as the Eating Attitudes Test (EAT; Garner, Olmstead, Bohr, & Garfinkel, 1982) and the Eating Disorder Inventory (EDI; Garner et al., 1983). However, these constructs do not assess muscularity-oriented body image concerns. The most commonly used silhouette measures provide a range from thin to obese and do not display muscularity, whereas the body dissatisfaction measures tend to be oriented toward dissatisfaction about being fatter or bigger than the person would like. The attitudes and behaviors associated with anorexia and bulimia also appear to be unrelated to the drive for muscularity (McCreary & Sasse, 2000; for a more detailed discussion of adiposity-based body image measurement tools, see Thompson et al., 1999).

If the drive for muscularity is to be studied thoroughly (e.g., antecedents, consequences, correlates, developmental sequelae), researchers must have a way to measure the construct. Measures of people's desire to be more muscular have been developed only recently. One tool that has displayed promise is a variation on the body image silhouette method. The Somatomorphic Matrix (SMM; Gruber, Pope, Borowiecki, & Cohane, 1999) is a matrix of silhouettes whose pictures vary along both muscularity and adiposity dimensions (see also Cafri & Thompson, 2004b). The silhouette at one extreme has the lowest levels of both body fat and muscularity. The silhouettes then increase in fixed amounts of both body fat and muscularity until they reach the final silhouette, which has the highest levels of body fat and muscularity. Participants view the silhouettes and make a series of choices, typically selecting the silhouette they feel best represents themselves as they are now, how they ideally would like to be, and how members of the other sex (or same sex, depending on sexual orientation) might ideally like them to be. Some researchers compare the self and ideal ratings directly, whereas others compute the discrepancy between current and ideal selves and use these scores as the dependent variables (see Cafri, van den Berg, & Brannick [2005] and Edwards [2002] for a discussion of the limitations of using discrepancy scores).

Although other researchers have developed muscularity-based silhouettes (e.g., Frederick et al., 2005; Furnham, Titman, & Sleeman, 1994; Lynch & Zellner, 1999; Thompson & Tantleff, 1992; Tucker, 1982), those silhouettes vary only in muscularity. Yet on most bodies, muscularity and adiposity coexist, giving the SMM procedure more face validity than the other measures. Where the SMM may lack validity is for individuals with higher levels of body fat because it is difficult for people to assess exactly how much muscle mass is hidden under the layer of fat. Thus, the extent to which these people can accurately determine their levels of muscularity (as opposed to the more readily observable body fat) needs to be determined empirically.

This issue aside, the SMM has been used fairly extensively in recent years, in part because it allows researchers to quantify, in kilograms and percentages, just how much muscle and body fat, respectively, people want to gain or lose. The SMM has been used in both North American and European settings (e.g., Cafri & Thompson, 2004b; Olivardia et al., 2004; Pope et al., 2000), as well as in a sample of Samoan men (Lepinski & Pope, 2002). This latter study is especially interesting, because even among the men on this isolated Pacific island, the trend was that respondents wanted an average of 11 kg more muscle than they currently perceived themselves to have; this desire was, in part, due to a perception that the women in their culture wanted them to look that way. These findings closely mimic those with North American and European men.

A second approach to measuring the drive for muscularity has been to develop pencil-and-paper questionnaires. Three such questionnaires have been developed to date: the Drive for Muscularity Scale (DMS; McCreary & Sasse, 2000), the Swansea Muscularity Attitudes Questionnaire (SMAQ; S. Edwards & Launder, 2000), and the Drive for Muscularity Attitudes Questionnaire (DMAQ; Morrison, Morrison, Hopkins, & Rowan, 2004). The SMAQ and the DMAQ contain 20 and 8 items, respectively, and measure muscularity attitudes. Both of these questionnaires have undergone only limited validation. The factor structure of the SMAQ was shown to consist of two lower-order factors: the drive for muscularity (e.g., "I would like to be more muscular in the future") and positive attributes of muscularity (e.g., "Being muscular gives me confidence"). Slightly more validation work was done on the DMAQ; Morrison et al. (2004) showed that the DMAQ is unidimensional and that muscularity attitudes are associated with poorer appearance self-esteem and greater levels of vanity.

A limitation to the SMAQ and DMAQ is that they were developed using samples of only men, suggesting they were created for use only with men. However, as I noted earlier, some women may experience the drive for muscularity, just as some men may experience a drive to be thin. The wording of some of the items on these scales is especially problematic; these items would have to be rewritten for use by women (e.g., the DMAQ item "When I see a guy who is really muscular, it inspires me to get bigger myself"). The DMS, however, was developed using both male and female participants and is intended for use by both genders. Furthermore, the DMS has undergone the most thorough validation of the three scales, and it has been used the most extensively (e.g., Cafri & Thompson, 2004a). For these reasons, I describe the scale, its reliability, and its validity in more detail in the next section. For a more detailed discussion of measurement issues associated with assessment tools for the drive for muscularity, see chapter 5 in this volume.

DEVELOPMENT OF THE DRIVE FOR MUSCULARITY SCALE

The DMS (McCreary & Sasse, 2000) was developed as a 15-item, self-report measure of people's perceptions of how muscular they are or want to be, as well as the behaviors that they engage in to become muscular. The scale's developers chose items for the DMS by polling men and women who were actively involved in weight training at a local gym and by examining the content of weight training magazines. On the basis of the scale's initial psychometric properties, as well as comments from respondents, McCreary and Sasse (2000) changed the wording of four items to more acutely focus on muscularity. Exhibit 4.1 contains the final version of the DMS, including general instructions to respondents. One item on the DMS (item 10, "I think about taking anabolic steroids") showed very little variability in samples of high school and university students and may be removed from the scale (McCreary, Sasse, Saucier, & Dorsch, 2004), resulting in a common set of 14 items.

Each item on the DMS is scored on a 6-point scale ranging from *always* (1) to *never* (6). However, because higher scores on the DMS are intended to indicate higher levels of the drive for muscularity, all DMS items need to be reverse coded before the scale is scored. McCreary and colleagues typically computed the overall average of the DMS items for each respondent, although some body image researchers prefer to compute scale totals (e.g., Cafri

EXHIBIT 4.1
The Drive for Muscularity Scale

Please read each item carefully and then, for each one, circle the number that best applies to you.

1	2	3	4	5	6
Always	Very often	Often	Sometimes	Rarely	Never

1.	I wish that I were more muscular.	1 2 3 4 5 6
2.	I lift weights to build up muscle.	1 2 3 4 5 6
3.	I use protein or energy supplements.	1 2 3 4 5 6
4.	I drink weight-gain or protein shakes.	1 2 3 4 5 6
5.	I try to consume as many calories as I can in a day.	1 2 3 4 5 6
6.	I feel guilty if I miss a weight training session.	1 2 3 4 5 6
7.	I think I would feel more confident if I had more muscle mass.	1 2 3 4 5 6
8.	Other people think I work out with weights too often.	1 2 3 4 5 6
9.	I think that I would look better if I gained 10 pounds in bulk.	1 2 3 4 5 6
10.	I think about taking anabolic steroids.[a]	1 2 3 4 5 6
11.	I think that I would feel stronger if I gained a little more muscle mass.	1 2 3 4 5 6
12.	I think that my weight training schedule interferes with other aspects of my life.	1 2 3 4 5 6
13.	I think that my arms are not muscular enough.	1 2 3 4 5 6
14.	I think that my chest is not muscular enough.	1 2 3 4 5 6
15.	I think that my legs are not muscular enough.	1 2 3 4 5 6

Note. Items 2, 3, 4, 5, 6, 8, 10, and 12 form the DMS behavioral subscale. Items 1, 7, 9, 11, 13, 14, and 15 form the DMS attitude subscale.
[a]This item can be included in or removed from the DMS at the researcher's discretion.

& Thompson, 2004a). Either procedure can be used because there is no mathematical difference between the two procedures; a mean is just a mathematical transformation of a sum.

The developers intended the DMS to be used as a single-score questionnaire. As it currently stands, the scale's psychometric properties support this use. However, my colleagues and I also have been aware that the attitude and behavior items included on the DMS may load on different factors in a factor analysis. This consideration is important because it may allow researchers to differentiate the antecedents and consequences of muscularity attitudes from those of the behaviors in which people engage to become muscular. It may also be important to separate the two types of item in certain situations. For example, when studying whether viewing muscular visual images affects men's drive for muscularity, it makes sense not to include the behavioral items in the dependent measure, because those would not change between the typical 10- to 30-minute pre- and posttest period (those researchers examining longer-term changes, however, may want to keep both subscales). The two-factor structure of the DMS is described later in this chapter in the discussion of its construct validity.

The DMS was created using general scale construction techniques. My colleague and I were especially informed by Nunnally and Bernstein's (1994) excellent overview on scale reliability and validity as well as by past research on the drive for thinness and a thinness-oriented approach to eating. One of the first decisions we made when creating the DMS was to incorporate a diverse group of attitudes and behaviors into the scale, as Garner et al. (1982) did when they developed the EAT (one of the most commonly used measures of a desire to be thinner). This structure also is in line with recommendations by Nunnally and Bernstein, who noted that items on a questionnaire should be sampled from the widest possible population of items for that construct. By limiting the DMS to measuring only attitudes, we would not be tapping into the fullest meaning of the drive for muscularity (i.e., someone with a high drive in this domain not only should possess higher drive for muscularity attitudes but also should be engaging in behaviors that will make him or her muscular). Yet combining attitudes and behaviors into a single construct can be difficult, because attitudes do not always correlate with behaviors (Ajzen, 2001). If someone was to create a questionnaire containing attitudes and behaviors that were poorly correlated with each other, the lack of correlation between these two types of items would lower the scale's corrected item–total correlations (which should be above .30; Nunnally & Bernstein, 1994) and its coefficient alpha.

The second way in which Nunnally and Bernstein (1994) influenced our thinking was with regard to the scoring procedure. The DMS uses a reverse-direction scoring procedure for all items but does not use any reverse-worded items. Using reverse-worded items on questionnaires is common, especially in longer scales, because they help to avoid response acquiescence (e.g., Marsh, 1996). However, research has shown that when reverse-worded items are used in smaller scales, they often create psychometric problems (Nunnally & Bernstein, 1994; Spector, Van Katwyk, Brannick, & Chen, 1997). The biggest issue is that the reverse-worded items in shorter scales often have lower item-level reliability (i.e., poorer corrected item–total correlations) and, as a result, contribute poorly to the scale's overall reliability. Also, in exploratory factor analyses, reverse-worded items often cluster together into a method factor, as opposed to contributing to the content-oriented factor. Thus, to avoid any possible method contamination of the DMS, a reverse-direction scoring procedure was used. This procedure keeps the rating scale salient to the respondent because it is counterintuitive and, in combination with the short length of the questionnaire, helps to protect against response acquiescence.

Reliability of the Drive for Muscularity Scale

The DMS has shown consistently good reliability in both the original 15-item version and the 14-item version (with the question about possible future anabolic steroid use removed). The three most important aspects of reliability are internal consistency, corrected item–total correlations, and test–retest reliability. For internal consistency, alpha coefficients above .80 are indicative of a scale's acceptable reliability. Among male respondents, the DMS has had alpha reliability estimates ranging from .85 to .91 in published reports (Cafri & Thompson, 2004a; Davis, Karvinen, & McCreary, 2005; Mahalik et al., 2003; McCreary et al., 2004; McCreary, Saucier, & Courtenay, 2005). The alpha coefficients have been equally high in reports presented at conferences but not yet published (e.g., Baxter & von Ranson, 2004; Holden, McCreary, & Davis, 2002; McCreary, Dorsch, & Rennebohm, 2001). For female respondents (e.g., McCreary et al., 2004, 2005), reliability estimates have been above .80. With regard to the second criterion for measuring reliability, McCreary et al. (2004) reported corrected item–total correlations of .37 to .65. These are well within the range recommended by Nunnally and Bernstein (1994). Finally, Cafri and Thompson (2004a) reported high 7- to 10-day test–retest correlations in a sample of men: .93 for the entire scale, .84 for the muscularity attitudes, and .96 for the muscularity behaviors.

Construct Validity of the Drive for Muscularity Scale

Construct validity is a general form of validity that indicates the degree to which an operationalized measure reflects the theoretical construct that it was created to measure. There are several ways to demonstrate the construct validity of the DMS, but I will concentrate on two: factor structure and social desirability bias.

Factor Structure

To determine the construct validity of the DMS via its underlying factor structure, McCreary et al. (2004) conducted exploratory factor analyses (EFAs) of the 15-item DMS using a combined sample of male and female high school and university students. The initial two EFAs revealed that the attitudes and behaviors formed separate lower-order subscales for the men but not for the women. An examination of the factor loadings suggests that the main gender differences are among the behaviors: Women appeared to use different behavioral strategies than men when it came to gaining muscle mass. This difference may be a function of the genders using muscularity to serve two different purposes: For women, weight training might help them look thinner because the toned look gained through weight training helps them show off their lack of body fat; for men, the drive for muscularity appears to be about becoming big, which, in turn, influences many other aspects of men's self-image (Grogan & Richards, 2002; Weinke, 1998).

Among the men, the two lower-order DMS factors were not orthogonal. McCreary et al. (2004) showed that the two subscales were correlated at .43 (r^2 = .19). In a separate study, Cafri and Thompson (2004a) reported a correlation of .48 (r^2 = .23) between the two DMS subscales. Because of this correlation, McCreary et al. explored whether the two lower-order factors loaded on a single, higher-order DMS factor. Evidence for this higher-order factor structure would provide further support for the use of a single DMS summary score for both genders. A single-factor, higher-order model emerged for both men and women.

Whether the two-factor, lower-order structure is evident in all potential samples of men and women needs to be determined empirically. Of specific interest is what the factor structure would be in samples of men and women who are frequent weight trainers. P. Choi (personal communication, October 27, 2004) explored the factor structure of the DMS in a sample of frequent weight trainers, 20 of whom admitted to using AAS, and found that the two-factor structure McCreary et al. (2004) reported did not emerge. Rather, Choi and her colleagues found that the attitude and behavioral items were much more highly correlated, resulting in a single-factor structure for the DMS. Whether this result can be replicated in samples of weight-training women and whether this structure holds true only for weight trainers or generalizes to other athletes need to be determined in future research.

Social Desirability Bias

To date, two studies have explored the association between socially desirable responding and the DMS. Duggan and McCreary (2004) asked a self-selected sample of heterosexual and homosexual men to complete the Balanced Inventory of Desirable Responding (BIDR; Paulhus, 1991) in addition to the DMS and no significant correlations between the two measures for either group of men was found. In a sample of undergraduate men, Tylka, Bergeron, and Schwartz (2005) reported nonsignificant correlations between the BIDR and the attitude and behavioural subscales of the DMS.

Concurrent Validity of the Drive for Muscularity Scale

In this context, tests of concurrent validity assess the extent to which DMS scores differ between groups that they should theoretically be able to distinguish between. Concurrent validity can be determined best by using a known-groups procedure. One of the most salient known-group differences would be between either men and women or boys and girls. Gender-based group differences have been found for both the overall DMS scale score and for many of the individual DMS items (e.g., McCreary & Sasse, 2000; McCreary et al., 2004, 2005). Researchers have shown significant gender differences on 12 of the 15 items (McCreary et al., 2004), as well as on the overall DMS score (Baxter & von Ranson, 2004; Cafri & Thompson, 2004a; McCreary et al., 2004, 2005). Men scored higher than women when the differences were significant.

A second known-groups comparison is between those who weight train and those who do not. Initially, McCreary and Sasse (2000) showed a positive correlation of .24 between DMS scores and the number of times each week the respondents typically engaged in weight training activities. How-ever, Baxter and von Ranson (2004) observed that men and women who weight trained during the previous 6 months scored significantly higher on the overall DMS than a group who had not weight trained in the same time period. Other researchers have shown significant differences between those who weight train regularly (three or more times per week) and those who weight train less regularly (Arbour & Martin-Ginis, 2004) or who do not weight train at all (Rutsztein et al., 2004).

A third known-groups comparison would be between weight trainers who abuse AAS and those who do not. To date, only one study has made this comparison. Choi, Pitts, and Grixti (2005) compared a group of AAS users with a group of non–AAS users who had been matched with the AAS users on both age and the gym they worked out at. The AAS users scored signifi-cantly higher on the DMS than the non–AAS-using group.

A final comparison would be between athletes who play sports requir-ing them to be lean (e.g., gymnastics, wrestling, cross-country running) and those who play sports requiring them to be muscular (e.g., ice hockey, base-ball, lacrosse). In a large study of college varsity athletes, J. Carter (personal communication, May 17, 2005) compared the two groups on both the over-all DMS score and the two subscales. Her findings revealed that athletes who played lean sports had significantly lower scores on the DMS than those who played muscular sports and that this difference could be found in both male and female athletes.

Convergent Validity of the Drive for Muscularity Scale

Convergent validity examines the degree to which the DMS is associ-ated with other constructs that it theoretically should be associated with. This section explores the DMS's convergent validity in four areas: (a) asso-ciations with similar measures, (b) correlations with measures of psychologi-cal well-being, (c) correlations with personality and individual difference measures, and (d) correlations with measures of masculinity.

The Drive for Muscularity Scale and Other Measures of Muscularity

Cafri and Thompson (2004a) explored the relationships among several measures of muscularity (DMS, muscularity-based figure silhouettes, adipos-ity-based figure silhouettes, and the SMM) in a sample of male and female college students. Using both bivariate correlations and regression analysis, they found very few significant relationships among muscularity measures, with the strongest being the relationship between the DMS Behavior and Attitude subscales.

In the only study that has looked at the relationship between the DMS and another self-report, pencil-and-paper muscularity measure, Baxter and von Ranson (2004) examined the correlation between the DMS and the

SMAQ (Edwards & Launder, 2000) in a sample of college-age men and women. To make the SMAQ appropriate for women, the wording of several items had to be slightly altered. They reported a significant correlation ($r = .83$) between the two measures, although they did not break down the correlations by gender.

The Drive for Muscularity Scale and Correlations With Measures of Psychological Well-Being

In our original scale development article, DMS scores were correlated with higher levels of depressive symptoms and lower levels of self-esteem, but only among the boys (McCreary & Sasse, 2000). The way gender interacted with the association between DMS scores and psychological well-being made sense in light of similar findings we had observed in the association between male gender-typed traits, attitudes, and stressors and alcohol use and alcohol problems (McCreary, Newcomb, & Sadava, 1999). That is, because of its socially prescribed nature, we expected the drive for muscularity to be more salient for boys and men and thus more closely linked to their sense of self. Because of this differential salience, it makes sense that a higher score on the Drive for Muscularity Scale should be associated with poorer psychological well-being for boys and men than for girls and women.

In another study, McCreary et al. (2001) explored the associations between results on the DMS and the EAT, self-esteem, and social physique anxiety. The authors hypothesized a model in which self-esteem would mediate the relationships between DMS and EAT scores, on the one hand, and social physique anxiety, on the other hand. For boys, this mediational model worked well: Higher DMS and EAT scores were associated with lower levels of self-esteem, which in turn were associated with higher levels of social physique anxiety; the initial correlations between EAT and DMS scores and social physique anxiety were reduced to zero. However, for girls, mediation did not occur: The association between DMS and self-esteem was not significant, and the direct paths between EAT and DMS scores and social physique anxiety were still significant.

Other studies have explored the associations between the DMS and well-being only among men. For example, Jacobs, Picot, and Lilenfeld (2004) found a strong negative association between DMS scores and self-esteem in their sample of homosexual men. This association was present even after controlling for EAT, drive for thinness (DT), body dissatisfaction (BD), and media internalization scores. Additionally, Duggan and McCreary (2004) reported positive correlations between DMS scores and social physique anxiety in both homosexual and heterosexual men.

The Drive for Muscularity Scale and Personality and Individual Difference Traits

Only two studies have explored associations between DMS scores and personality traits. Holden et al. (2002), for example, showed that appearance orientation was positively associated with DMS scores in a sample of college men. Davis et al. (2005) replicated and extended this study, exploring the associations among the drive for muscularity and five personality and individual difference dimensions: neuroticism, narcissism, self-oriented perfectionism, appearance orientation, and fitness orientation. Davis et al. observed that four of the five dimensions uniquely predicted DMS scores; only narcissism was not a significant predictor. The beta values for the significant associations were positive, with higher levels of neuroticism, perfectionism, and appearance and fitness orientation being associated with higher levels of the drive for muscularity.

The Drive for Muscularity Scale and Measures of Masculinity

Qualitative researchers have shown that men think being more muscular makes them look and feel more masculine and that muscular men are more masculine (e.g., Grogan & Richards, 2002). McCreary et al. (2005) explored this question empirically. In their first study, they observed that male gender-typed traits and behaviors predicted DMS scores: The higher the drive for muscularity, the more agentic and unmitigated agentic traits the respondents reported having and the more male-stereotypic behaviors they reported engaging in. In the second study, they showed that men with more traditional attitudes about the male gender role, as well as those experiencing more gender role conflict (i.e., with regard to society's expectations that men be successful, powerful, and competitive and that finding a balance between work and leisure is difficult) tended to score more highly on the DMS.

Mahalik et al. (2003) conducted another study looking at the association between the DMS and masculinity. They showed that higher scores on the DMS were associated with a greater perceived need to conform to society's male role norms (i.e., the socially prescriptive norms for how men are expected to act). In addition to the correlation between the DMS and the overall Conformity to Masculine Norms (CMNI) scale score, Mahalik et al. also reported a significant correlation between the DMS and the CMNI's Winning subscale, which suggests that men with a higher drive for muscularity also have a higher desire to win over others, perhaps even at all costs.

Discriminant Validity of the Drive for Muscularity Scale

Discriminant validity explores the degree to which the DMS is uncorrelated with measures with which it should not theoretically be correlated. In this case, the DMS should not be highly correlated with measures of the drive for thinness. That is, the drive for muscularity is not the opposite of the drive for thinness (i.e., being big vs. being small); rather, it is something distinct, and this conceptual independence should be reflected in low correlations between the two types of measures. However, because people with high levels of muscularity want to show those muscles off to others, they also need to have a relatively low level of body fat. Because of this consideration, there should be a certain degree of association between the two constructs.

To date, several studies have borne out these expectations, demonstrating that the DMS has good discriminant validity. McCreary and Sasse (2000) found that DMS and EAT (Garner et al., 1982) scores were uncorrelated among girls but positively correlated among boys ($r = .37$). Tylka et al. (2005) expanded on this finding and showed that EAT scores were correlated with both the attitude ($r = .22$) and behaviour ($r = .20$) subscales of the DMS. In addition, the thinness-oriented Body Dissatisfaction subscale of the EDI (Garner et al., 1983) and the DMS were uncorrelated in both genders. Baxter and von Ranson (2004) reported a nonsignificant correlation between the DMS and the DT subscale of the EDI. However, Duggan and McCreary (2004) reported a positive correlation ($r = .31$) between the DMS and the EAT, but only among homosexual men; the correlation was not significant among the sample's heterosexual men. Similarly, Jacobs et al. (2004) found a significant association between these two scales in a sample of homosexual men.

Limitations and Future Research Directions

Recently created measures of the drive for muscularity (e.g., DMS, SMM) have filled an important void in the study of men's body image: Men's body image could not be adequately assessed using instruments that focussed a thinness-oriented construct, because that dimension was less relevant to them. To measure men's body images in a socially salient way meant asking them about their desire to be big and muscular (i.e., the drive for muscularity construct). The DMS has become the most validated measure of the drive for muscularity construct. It has been used in a number of populations, including high school and college students, athletes and nonathletes, men and women, and homosexual and heterosexual men.

However, there are limitations to the existing body of research exploring the drive for muscularity. First, the majority of the research done to date has been correlational in nature. Furthermore, there have been few attempts to develop the ideas behind the drive for muscularity construct using an experimental procedure. For example, is the drive for muscularity malleable? Can a group with a low drive for muscularity increase their DMS scores, and if so, how? Second, further research needs to be conducted on the antecedents and consequences of the drive for muscularity. As an example, how is muscle dysmorphia (Pope, Gruber, Choi, Olivardia, & Phillips, 1997) related to the drive for muscularity? Is it an extreme form of the drive for muscularity, or is it a clinical disorder that is only tangentially associated with the drive for muscularity construct? Research by Maida and Armstrong (2005) suggests that scores above the DMS midpoint are predictive of being diagnosed with muscle dysmorphia. A third question concerns individual differences in the desire to be muscular. At this point in the research, even a basic question, such as "What are similarities and differences between those high in the drive for muscularity and those who are low in the drive for muscularity?" needs to be considered.

CONCLUSION

The drive for muscularity is an important component of men's self-image. Right now, theorists and researchers are at the beginning of the long path that will lead to a better understanding of individual differences in men's body image perceptions and body-related behaviors. Luckily, there are many years of women's body image research to draw on. However, it is apparent that a focus on women's body image issues can cloud one's judgment of men's body image issues. The strategies researchers have used in the past may not translate to this new area. Thus, researchers need to be open-minded and creative.

REFERENCES

Ajzen, I. (2001). Nature and operation of attitudes. *Annual Review of Psychology, 52,* 27–58.

Arbour, K. P., & Martin-Ginis, K. A. (2004, October). *Lifting satisfaction: The relationship between young men's weight-training participation, muscle building confidence, and behavior.* Paper presented at the annual meeting of the Canadian Society for Psychomotor Learning and Sport Psychology, Saskatoon, Saskatchewan, Canada.

Baxter, A. E., & von Ranson, K. M. (2004, April). *Validation of the Drive for Muscularity Scale in university men and women.* Paper presented at the International Conference on Eating Disorders, Orlando, FL.

Cafri, G., Strauss, J., & Thompson, J. K. (2002). Male body image: Satisfaction and its relationship to well-being using the Somatomorphic Matrix. *International Journal of Men's Health, 1,* 215–231.

Cafri, G., & Thompson, J. K. (2004a). Evaluating the convergence of muscle appearance attitude measures. *Assessment, 11,* 224–229.

Cafri, G., & Thompson, J. K. (2004b). Measuring male body image: A review of current methodology. *Psychology of Men and Masculinity, 5,* 18–29.

Cafri, G., Thompson, J. K., Ricciardelli, L., McCabe, M., Smolak, L., & Yesalis, C. (2005). Pursuit of the muscular ideal: Physical and psychological consequences and putative risk factors. *Clinical Psychology Review, 25,* 215–239.

Cafri, G., van den Berg, P., & Brannick, M. (2005). *What have the difference scores not been telling us? A critique and proposed alternative to the use of self–ideal discrepancy in the assessment of body image.* Unpublished manuscript.

Carpenter, K. M., Hasin, D. S., Allison, D. B., & Faith, M. S. (2000). Relationships between obesity and DSM–IV major depressive disorder, suicide ideation, and suicide attempts: Results from a general population study. *American Journal of Public Health, 90,* 251–257.

Cash, T. F. (1994). *The Multidimensional Body–Self Questionnaire* (unpublished test manual). Norfolk, VA: Old Dominion University.

Choi, P. Y. L., Pitts, M., & Grixti, L. (2005, August). *How do anabolic steroid users differ from non-users? A case–control study.* Paper presented at the annual meeting of the International Society for Sport Psychology, Sydney, Australia.

Davis, C., Karvinen, K., & McCreary, D. R. (2005). Personality correlates of a drive for muscularity in young men. *Personality and Individual Differences, 39,* 349–359.

Drewnowski, A., & Yee, D. K. (1987). Men and body image: Are males satisfied with their body weight? *Psychosomatic Medicine, 49,* 626–634.

Duggan, S. L., & McCreary, D. R. (2004). Body image, eating disorders and drive for muscularity in gay and heterosexual men: The influence of media images. *Journal of Homosexuality, 47,* 45–58.

Edwards, J. R. (2002). Alternatives to difference scores: Polynomial regression and response surface methodology. In F. Drasgow & N. W. Schmitt (Eds.), *Advances in measurement and data analysis* (pp. 350–400). San Francisco: Jossey-Bass.

Edwards, S., & Launder, C. (2000). Investigating muscularity concerns in male body image: Development of the Swansea Muscularity Attitudes Questionnaire. *International Journal of Eating Disorders, 28,* 120–124.

Feingold, A., & Mazzella, R. (1998). Gender differences in body image are increasing. *Psychological Science, 9,* 190–195.

Frederick, D. A., Fessler, D. M. T., & Haselton, M. G. (2005). Do representations of male muscularity differ in men's and women's magazines? *Body Image, 2,* 81–86.

Furnham, A., Titman, P., & Sleeman, E. (1994). Perception of female body shapes as a function of exercise. *Journal of Social Behavior and Personality, 9,* 335–352.

Garner, D. M., Olmstead, M. P., Bohr, Y., & Garfinkel, P. (1982). The Eating Attitudes Test: Psychometric features and clinical correlates. *Psychological Medicine, 12,* 871–878.

Garner, D. M., Olmstead, M. P., & Polivy, J. (1983). Development and validation of a multidimensional eating disorder inventory for anorexia nervosa and bulimia. *International Journal of Eating Disorders, 2,* 15–34.

Grogan, S., & Richards, H. (2002). Body image: Focus groups with boys and men. *Men and Masculinities, 4,* 219–232.

Gruber, A. J., Pope, H. G., Jr., Borowiecki, J. J., & Cohane, G. (2000). The development of the Somatomorphic Matrix: A biaxial instrument for measuring body image in men and women. In K. I. Norton, T. S. Olds, & J. Dollman (Eds.), *Kinanthropometry VI* (pp. 221–231). Adelaide, Australia: International Society for the Advancement of Kinanthropometry.

Harrison, K. (2003). Television viewers' ideal body proportions: The case of the curvaceously thin woman. *Sex Roles, 48,* 255–264.

Holden, R., McCreary, D. R., & Davis, C. (2002, August). *Predicting the drive for muscularity in young men.* Paper presented at the annual meeting of the American Psychological Association, Chicago.

Huenemann, R. L., Shapiro, L. R., Hampton, M. C., & Mitchell, B. (1966). A longitudinal study of gross body composition and body confirmation and their association with food and activity in a teen-age population. *American Journal of Clinical Nutrition, 18,* 325–338.

Huon, G. F., & Brown, L. (1986). Attitude correlates of weight control among secondary school boys and girls. *Journal of Adolescent Health Care, 7,* 178–182.

Jacobi, L., & Cash, T. F. (1994). In pursuit of the perfect appearance: Discrepancies among self–ideal perceptions of multiple physical attributes. *Journal of Applied Social Psychology, 24,* 379–396.

Jacobs, C., Picot, A. K., & Lilenfeld, L. R. (2004, May). *Drive for muscularity as a predictor of eating pathology and body image among gay men.* Paper presented at the 12th International Conference on Eating Disorders, Orlando, FL.

Jones, D. C. (2001). Social comparison and body image: Attractiveness comparisons to models and peers among adolescent boys and girls. *Sex Roles, 45,* 645–664.

Kelly, J. T., & Patten, S. E. (1985). Adolescent behaviors and attitudes toward weight. In J. E. Mitchell (Ed.), *Anorexia nervosa and bulimia: Diagnosis and treatment* (pp. 191–204). Minneapolis: University of Minnesota Press.

Leit, R. A., Gray, J. J., & Pope, H. G. (2002). The media's representation of the ideal body: A cause for muscle dysmorphia? *International Journal of Eating Disorders, 31,* 334–338.

Leit, R. A., Pope, H. G., & Gray, J. J. (2001). Cultural expectations of muscularity in men: The evolution of *Playgirl* centerfolds. *International Journal of Eating Disorders, 29,* 90–93.

Lepinski, J. P., & Pope, H. G. (2002). Body ideals in young Samoan men: A comparison with men in North America and Europe. *International Journal of Men's Health, 1,* 163–171.

Leslie, E., Owen, N., & Sallis, J. F. (1999). Inactive Australian college students' preferred activities, sources of assistance, and motivators. *American Journal of Health Promotion, 13,* 197–199.

Lynch, S. M., & Zellner, D. A. (1999). Figure preferences in two generations of men: The use of figure drawings illustrating differences in muscle mass. *Sex Roles, 40,* 833–843.

Mahalik, J. R., Locke, B. D., Ludlow, L. H., Diemer, M. A., Scott, R. P. J., Gottfried, M., & Freitas, G. (2003). Development of the Conformity to Masculine Norms Inventory. *Psychology of Men and Masculinity, 4,* 3–25.

Maida, D. M., & Armstrong, S. L. (2005). The classification of muscle dysmorphia. *International Journal of Men's Health, 4,* 73–91.

Marsh, H. W. (1996). Positive and negative global self-esteem: A substantively meaningful distinction or artifactors? *Journal of Personality and Social Psychology, 70,* 810–819.

McCabe, M. P., & Ricciardelli, L. A. (2003). A longitudinal study of body change strategies among adolescent males. *Journal of Youth and Adolescence, 32*, 105–113.

McCreary, D. R. (2002). Gender and age differences in the relationship between body mass index and perceived weight: Exploring the paradox. *International Journal of Men's Health, 1*, 31–42.

McCreary, D. R., Dorsch, K. D., & Rennebohm, J. (2001, August). *Exploring body image perceptions in adolescent boys and girls.* Paper presented at the annual meeting of the American Psychological Association, San Francisco.

McCreary, D. R., Newcomb, M. D., & Sadava, S. W. (1999). The male role, alcohol use, and alcohol problems: A structural modeling examination in adult women and men. *Journal of Counseling Psychology, 46*, 109–124.

McCreary, D. R., & Sadava, S. W. (1999). TV-viewing and self-perceived health, weight, and physical fitness: Evidence for the cultivation hypothesis. *Journal of Applied Social Psychology, 29*, 2342–2361.

McCreary, D. R., & Sadava, S. W. (2001). Gender differences in relationships among perceived attractiveness, life satisfaction, and health in adults as a function of body mass index and perceived weight. *Psychology of Men and Masculinity, 2*, 108–116.

McCreary, D. R., & Sasse, D. K. (2000). Exploring the drive for muscularity in adolescent boys and girls. *Journal of American College Health, 48*, 297–304.

McCreary, D. R., & Sasse, D. K. (2002). Gender differences in high school students' dieting behavior and their correlates. *International Journal of Men's Health, 1*, 195–213.

McCreary, D. R., Sasse, D. K., Saucier, D. M., & Dorsch, K. D. (2004). Measuring the drive for muscularity: Factorial validity of the Drive for Muscularity Scale in men and women. *Psychology of Men and Masculinity, 5*, 49–58.

McCreary, D. R., Saucier, D. M., & Courtenay, W. H. (2005). The drive for muscularity and masculinity: Testing the associations among gender role traits, behaviors, attitudes, and conflict. *Psychology of Men and Masculinity, 6*, 83–94.

Mishkind, M. E., Rodin, J., Silberstein, L. R., & Striegel-Moore, R. H. (1986). The embodiment of masculinity: Cultural, psychological, and behavioral dimensions. *American Behavioral Scientist, 29*, 545–562.

Moore, D. C. (1990). Body image and eating behavior in adolescent boys. *American Journal of Diseases in Children, 144*, 475–479.

Morrison, T. G., Morrison, M. A., Hopkins, C., & Rowan, E. T. (2004). Muscle mania: Development of a new scale examining the drive for muscularity in Canadian males. *Psychology of Men and Masculinity, 5*, 30–39.

Must, A., Spadano, J., Coakly, E. H., Field, A. E., Colditz, G., & Dietz, W. H. (1999). The disease burden associated with overweight and obesity. *Journal of the American Medical Association, 282*, 1523–1529.

Muth, J. L., & Cash, T. F. (1997). Body-image attitudes: What difference does gender make? *Journal of Applied Social Psychology, 27*, 1438–1452.

Nunnally, J. C., & Bernstein, I. H. (1994). *Psychometric theory* (3rd ed.). New York: McGraw-Hill.

O'Dea, J. A., & Abraham, S. (1999). Onset of disordered eating attitudes and behaviors in early adolescence: Interplay of pubertal status, gender, weight, and age. *Adolescence, 34,* 671–679.

O'Dea, J. A., & Rawstorne, P. R. (2001). Male adolescents identify their weight gain practices, reasons for desired weight gain, and sources of weight gain information. *Journal of the American Dietetic Association, 101,* 105–107.

Olivardia, R., Pope, H. G., Borowiecki, J. J., & Cohane, G. H. (2004). Biceps and body image: The relationship between muscularity and self-esteem, depression, and eating disorder symptoms. *Psychology of Men and Masculinity, 5,* 112–120.

Olivardia, R., Pope, H. G., Mangweth, B., & Hudson, J. I. (1995). Eating disorders in college men. *American Journal of Psychiatry, 152,* 1279–1285.

Paulhus, D. L. (1991). Measurement and control of response bias. In J. P. Robinson, P. R. Shaver, & L. S. Wrightsman (Eds.), *Measures of personality and social psychological attitudes* (pp. 17–59). New York: Academic Press.

Phillips, K. A., & Diaz, S. F. (1997). Gender differences in body dysmorphic disorder. *Journal of Nervous and Mental Disease, 185,* 570–577.

Pope, H. G., Gruber, A. J., Choi, P., Olivardia, R., & Phillips, K. A. (1997). Muscle dysmorphia: An underrecognized form of body dysmorphic disorder. *Psychosomatics, 38,* 548–557.

Pope, H. G., Gruber, A. J., Mangweth, B., Bureau, B., deCol, C., Jouvent, R., & Hudson, J. I. (2000). Body image perception among men in three countries. *American Journal of Psychiatry, 157,* 1297–1301.

Pope, H. G., Olivardia, R., Gruber, A., & Borowiecki, J. (1999). Evolving ideals of male body image as seen through action toys. *International Journal of Eating Disorders, 26,* 65–72.

Raudenbush, B., & Zellner, D. A. (1997). Nobody's satisfied: Effects of abnormal eating behaviors and actual and perceived weight status on body image satisfaction in males and females. *Journal of Social and Clinical Psychology, 16,* 95–110.

Rosen, J. C., & Gross, J. (1987). Prevalence of weight reducing and weight gaining in adolescent girls and boys. *Health Psychology, 6,* 131–147.

Rutsztein, G., Casquet, A., Leonardelli, E., López, P., Macchi, M., Marola, M. E., & Redondo, G. (2004). Imagen corporal en hombres y su relación con la dismorfia muscular [Body image in men and its relationship with muscle dysmorphia]. *Revista Argentina de Psicología Clínica, 13,* 119–131.

Silverstein, B., Perdue, L., Peterson, B., & Kelly, E. (1986). The role of the mass media in promoting a thin standard of bodily attractiveness for women. *Sex Roles, 14,* 519–532.

Spector, P. E., Van Katwyk, P. T., Brannick, M. T., & Chen, P. Y. (1997). When two factors don't reflect two constructs: How item characteristics can produce artifactual factors. *Journal of Management, 23,* 659–677.

Stice, E. (2002). Risk and maintenance factors for eating pathology: A meta-analytic review. *Psychological Bulletin, 128,* 825–848.

Stunkard, A. J., Sorenson, T., & Schulsinger, F. (1983). Use of the Danish adoption register for the study of obesity and thinness. In S. S. Kety, L. P. Rowland, R. L. Sidman, & S. W. Mathysse (Eds.), *The genetics of neurological and psychiatric disorders* (pp. 115–120). New York: Raven Press.

Thompson, J. K., Heinberg, L. J., Altabe, M., & Tantleff-Dunn, S. (1999). *Exacting beauty: Theory, assessment, and treatment of body image disturbance.* Washington, DC: American Psychological Association.

Thompson, J. K., & Tantleff, S. (1992). Female and male ratings of upper torso: Actual, ideal, and stereotypical conceptions. *Journal of Social Behavior and Personality, 7,* 345–354.

Tucker, L. A. (1982). Relationship between perceived somatotype and body cathexis of college males. *Psychological Reports, 50,* 983–989.

Tucker, L. A. (1983). Muscular strength: A predictor of personality in males. *Journal of Sports Medicine, 23,* 213–220.

Tucker, L. A. (1987). Effect of weight training on body attitudes: Who benefits most? *Journal of Sports Medicine, 27,* 70–78.

Tylka, T. L., Bergeron, D., & Schwartz, J. P. (2005). Development and psychometric evaluation of the Male Body Attitudes Scale (MBAS). *Body Image, 2,* 161–175.

Weinke, C. (1998). Negotiating the male body: Men, masculinity, and cultural ideals. *Journal of Men's Studies, 6,* 255–282.

5

MEASUREMENT OF
THE MUSCULAR IDEAL

GUY CAFRI AND J. KEVIN THOMPSON

A thin ideal of beauty is overwhelmingly the body ideal aspired to by women and girls in Westernized cultures, and eating disorders are important clinical outcomes related to this body ideal (Thompson, Heinberg, Altabe, & Tantleff-Dunn, 1999). In contrast, a muscular ideal is aspired to by most men and boys (Cafri & Thompson, 2004c; see also chaps. 4 and 10, this volume), although some women want to be more muscular as well (see also chap. 11, this volume). Pope and colleagues identified a clinical disorder that corresponds to a pathological preoccupation with the pursuit of a muscular ideal, once referred to as *reverse anorexia* but now known as *muscle dysmorphia* (Pope, Gruber, Choi, Olivardia, & Phillips, 1997; Pope, Katz, & Hudson, 1993). In muscle dysmorphia, a subtype of body dysmorphic disorder (BDD), a person typically experiences cognitive symptoms that include extreme body dissatisfaction and obsessive thoughts of not being sufficiently muscular, as well as behavioral symptoms like substance abuse (e.g., anabolic steroids), strict attention to dieting, and compulsive weight lifting and mirror checking (see chap. 6, this volume).

This chapter discusses existing methods for the assessment of body image and muscle dysmorphia. The chapter is broadly divided into two sections, body image and muscle dysmorphia. Body image is discussed separately from muscle dysmorphia because even though the former is a central symptom of the latter, a muscular body image is an important area of study in its own right, and many studies have examined body image independently from its clinical implications. The section on body image discusses two types of self-report questionnaire measures of body image: Likert-scale and silhouette measures. Although the measures presented in the body image section have not been validated for use with muscle dysmorphia (with the exception of a study conducted with the Drive for Muscularity Scale [DMS]; McCreary & Sasse, 2000), they should be used in the future if evidence supports their validity in this population. In the section on muscle dysmorphia, we discuss assessment using semistructured interviews and self-report questionnaire measures. Given that muscle dysmorphia is considered a subtype of body dysmorphic disorder, several of the assessment tools that are discussed are measures of BDD, whereas others are more specific measures of symptoms related to muscle dysmorphia. In both the body image and muscle dysmorphia sections, we discuss limitations and provide recommendations for assessment.

MEASURES OF BODY IMAGE

Measures of muscular body image that are currently available include several Likert-based measures and silhouette scales. Measurement of a muscular body image consists of assessment not only of muscularity but of body fat as well, given that body fat determines the extent to which muscles are visible (Cafri & Thompson, 2004c). Moreover, we recently identified a person who demonstrated clinical levels of cognitive–behavioral disturbance related to the perception that he had too much body fat and was not sufficiently lean. The case is presented in Exhibit 5.1 and supports our recommendation that body image related to body fat and leanness be examined when assessing a muscular ideal. Therefore, we review measures that have content specifically assessing muscularity, body fat, or both. We do not review measures that are more generic (e.g., Appearance Evaluation subscale of the Multidimensional Body–Self Relations Questionnaire; Brown, Cash, & Mikulka, 1990) or assess disturbed body image as it relates to eating disorders (e.g., Body Dissatisfaction subscale of the Eating Disorder Inventory; Garner, 1991). Although such measures may tap some dimension of body image related to muscularity, this has yet to be shown empirically.

Likert-Based Measures

The Swansea Muscularity Attitudes Questionnaire (SMAQ; Edwards & Launder, 2000) is a 20-item measure containing two dimensions: (a) attitudes and behaviors related to becoming more muscular (drive for muscular-

EXHIBIT 5.1
Case Description

The psychologist conducted a semistructured interview with Mr. A using the Structured Clinical Interview for the *Diagnostic and Statistical Manual of Mental Disorders, Fourth Edition, Text Revision* (First et al., 2002) and the BDDDM (Phillips, 1996). At the time of the interview, he was 6 feet 0 inches and 165 pounds (body mass index [BMI] = 22.4). He reported few current muscle dysmorphia symptoms, but described numerous symptoms from ages 16 through 19. The predominant feature was a preoccupation with the idea that he had too much body fat, which obscured the visibility of his muscles. This preoccupation significantly impaired Mr. A's social, occupational, physical, and mental health functioning.

At age 16, he weighed 250 pounds (BMI = 33.9), which meets obesity criteria, although he described himself as being muscular at that time. He reported lifting weights 4 hours per day and dieting to gain weight. Thereafter, he had a desire to reduce his body fat, which led to continued weight training and abuse of diet pills containing ephedra (up to 16 pills per day). After 4 months, Mr. A was hospitalized and diagnosed with advanced Crohn's disease precipitated by ephedra abuse. Mr. A dieted and weight trained without using ephedra for the next 2 years, losing over 100 pounds. At age 18, he weighed 145 pounds (BMI = 19.7). Mr. A's symptoms subsided at age 19. He appeared to have poor insight and little motivation to change when he was symptomatic, but he had good retrospective insight and very few symptoms at the time of his report.

Mr. A also reported a substantial history of psychopathology, including past major depressive disorder, current panic disorder, current alcohol abuse, past cocaine and cannabis dependence, and current cannabis abuse. Mr. A also reported using two forms of testosterone precursors, Sterabol and 1-AD.

ity; DFM) and (b) perceived positive attributes of becoming more muscular (PAM). Each subscale has good reliability (Cronbach's α DFM = .94, Cronbach's α PAM = .91), but there is no information regarding the scale's validity other than the fact that the scale was developed via exploratory factor analysis, which in part attests to its construct validity (Edwards & Launder, 2000).

The DMS (McCreary & Sasse, 2000) is a 15-item measure with a six-point response format that assesses attitudes and behaviors related to a muscular appearance. The overall scale has good internal consistency, test–retest reliability, and construct validity for men and women (see chap. 4, this volume). The total scale score should not be used as an indicator of body image, however, because it includes both body image and behavioral items. A factor analysis supported this point for men but not women, finding that the DMS consisted of two factors, body image and behaviors (McCreary, Sasse, Saucier, & Dorsch, 2004). High internal consistencies, test–retest reliabilities, and construct validity (based on exploratory factor analysis and convergent validity coefficients) among men has been found for these subscales as well (see chap. 4, this volume).

The Drive for Muscularity Attitudes Questionnaire (DMAQ; Morrison, Morrison, Hopkins, & Rowan, 2004) is an eight-item measure (including reverse-worded items) that assesses attitudes related to a muscular appearance. The scale has appropriate internal consistency (Cronbach's α = .82–.84) and construct validity for men, the latter established through exploratory factor analysis and convergent validity (Morrison et al., 2004).

The Male Body Attitudes Scale (MBAS; Tylka, Bergeron, & Schwartz, 2005) is a 24-item measure (including reverse-worded items) that assesses body image related to muscularity, body fat, body shape, and height. Among men, the scale has demonstrated adequate reliability for its total score and subscales (Cronbach's á = .80–.94; test–retest r = .81–.94), as well as validity through exploratory and confirmatory factor analysis (although a complete measurement model was not evaluated), convergent and discriminant validity, and concurrent validity (Tylka et al., 2005).

Although these measures are quite new, we are able to provide several guidelines regarding their use. First, the SMAQ has been criticized on several grounds, including its exclusive use of positively worded items, lack of information regarding validity, inappropriate method of factor rotation when conducting exploratory factor analysis and excessive cross loading of several of the items, and item redundancy (Morrison et al., 2004). Given these criticisms, we suggest not using this scale.

With respect to the DMS, DMAQ, and MBAS, all three measures can effectively be used in the assessment of a muscular body image. With respect to the DMS, a particular strength is that it has been used more extensively than the DMAQ and MBAS, yielding greater confidence in its reliability and validity. However, most of the research has been with the total scale score rather than the body image subscale score, which is the only component that is relevant in assessing a muscular body image. Another benefit of the DMS is that its psychometric properties have been evaluated for both genders, which is not true for either the DMAQ or MBAS.

One criticism of the DMS is its exclusive use of positively worded items, which may produce a response set bias (Morrison et al., 2004). Including reverse-worded items, however, may produce other psychometric problems in scales with few items (see arguments in chap. 4, this volume). Therefore, use of reverse-worded items, as is the case with the DMAQ and the MBAS, may not necessarily yield improved measurement. Finally, the MBAS is the only measure that assesses a dimension of attitudes relevant to body fat and body shape, which may be important in achieving a more comprehensive assessment of body image related to a muscular ideal.

Silhouette Measures

Before reviewing the silhouette measures, it is important to consider their benefits and limitations. Secondary analysis of existing data sets with silhouette ratings of muscularity for men (Cafri & Thompson, 2004b; Cafri, van den Berg, & Thompson, 2006) and thin ideal ratings of women (Wertheim, Paxton, & Tilgner, 2004) suggests that these scales are useful because they add incrementally to the prediction of outcome behaviors related to a poor body image beyond using Likert measures of body image. Therefore, we suggest that researchers use both Likert and silhouette measures. With respect to the limitations, difference scores have typically been used to analyze data from these measures, which is problematic because difference scores are often less reliable than the individual ratings and produce certain problems (e.g., attenuating the measure's association with other variables; Cafri, Brannick, & van den Berg, 2006). In spite of this limitation, statistically significant correlations have often been observed between the discrepancy score and other measures (e.g., Likert measures of body image), which we cite in this chapter because they attest to scale validity. Moreover, the problems with using difference scores can be subverted through using individual ratings as the indicator variables (Cafri, Brannick, et al., 2006). Finally, we chose to exclude several scales that could be used to assess a muscular appearance (Breast–Chest Rating Scale, Thompson & Tantleff, 1992; Male Figure Drawings, Lynch & Zellner, 1999; Muscularity Rating Scale, Furnham, Titman, & Sleeman, 1994; Perceived Somatotype Scale, Tucker, 1982) because of criticisms that include such methodological concerns as scale coarseness and method of figure presentation (Cafri & Thompson, 2004c).

The Somatomorphic Matrix (SM) is a bidimensional computerized body image test that can assess self and ideal body image related to muscularity and body fat (Gruber, Pope, Borowiecki, & Cohane, 1999). For each gender, the test consists of 100 images arranged in a 10 by 10 matrix, representing 10 degrees of adiposity and 10 degrees of muscularity. Among college men and women, several of the ratings have yielded test–retest reliabilities that are less than adequate, in particular the discrepancy scores (i.e., self–ideal ratings), which were substantially lower than the point estimates of the individual ratings (see Table 5.1). In support of the measure's construct validity, the images used correspond to particular fat-free mass indexes and body fat percentages (Gruber et al., 1999). Evidence for convergent and concurrent validity using the discrepancy score is available (e.g., Cafri, Strauss, & Thompson, 2002; Cafri & Thompson, 2004b).

The Somatomorphic Matrix Modification (SMM) is a paper-and-pencil modification to the Somatomorphic Matrix (Cafri & Thompson, 2004c). The first modification consisted of 32 figures, transposed from the original measure on a 2 foot by 3 foot poster board, strategically placed in a matrix so that the measure covers the same domain as the 100 figures found in the original Somatomorphic Matrix (Cafri & Thompson, 2004c). A more recent version of this scale consists of 16 figures (covering the same domain) and placed on an 11 inch by 17 inch sheet of paper (Cafri & Thompson, 2004a). Data on the reliability of these modifications are quite similar to the original (Table 5.1). There is also evidence for validity of the 16-figure version among adolescent boys, with statistically significant correlations between

TABLE 5.1
Test–Retest Reliability of the Somatomorphic Matrix and Its Modifications

Ratings	Original Somatoform Matrix, women (n = 32)[a]	Original Somatoform Matrix, men (n = 31)[a]	Somatoform Matrix Modification, 32 figures[b]	Somatoform Matrix Modification, 16 figures[c]
Self muscularity	.54	.78	.80	.76
Ideal muscularity	.55	.55	.64	.70
Self body fat	.75	.64	.72	.77
Ideal body fat	.39	.79	.58	.53
Self–ideal muscularity	.35	.34	.54	.30
Self–ideal body fat	.56	.57	.45	.51

[a]Results published by Cafri, Roehrig, and Thompson (2004). [b]Results based on the responses of men in the Cafri et al. (2004) sample. [c]Results based on a subsample of 66 adolescent boys from the Cafri, van den Berg, et al. (2006) sample.

individual ratings and measures of body image (e.g., body image subscale of the DMS), media influence, symptoms of muscle dysmorphia, and other behaviors related to the pursuit of muscularity (Cafri, 2005).

The Bodybuilder Image Grid, original and scaled (BIG–O and BIG–S, respectively; Hildebrandt, Langenbucher, & Schlundt, 2004), is another silhouette measure. The scale is a paper-and-pencil measure that has figures arranged in a 6 × 5 matrix with body fat and muscularity varying on two separate dimensions (i.e., six degrees of body fat and five degrees of muscularity). Test–retest reliability of ratings on the scale is adequate, but the original version yielded better reliability estimates than the scaled version among a sample of college men (original rs .77–.96), with higher estimates obtained with weight-lifting men (original rs .84–.94; Hildebrandt et al., 2004). The figures in the measure were created in a manner very similar to the Somatomorphic Matrix, supporting its construct validity (Hildebrandt et al., 2004). Also attesting to scale validity is satisfactory convergent and discriminant validity and concurrent validity of individual ratings with other measures of body image and bodybuilding behaviors (Hildebrandt et al., 2004).

This review of silhouette-based measures suggests several points about future assessment of a muscular body image. First, a strength of the SM, the SMM, and the BIG–O is their ability to evaluate body image attitudes related to both muscularity and body fat. Among the reviewed measures, the BIG–O appears to have higher estimates of test–retest reliability than the SM and the SMM for individual items, which supports its continued use.[1]

---

[1]Comparison of test–retest reliability across measures is limited by differences in sample characteristics and very small sample sizes, leading to very large confidence intervals.

However, the figures in the BIG–O appear awkward and unrealistic, which may lead to lower validity coefficients. A notable limitation of the BIG–O and the SMM is their exclusive ability to assess body image attitudes of men; only the SM can be used as a measure of female body image related to a muscular ideal. A limitation of all three silhouette scales is the lack of data regarding their psychometric properties. Future research needs to examine the test–retest reliability of these measures using larger sample sizes, internal consistency through use of multiple items to assess self and ideal dimensions of body image (Cafri, Brannick, et al., 2006), and validity via correlations with other measures of body image and other relevant outcome variables. Regardless of the type of silhouette measure selected, it is important to use individual item scores rather than the difference score as the unit of analysis (Cafri, Brannick, et al., 2006).

MEASURES OF MUSCLE DYSMORPHIA

Muscle dysmorphia can be assessed using semistructured interviews and self-report questionnaire measures. As we mentioned in the introduction to this chapter, several of the assessment tools we discuss in this section are measures of body dysmorphic disorder, whereas others are more specific measures of symptoms related to muscle dysmorphia. Using BDD measures for the assessment of muscle dysmorphia is reasonable given that muscle dysmorphia is a proposed subtype of BDD. One concern, however, is that measures of BDD may not offer sufficient information on specific symptoms of muscle dysmorphia and, as one consequence, may not be sufficiently sensitive to detect the presence of muscle dysmorphia. For instance, if one compares the diagnostic criteria for the *Diagnostic and Statistical Manual of Mental Disorders, Fourth Edition* (American Psychiatric Association, 1994) with the research criteria of muscle dysmorphia proposed by Pope et al. (1997; see Table 5.2), it is clear that there are similarities but some disparities as well. Therefore, whenever possible, it may be useful to include measures of both BDD and muscle dysmorphia when assessing symptoms of muscle dysmorphia.

Semistructured Interviews

The Body Dysmorphic Disorder Diagnostic Module (BDDDM) is an interview based on the diagnostic criteria in the fourth edition of the *Diagnostic and Statistical Manual of Mental Disorders* (American Psychiatric Association, 1994) that is designed similar to other SCID modules (First et al., 2002) to determine whether a diagnosis of body dysmorphic disorder is appropriate (Phillips, 1996). There is evidence for the reliability of the measure based on interrater agreement (kappa = .96; Phillips, 1996). There is evidence indicating that men with muscle dysmorphia met criteria for BDD

TABLE 5.2
Diagnostic Criteria for Body Dysmorphic Disorder and Proposed
Research Criteria for Muscle Dysmorphia

Diagnostic criteria for body dysmorphic disorder[a]	Proposed research criteria for muscle dysmorphia[b]
1. The person has a preoccupation with an imagined defect in appearance; if a slight physical anomaly is present, the person's concern is markedly excessive.	1. The person has a preoccupation with the idea that his or her body is not sufficiently lean and muscular. Characteristic associated behaviors include long hours of lifting weights and excessive attention to diet.
2. The preoccupation causes clinically significant distress or impairment in social, occupational, or other important areas of functioning.	2. The preoccupation causes clinically significant distress or impairment in social, occupational, or other important areas of functioning, as demonstrated by at least two of the following four criteria: a. The individual gives up important social, occupational, or recreational activities because of a compulsive need to maintain his or her workout and diet schedule. b. The individual avoids situations in which his or her body is exposed to others or endures such situations only with marked distress or intense anxiety. c. The individual's preoccupation with the inadequacy of body size or musculature causes clinically significant distress or impairment in social, occupational, or other important areas of functioning. d. The individual continues to work out, diet, or use ergogenic (performance-enhancing) substances despite knowledge of adverse physical or psychological consequences.
3. The preoccupation is not better accounted for by another mental disorder (e.g., dissatisfaction with body shape and size in anorexia nervosa).	3. The primary focus of the preoccupation is on being too small or inadequately muscular, as distinguished from fear of being fat, as in anorexia nervosa, or a primary preoccupation only with other aspects of appearance, as in other forms of body dysmorphic disorder.

[a]From the *Diagnostic and Statistical Manual of Mental Disorders, Fourth Edition, Text Revision* (American Psychiatric Association, 2000). [b]From Pope et al. (1997).

in the study by Olivardia, Pope, and Hudson (2000) based on responses to this measure, whereas weight lifting control participants did not (R. Olivardia, personal communication, August 30, 2005).

The BDD modification of the Yale–Brown Obsessive–Compulsive Scale (Y–BOCS) is a 12-item interview that assesses severity of BDD symptoms (Phillips, 1996). The items assess BDD-related thoughts, behaviors, insight, and avoidance. The scale is reported to have acceptable psychometric properties, and norms are provided for individuals who have BDD (12-item M =

28.5, *SD* = 7.8; Phillips, 1996). There is evidence that men with muscle dysmorphia in the study by Olivardia et al. (2000) scored significantly higher than weight-lifting control participants on this measure (R. Olivardia, personal communication, August 30, 2005).

The Body Dysmorphic Disorder Examination (BDDE) is a 34-item interview that can be used for a diagnosis of BDD and can provide information regarding symptom characteristics and severity (Rosen & Reiter, 1996). The content of the interview includes preoccupation or negative evaluation of appearance, self-consciousness, excessive importance given to appearance in self-evaluation, avoidance of social situations or activities, camouflaging of appearance, and body-checking behavior. The interview has evidence for reliability (Cronbach's α = .81–.93; 2-week test–retest r = .87–.94), interrater reliability (intraclass r = .86–.99; Rosen & Reiter, 1996). The interview also has evidence of concurrent validity, criterion group validity, and treatment validity (Rosen & Reiter, 1996). No studies have been conducted with this measure among people with muscle dysmorphia.

The Muscle Dysmorphia Symptom Questionnaire (MDSQ) is a five-item interview that can be used to obtain detailed information regarding specific symptoms of muscle dysmorphia. Demonstrating criterion group validity are data indicating that the items discriminate participants with muscle dysmorphia from weight-lifting control participants (Olivardia et al., 2000).

The four reviewed measures can be used to assess symptoms of muscle dysmorphia. The BDDDM is particularly useful in making a diagnosis of muscle dysmorphia, the BDD modification of the Y–BOCS and MDSQ are useful for obtaining information regarding symptom characteristics and severity, and the BDDE can be used for both purposes. Moreover, although the reported psychometric properties of these scales are all quite favorable, the BDDE is the most extensively evaluated in terms of reliability and validity. A limitation of the BDDE is that it has not been used in a sample of people with muscle dysmorphia; therefore, its validity in this population is unknown.

Self-Report Questionnaire Measures

The Body Dysmorphic Disorder Questionnaire (BDDQ) is a 15-item measure that can be used to screen people for BDD. This measure consists of questions requiring yes-or-no responses, with yes responses followed up with successive questions with yes-or-no responses and questions with free-response options. Attesting to its validity, this scale has shown satisfactory agreement with diagnoses of BDD using the BDDDM on a sample of 66 psychiatric patients (sensitivity 100%, specificity 89%; Phillips, 1996).

The Body Dysmorphic Disorder Examination—Self Report (BDDE–SR) is the self-report version of the BDDE clinical interview. It is designed to measure the same symptoms of body dysmorphic disorder but without the necessity of an interview. The BDDE–SR has good reliability (Cronbach's α = .94;

test–retest r = .90) and validity with nonclinical and clinical populations (Rosen & Reiter, 1994).

The Body Image Rating Scale (BIRS) was designed to assess the presence and severity of body dysmorphic disorder and its associated features among adolescents (Mayville, Katz, Gipson, & Cabral, 1999). The scale consists of 15 items in a Likert format that focus on cognitive, affective, and behavioral features of BDD. Among adolescents, the scale has excellent reliability (Cronbach's α = .93; test–retest reliability r = .86) and validity (Mayville et al., 1999).

The Muscle Appearance Satisfaction Scale (MASS; Mayville, Williamson, White, Netemeyer, & Drab, 2002) consists of 19 items rated on a seven-point Likert scale. The items can be separated into five subscales: bodybuilding dependence, appearance checking, substance use susceptibility, injury, and muscle satisfaction. These subscales have adequate reliability (Cronbach's α = .74–.79; test–retest reliability r = .76–.89) and construct validity, established through exploratory and confirmatory factor analysis and convergent and divergent validity (Mayville et al., 2002).

The Muscle Dysmorphic Disorder Inventory (MDDI; Hildebrandt et al., 2004) consists of 13 items rated on a five-point Likert scale. The items assess three distinct factors related to muscle dysmorphia symptoms: desire for size, appearance intolerance, and functional impairment. Each factor has adequate reliability (Cronbach's α = .77–.85; test–retest reliability r = .81–.87) and construct validity, established via exploratory factor analysis and convergent validity (Hildebrandt et al., 2004).

The absence of research attesting to the utility of these measures, due in large part to their novelty, precludes the establishment of firm guidelines regarding their use. One critical piece of missing information for all the measures is validation with people who actually have muscle dysmorphia. Therefore, these scales currently have limited use. None of these scales directly assess steroid use aimed at increasing muscularity, which is not only a symptom of muscle dysmorphia but also a primary health concern (Cafri, Thompson, et al., 2005; Olivardia et al., 2000; Pope et al., 1997). One approach to the assessment of substance use is that taken by large-scale surveys. For instance, with respect to steroid use, an item is typically worded in the following way: "On how many occasions (if any) have you taken steroids on your own—that is, without a doctor telling you to take them?" (Johnston, O'Malley, & Bachman, 2003, p. 40). The response format usually consists of an ordinal scale (e.g., 0, 1–2, 3–5, 6–9, 10–19, 20+), and the question can be adapted to assess use over the course of the respondent's lifetime, the past year, and the past 30 days (i.e., current use; Johnston et al., 2003). Another adaptation of the item may consist of modifying the response scale; for instance, with steroids, one can change the scale to the number of months the respondent used the drug, because steroids are often taken in monthly cycles. In some cases, it might be appropriate to add chemical, herbal, or name brands to help respondents identify whether they have used a substance (e.g., Cafri, van den Berg, et al., 2006; Kanayama, Gruber, Pope, Borowiecki, & Hudson, 2001). It is difficult to speculate about the reliability and validity of such substance use items, because they have not been subject to extensive psychometric evaluation; these behaviors are illegal and stigmatized, which limits the extent that validity and reliability data can be collected. Indirect evidence indicates that items assessing illicit anabolic steroid use are reliable over time but less than perfectly valid because underreporting may be a problem (Yesalis, Bahrke, Kopstein, & Barsukiewicz, 2000).

CONCLUSION

We make several recommendations for future assessment on the basis of the reviewed literature. With respect to the assessment of a muscular body image, we suggest using both a Likert measure, either the body image subscale of the DMS or the DMAQ, and a silhouette measure, such as the SM, the SMM, and the BIG–O. The MBAS can also assess a body fat dimension, as can the silhouette measures, which is useful in assessing desire for a muscular appearance more generally.

With respect to assessment of muscle dysmorphia symptoms, the BDDDM and the BDD modification of the Y–BOCS have the most research support and hence are recommended for use in future studies, although future studies may find that the other reviewed measures are useful as well. Particularly lacking are survey methods validated on clinical samples of men with muscle dysmorphia. Certainly, a great deal more research is necessary in the area of assessment related to a muscular body image and symptoms of muscle dysmorphia.

REFERENCES

American Psychiatric Association. (1994). *Diagnostic and statistical manual of mental disorders* (4th ed.). Washington, DC: Author.

American Psychiatric Association. (2000). *Diagnostic and statistical manual of mental disorders* (4th ed.; text rev.). Washington, DC: Author.

Brown, T. A., Cash, T. F., & Mikulka, P. J. (1990). Attitudinal body image assessment: Factor analysis of the Body–Self Relations Questionnaire. *Journal of Personality Assessment, 55,* 135–144.

Cafri, G. (2005). [Convergence data for the 16-figure modification of the Somatomorphic Matrix]. Unpublished raw data.

Cafri, G., Brannick, M. T., & van den Berg, P. (2006). *What have the difference scores not been telling us? A critique of the use of self–ideal discrepancy in the assessment of body image and an evaluation of alternatives*. Manuscript submitted for publication.

Cafri, G., Roehrig, M., & Thompson, J. K. (2004). Reliability assessment of the Somatomorphic Matrix. *International Journal of Eating Disorders, 35,* 597–600.

Cafri, G., Strauss, J., & Thompson, J. K. (2002). Male body image: Satisfaction and its relationship to well-being using the Somatomorphic Matrix. *International Journal of Men's Health, 1,* 215–231.

Cafri, G., & Thompson, J. K. (2004a). *Development of a modified version of the Somatomorphic Matrix.* Unpublished measure.

Cafri, G., & Thompson, J. K. (2004b). Evaluating the convergence of muscle appearance attitude measures. *Assessment, 11,* 224–229.

Cafri, G., & Thompson, J. K. (2004c). Measuring male body image: A review of the current methodology. *Psychology of Men and Masculinity, 5*(1), 18–29.

Cafri, G., Thompson, J. K., Ricciardelli, L., McCabe, M., Smolak, L., & Yesalis, C. E. (2005). Pursuit of the muscular ideal: Physical and psychological consequences and putative risk factors. *Clinical Psychology Review, 25,* 215–239.

Cafri, G., van den Berg, P., & Thompson, J. K. (2006). Pursuit of muscularity in adolescent boys: Relations among biopsychosocial variables and clinical outcomes. *Journal of Clinical Child and Adolescent Psychology, 35,* 283–291.

Edwards, S., & Launder, C. (2000). Investigating muscularity concerns in male body image: Development of the Swansea Muscularity Attitudes Questionnaire. *International Journal of Eating Disorders, 28,* 120–124.

First, M. B., Spitzer, R. L., Gibbon, M., & Williams, J. B. W. (2002). *Structured Clinical Interview for the DSM–IV–TR Axis I Disorders, Research version, patient edition.* New York: Biometrics Research/New York State Psychiatric Institute.

Furnham, A., Titman, P., & Sleeman, E. (1994). Perception of female body shapes as a function of exercise. *Journal of Social Behavior and Personality, 9,* 335–352.

Garner, D. M. (1991). *Eating disorder inventory—2 professional manual.* Odessa, FL: Psychological Assessment Resources.

Gruber, A. J., Pope, H. G., Borowiecki, J., & Cohane, G. (1999). The development of the Somatomorphic Matrix: A bi-axial instrument for measuring body image in men and women. In T. S. Olds, J. Dollman, & K. I. Norton (Eds.), *Kinanthropometry VI* (pp. 217–231). Sydney, Australia: International Society for the Advancement of Kinanthropometry.

Hildebrandt, T., Langenbucher, J., & Schlundt, D. G. (2004). Muscularity concerns Among men: Development of attitudinal and perceptual measures. *Body Image, 1,* 169–181.

Johnston, L. D., O'Malley, P. M., & Bachman, J. G. (2003). *Monitoring the future national results on adolescent drug use: Overview of key findings, 2002* (NIH Publication No. 03-5374). Bethesda, MD: National Institute on Drug Abuse.

Kanayama, G., Gruber, A. J., Pope, H. G., Borowiecki, J. J., & Hudson, J. I. (2001). Over-the-counter drug use in gymnasiums: An underrecognized substance abuse problem? *Psychotherapy and Psychosomatics, 70,* 137–140.

Lynch, S. M., & Zellner, D. A. (1999). Figure preferences in two generations of men: The use of figure drawings illustrating differences in muscle mass. *Sex Roles, 40,* 833–843.

Maida, D. M., & Armstrong, S. L. (2005). The classification of muscle dysmorphia. *International Journal of Men's Health, 4,* 73–91.

Mayville, S., Katz, R. C., Gipson, M. T., & Cabral, K. (1999). Assessing the prevalence of body dysmorphic disorder in an ethnically diverse group of adolescents. *Journal of Child and Family Studies, 8,* 357–362.

Mayville, S. B., Williamson, D. A., White, M. A., Netemeyer, R., & Drab, D. L. (2002). Development of the Muscle Appearance Satisfaction Scale: A self-report measure for the assessment of muscle dysmorphia symptoms. *Assessment, 9,* 351–360.

McCreary, D. R., & Sasse, D. K. (2000). An exploration of the drive for muscularity in adolescent boys and girls. *Journal of American College Health, 48,* 297–304.

McCreary, D. R., Sasse, D. K., Saucier, D. M., & Dorsch, K. D. (2004). Measuring the drive for muscularity: Factorial validity of the drive for muscularity scale in men and women. *Psychology of Men and Masculinity, 5,* 49–58.

Morrison, T. G., Morrison, M. A., Hopkins, C., & Rowan, E. T. (2004). Muscle mania: Development of a new scale examining the drive for muscularity in Canadian males. *Psychology of Men and Masculinity, 5,* 30–39.

Olivardia, R., Pope, H. G., & Hudson, J. I. (2000). Muscle dysmorphia in male weightlifters: A case–control study. *American Journal of Psychiatry, 157,* 1291–1296.

Phillips, K. A. (1996). *The broken mirror.* New York: Oxford University Press.

Pope, H. G., Gruber, A., Choi, P., Olivardia, R., & Phillips, K. (1997). Muscle dysmorphia: An underrecognized form of body dysmorphic disorder. *Psychosomatics, 38,* 548–557.

Pope, H., Katz, D., & Hudson, J. (1993). Anorexia nervosa and "reverse anorexia" among 108 male bodybuilders. *Comprehensive Psychiatry, 34,* 406–409.

Rosen, J. C., & Reiter, J. (1994). *Instructions to users of the Body Dysmorphic Disorder Examination—Self Report (BDDE–SR).* Unpublished manual.

Rosen, J. C., & Reiter, J. (1996). Development of the Body Dysmorphic Disorder Examination. *Behaviour Research and Therapy, 34,* 755–766.

Thompson, J. K., Heinberg, L., Altabe, M., & Tantleff-Dunn, S. (1999). *Exacting beauty.* Washington, DC: American Psychological Association.

Thompson, J. K., & Tantleff, S. (1992). Female and male ratings of upper torso: Actual, ideal, and stereotypical conceptions. *Journal of Social Behavior and Personality, 7,* 345–354.

Tucker, L. A. (1982). Relationship between perceived somatotype and body cathexis of college males. *Psychological Reports, 50,* 983–989.

Tylka, T. L., Bergeron, D., & Schwartz, J. P. (2005). Development and psychometric evaluation of the Male Body Attitudes Scale (MBAS). *Body Image, 2,* 161–175.

Wertheim, E. H., Paxton, S. J., & Tilgner, L. (2004). Test–retest reliability and construct validity of Contour Drawing Rating Scale scores in a sample of early adolescent girls. *Body Image, 1*, 199–205.

Yesalis, C. E., Bahrke, M. S., Kopstein, A. N., & Barsukiewicz, C. K. (2000). Incidence of anabolic steroid use: A discussion of methodological issues. In C. E. Yesalis (Ed.), *Anabolic steroids in sports and exercise* (pp. 73–114). Champaign, IL: Human Kinetics.

III

MEDICAL ISSUES, TREATMENT, AND PREVENTION

6

MUSCLE DYSMORPHIA: CHARACTERISTICS, ASSESSMENT, AND TREATMENT

ROBERTO OLIVARDIA

Images of young women are typically conjured up when one hears the phrase "body image disorder." The idea of a man as the subject of this description still surprises and baffles many. Although women make up the majority of eating disorder patients, men account for 16% of eating-disordered individuals (Andersen, 1999). Unlike eating disorders, wherein the target area is reducing body fat, more and more men are targeting an ideal of increasing muscularity and decreasing body fat (Cafri & Thompson, 2004). Although there is nothing wrong with a healthy pursuit of muscularity and being fit, there exists a clinical phenomenon on the severe end of this continuum that is anything but healthy. Muscle dysmorphia is a pathological preoccupation with muscularity in which men fear that they look too small, skinny, or weak (Olivardia, 2001).

HISTORY OF THE MUSCLE DYSMORPHIA CONCEPT

Before the term *muscle dysmorphia* entered the clinical lexicon, researchers were describing "reverse anorexia" among 108 male bodybuilders (H. G.

Pope, Katz, & Hudson, 1993). It is interesting to note that four of the men had histories of anorexia nervosa (3.7%)—a rate far higher than the 0.02% rate typically reported among U.S. men. These men, along with five others in the sample (8.3% in total), described having "the opposite of anorexia." Instead of fearing fat, they were anxious about the thought of losing muscle. By objective standards, these men were very large and muscular and had low body fat composition. They described this preoccupation as affecting their social lives. In 1997, researchers further studied this phenomenon, coined the term *muscle dysmorphia,* and formalized its symptoms to better describe this condition (H. G. Pope, Gruber, Choi, Olivardia, & Phillips, 1997).

MUSCLE DYSMORPHIA SYMPTOMS AND CLASSIFICATION

H. G. Pope and colleagues (1997) conceptualized the symptoms of muscle dysmorphia as follows:

1. The person has a preoccupation with the idea that his or her body is not sufficiently lean or muscular.
2. At least two of the following four criteria are met: (a) The individual frequently gives up important social, occupational, or recreational activities because of a compulsive need to maintain his or her workout schedule or diet schedule; (b) the individual avoids situations in which his or her body is exposed to others or endures such situations only with marked distress or intense anxiety; (c) the preoccupation with the inadequacy of body size or musculature causes clinically significant distress or impairment in social, occupational, or other important areas of functioning; and (d) the individual continues to work out, diet, or use performance-enhancing substances despite knowledge of adverse physical and psychological consequences.
3. The primary focus of the preoccupation and behavior is on being too small or inadequately muscular and not on being fat, as in anorexia nervosa, or on other aspects of appearance, as in other forms of body dysmorphic disorder.

Muscle dysmorphia was conceptualized as a subtype of body dysmorphic disorder (BDD; H. G. Pope et al., 1997). Individuals with BDD can be preoccupied with an aspect of their appearance such as their hair or skin. Muscle dysmorphia is basically BDD involving the physique. C. G. Pope, Pope, Menard, Fay, Olivardia, and Phillips (in press) found that 14 men with muscle dysmorphia resembled 49 men with BDD who did not have muscle dysmorphia in demographic features, BDD severity, delusionality, and number of non–muscle-related body parts of concern. Although research and clinical experience point to muscle dysmorphia as a BDD subtype in that symptoms involve a body image concern versus a general obsession, Chung (2001) asserted that muscle dysmorphia should be classified as an obsessive–compulsive disorder rather than a subtype of BDD. Further research will be needed to elucidate the true categorization of muscle dysmorphia.

Cognitive Aspects of Muscle Dysmorphia

The hallmark symptom of muscle dysmorphia involves the thought that one is not muscular or big enough, leading to a preoccupation and obsession with the body's physique (H. G. Pope et al., 2000). Many men with muscle dysmorphia actually have well-defined bodies and are often the envy of other men. However, they do not perceive themselves that way; they often distort their body image and see in the mirror someone who is scrawny, weak looking, or small.

John (age 23) was 5 feet 10 inches tall, weighed 210 pounds, and had 6% body fat. He stated, "I'm not sure what people see when they look at me, but they can't be seeing muscle because I don't have any. I lift and lift and can never seem to get big. I am doomed to be small my whole life." Even when their perception of their own bodies is congruent with the perception of other people, they may cognitively evaluate their appearance differently. Gregg (age 28) stated, "I know physically that I am muscular, but I am not muscular enough. I see the muscle, but it just doesn't look as good on me as it does on other people. I need to be bigger."

With respect to preoccupation, insight levels in men with muscle dysmorphia vary. One study found that 42% of a sample of men with muscle dysmorphia had "excellent" or "good" insight, 50% had "fair" or "poor" insight, and 8% lacked insight altogether (Olivardia, Pope, & Hudson, 2000). Thus, it can be very difficult for men with muscle dysmorphia to be convinced that their perception is inaccurate or their compulsive behaviors unwarranted.

A distorted body image leads them to constant thinking and anxiety about their appearance. Olivardia et al. (2000) found that men with muscle dysmorphia thought about being too small, not being big enough, or getting bigger approximately 5½ hours per day, compared with 40 minutes per day by a comparison group of weight lifters. These thoughts when beyond simply thinking about their bodies; these individuals were often tormented by the thoughts. They overvalued the importance of their appearance with respect to their sense of self, leading them to conclude that if they could not achieve the "perfect" body, they had failed as individuals. They reported having involuntary and intrusive thoughts about this issue: Sam (age 40) observed the following:

> I would get up in the morning and already wonder whether I lost muscle overnight while sleeping. I would rather be thinking about the day and

who I was going to see, et cetera. But instead, the thoughts always centered on my body. Throughout the day, I would think about everything I ate, every physical movement I did, and whether it contributed to muscle loss in any way. I would go to bed and pray that I would wake up and think about something else the next day. It's a treadmill I can't get off of.

These consuming thoughts result in a general distractibility among these men (H. G. Pope et al., 2000). It is difficult for them to concentrate and focus on any task or interpersonal exchange when their thoughts are occupied by their body image. Adam (age 18) described his distractibility as follows:

I totally looked like I had ADD [attention deficit disorder]. I couldn't pay attention in school. I got tested, and they said that I didn't have ADD. I was too embarrassed to tell anyone that the reason I couldn't focus was because my head was constantly thinking about how people, especially girls, were seeing me. Did I look bigger than that guy? Did this shirt make me look too skinny? Should I have done extra repetitions on the bench press last night? It goes on and on. I swear, time goes by so quickly when I am in "muscle mode."

The thoughts of men with muscle dysmorphia are highly prone to specific cognitive distortions (DiGregorio, 2005). For example, men with muscle dysmorphia often see their bodies in polarized ways, as reflected in the following typical statements:

- "If I lose an ounce of muscle, then I am the Pillsbury doughboy."
- "If I don't work out one day, I might as well give it all up."
- "If I eat too much fat, then I've blown it."
- "If I am not the biggest guy I know, then I am not big at all and might as well be the smallest guy in the room."

Because of the intense scrutiny men with muscle dysmorphia place on themselves, they project this judgment on others, leading them to endorse the distortion of mind reading in which if they see themselves as skinny and out of shape, then others must be seeing them that way, too. Their thought process leads them to scan their body for imperfections. They filter their body image through a negative lens, ignoring or discounting any positive aspects of their musculature and highlighting the negative aspects. Accepting compliments can be very difficult because of this way of thinking. Raimundo (age 32) explained,

Even when I just had a 3-hour workout and felt OK, I could go home, and one thing could throw it off. If someone compliments me, I don't believe it. I could make it negative in some way. I don't mean to. This woman at the gym said to me that I look good, and whatever I'm doing must be working. [Interviewer: Isn't that a positive comment?] Absolutely not. It just confirmed that people are noticing how big I am, and it made me think that I had to be smaller the day before, because if I was always big, why wouldn't she have complimented me earlier? It also put a lot of stress on me, because I felt I had to maintain my workouts or else she, and anyone else that notices me, will judge me if I lose some muscle.

Another common cognitive distortion is personalization, or feeling that others' actions somehow confirm the person's inaccurate perception. This distortion is also known as *referential thinking*, which is prevalent in psychotic disorders. However, the majority of men with muscle dysmorphia are not psychotic, although they may present that way, given the leaps they make in interpreting others' behaviors. For example, if someone were laughing at a distance, someone with muscle dysmorphia would automatically assume that the person was laughing at him. Angel (age 34) described it as follows:

> It got so bad that I couldn't be around people no more. I was at work and someone was talking about a gym he joined, and I assumed that was a hint that I should be working out more. There was a *Men's Fitness* magazine in the lobby of the building I worked at. I assumed that was put there to tell me that I am a joker if I think I could ever look like the guy on the cover. I know how crazy this sounds, but I can't help it. (*tearful*) I just can't control it.

Individuals with muscle dysmorphia feel they have little control over these thoughts, which further accentuate a feeling of helplessness and promote the use of various compulsive behaviors as a means of managing their anxiety and increasing their sense of control.

Behavioral Aspects of Muscle Dysmorphia

There are several behaviors associated with muscle dysmorphia. The most common is excessively working out and lifting weights. Clinical anecdotes suggest that some men may work out up to 5 hours per day (H. G. Pope et al., 2000). One study found that significantly more men with muscle dysmorphia than comparison weight lifters reported that they would be "extremely uncomfortable" if they missed a week at the gym (Olivardia et al., 2000). They may sacrifice important events to adhere to their workout schedule. One man missed an important job interview because he felt it would conflict with his workout schedule and cause his body to shrink. Men with muscle dysmorphia are often seen as "dedicated" weight lifters at the gym and are often complimented for their rigorous workouts. Igor (age 29) expressed the following:

> People assumed I loved working out. But honestly, I [expletive] hate it! I feel prisoner to it. If I don't do it, I'll feel like [expletive]. So I work out 4 hours a day, hating every minute of it. I don't feel the high everyone is talking about. I just feel the relief of not obsessing that night that I am turning into Jabba the Hut.

This sentiment is shared by other men with muscle dysmorphia. Those who positively endorse long hours of lifting often discuss the "self-medicating" aspect of it, feeling as if it helps manage symptoms of any comorbid disorders. When they do work out, they often exercise intensely and are highly prone to overtraining (Olivardia, 2001).

In addition, men with muscle dysmorphia pay excessive attention to their diet (Phillips, 2005). Phenomenologically, they share similar characteristics to anorexic women who count calories, experience difficulty eating out at restaurants because of a lack of information about the caloric content of the food, and are always thinking about food (Olivardia et al., 2000). The difference is that men with muscle dysmorphia do not want to fully restrict food; they are invested in finding the "perfect" formula of carbohydrates, fats, proteins, and vitamins to maximize their physiques. They often eat multiple times a day. Frank (age 35) described his eating habits as follows:

> I can't even tell you how many cans of tuna fish I ate in a week. They are good for protein, and protein is good for the muscles. I never eat out unless I have the caloric information. Some restaurants post that info online now, which is great. But it limits the places I can go. Most of the time, I am declining social invitations to go out to eat. I want to ensure that everything I put in my mouth is helping me in my goal to get bigger. If a food I eat decreases my muscle mass or does not increase it, then that is a food that no longer exists in my world.

A common behavior among individuals with muscle dysmorphia is checking mirrors and other reflective surfaces such as CDs and car windows (Olivardia, 2001). The motivation for constant checking is not vanity but rather anxiety. Because they are constantly thinking about how small they are, they seek out external validation or invalidation in hopes of easing the obsessive thinking. The result is that they check and recheck, never feeling the "just right" feeling they are looking for, feeling disappointed in themselves if they are not bigger than they feel they should be, and imagining how they would look if their biceps were bigger or abs were tighter. They report getting "stuck" sometimes in the mirror. Christopher (age 32) described this obsession as follows:

> I can't help it. Every time I pass a mirror, I need to check. I will make frequent trips to the bathroom just to check. I don't even really know what I'm expecting. I guess I am hoping that I will look big or, more, not look small. It never works. It's probably because I already have it set in my mind that I won't like what I see, and then presto! I don't like what I see. I could spend hours looking at every inch of my arms, legs, chest, and shoulders. Sometimes I realize that no one ever is inspecting my body like I am, but that thought goes out the window once I am in front of the mirror.

As a result of constant mirror checking, some choose to avoid mirrors altogether, neglecting to see themselves in mirrors even when it is appropriate (H. G. Pope et al., 2000).

Social avoidance is a common characteristic of people with muscle dysmorphia (H. G. Pope et al., 1997). Because they feel so discontented with their bodies, they often camouflage or conceal them. Examples include wearing heavy sweatshirts on hot days, refusing to wear shorts, not taking their shirts off at the beach, being housebound for periods of time, and going out of the house only at night. Others with muscle dysmorphia may wear tank tops or take their shirts off, but with marked anxiety and a hypervigilance about feedback from their environment.

Functioning at school or on the job may become severely compromised by muscle dysmorphia symptoms (Choi, Pope, & Olivardia, 2002; Phillips, O'Sullivan, & Pope, 1997; Ung, Fones, & Ang, 2000). Men have described being forced to drop out of school or quit jobs because of their inability to control their thoughts and behaviors related to muscle dysmorphia. One report noted that two men gave up lucrative and reputable jobs to work full time at a gymnasium so that they could satisfy their weight lifting compulsion (Olivardia et al., 2000). School performance also suffers, as described by Zeke (age 16):

> I would work out before and after school. Then one day, I worked out a bit more in the morning, which led to me being tardy to school by an hour. Then I would want to leave school an hour earlier to get a jump start on my workout. I was always self-conscious about how others saw me. I felt so small inside. It was too much to handle. My parents bought me a home gym for my basement, thinking that would prevent me from going to the gym, which it did. But then I couldn't leave the house because I was exercising so much. School was also hard to get through if I was sore and in pain from my last workout.

The interference caused by working out takes a toll on interpersonal relationships (H. G. Pope et al., 2000). Men with muscle dysmorphia often decline social invitations either because they want to be working out or because they don't feel particularly in shape. When they go out, they may be so self-conscious and immersed in their negative thoughts that they are not socially present, something friends often pick up on. Reassurance seeking is common in some people with muscle dysmorphia. Asking loved ones if they look big or if they are "bigger than that guy" tax companions, who quickly find out that nothing they say will help. Even though it doesn't help, the individual with muscle dysmorphia feels the need to continue asking, which I refer to as "verbal cocaine." Once reassurance is given to someone with muscle dysmorphia, he feels he needs it to feel OK. He quickly develops a tolerance for the relief reassurance brings, leading him to ask increasingly often and intensely. He may go out of his way to obtain reassurance. For example, in the words of Robert (age 33),

> I would ask my Dad once an hour whether he thought I was muscular. He would say yes, and it might have helped me for an hour, then I would accuse him of just saying that to appease me and to tell me the truth. It actually got to the point where I asked him more than 75 times in one hour! I don't really know what I was looking for. He kept telling me that I looked great. Finally, my Dad got exasperated and said, "You look like a wimp! Is that what you want to hear?!" I then felt that that was the truth all along and that everything else was a lie.

Situations involving intimacy and sex can be difficult because of the negative thoughts men with muscle dysmorphia have about their appearance (Olivardia, 2001). Fifty-four percent of men with muscle dysmorphia reported that they "find themselves in awkward sexual situations," compared with only 13% of comparison subjects (Olivardia et al., 2000). One man reported not being able to kiss his girlfriend for fear that she would transmit calories through her saliva. Another man abstained from sexual relations with his wife, fearing that he was wasting energy that could be reserved for the gym, and another could not engage in any intimacy with the lights on for fear that he would be rejected if his partner "really" saw what he looked like.

A common means in the desperate pursuit of muscularity is the use of anabolic steroids (Olivardia et al., 2000). One study found that almost 50% of men with muscle dysmorphia used steroids versus only 7% of comparison men, a large effect (Olivardia et al., 2000). It is interesting that 73% of the men who used steroids had muscle dysmorphia at least 1 year before the steroid use, 9% reported using steroids at least 1 year before the onset of muscle dysmorphia, and 18% reported the onset of muscle dysmorphia and steroid use within the same year. These findings suggest that steroid users should be assessed for underlying muscle dysmorphia symptoms. Even with knowledge of the host of adverse physical and psychological consequences associated with steroids (H. G. Pope & Brower, 1999), many individuals with muscle dysmorphia feel the price is worth it. Others are not properly educated about the havoc that steroids can wreak on one's health.

The effects of overtraining and excessive exercise also take their toll on the body. Men with muscle dysmorphia are at risk for various injuries, including broken bones, torn ligaments, hernias, and damaged joints (H. G. Pope et al., 1997). Given these criteria, gym owners and mental health professionals may encounter subclinical forms of muscle dysmorphia that still warrant concern. For example, a man may compulsively lift weights but not be embarrassed to take his shirt off; or a man who uses steroids but works out appropriately. A man's body image could be just as negative as someone with muscle dysmorphia, but he may express it differently. The individual may benefit from treatment, whether or not these subclinical forms of muscle dysmorphia may lead to clinical thresholds.

Demographic Features

Little is known about the demographic features of people with muscle dysmorphia. No formal epidemiological studies have been conducted to determine the prevalence of this condition. Estimates have cited a prevalence rate of at least several hundred thousand men who fulfill the full criteria and many other individuals who have subclinical experiences of muscle dysmorphia (H. G. Pope et al., 1997, 2000). Further research can better illustrate the true rates of this problem. What is clear is that muscle dysmorphia affects more men than women (H. G. Pope et al., 2000), although cases of women with muscle dysmorphia have been published in the literature (Gruber & Pope, 1999); this gender difference reflects the fact that muscularity is a societal ideal for men more than it is for women. One study found that the age of onset of muscle dysmorphia, on the basis of retrospective reports, was 19.4 ± 3.6 years (Olivardia et al., 2000). Anecdotally, however, men have reported having subclinical preoccupations with their body earlier. It is unclear whether this onset age is representative of groups outside this one particular study.

Comorbid Disorders

Muscle dysmorphia is associated with various Axis I disorders. Mood disorders commonly co-occur with muscle dysmorphia (Olivardia et al., 2000; H. G. Pope et al., 1997). Using the Structured Clinical Interview for *DSM–IV* Axis I Disorders (First, Spitzer, Gibbon, & Williams, 1995), Olivardia et al. (2000) found that 58% of men with muscle dysmorphia had a history of a mood disorder compared with only 20% of comparison men. Nearly one third of men with muscle dysmorphia had a lifetime anxiety disorder, such as obsessive–compulsive disorder, compared with only 3% of control participants. Eating disorders (past or current) occurred in approximately one third of men with muscle dysmorphia. No consistent sequence has been identified as to whether the muscle dysmorphia or the comorbid disorder occurs first (Olivardia et al., 2000). Studies have yet to assess the prevalence of personality disorders in muscle dysmorphia.

Etiological Theories of Muscle Dysmorphia

The hypothesized etiology of muscle dysmorphia follows a biopsychosocial model (Olivardia et al., 2000; H. G. Pope et al., 1997, 2000). BDD, including the muscle dysmorphia form of BDD, has been conceptualized as part of the spectrum of obsessive–compulsive disorders, which posits that disorders such as obsessive–compulsive disorder and muscle dysmorphia share an underlying biological or genetic predisposition (McElroy, Phillips, & Keck, 1994). These disorders share common phenomenological features and may run in families.

Psychologically, men with muscle dysmorphia appear to have low self-esteem. Anecdotal comments suggest that the drive for muscularity may be a means of compensating for a sense of inadequacy about one's masculinity (Mishkind, Rodin, Silberstein, & Striegel-Moore, 1986). A muscular body is culturally a powerful symbolic expression of one's manhood and sexual virility and is seen as inspiring the respect, admiration, and envy of others (both men and women). For some men, the purpose of being very muscular is to convey strength and power, causing others to be fearful or to feel intimidated. In contrast, a thin body is often associated with more emasculated characteristics (Andersen, Cohn, & Holbrook, 2000).

Peer experiences may also influence the development of a body image disorder (H. G. Pope et al., 2000). Men with muscle dysmorphia report having been very underweight or overweight as children and adolescents, for which they were harassed and teased, leading them to overly focus on their appearance and physique to cease the harassment.

A sociocultural theory of muscle dysmorphia has received the most attention. Men are being exposed to an increasing array of images in the media (e.g., advertisements, movie stars, athletes, action figures) that dictate that the muscular and fit body is the male ideal and that falling short of that ideal renders one unattractive (H. G. Pope et al., 2000). For example, in 1958, only 6% of male models in *Cosmopolitan* magazine were undressed in some way (compared with 17% of female models), but in 1998, 32% of male models were similarly undressed (compared with 27% of female models). Many of these photographs were used to sell products that had nothing to do at all with the human body (H. G. Pope et al., 2000). Leit, Pope, and Gray (2001) also found that the *Playgirl* centerfold has shed an average of 12 pounds of fat and gained an average of 27 pounds of muscle in the past 25 years. Many of these bodies are unattainable for the average man. However, the literature on men and body image is still in its infancy. It is important to emphasize that although the media may greatly affect how men view their bodies (Cafri, van den Berg, & Thompson, 2006; Leit, Gray, & Pope, 2002; Morrison, Morrison, & Hopkins, 2003), it would be inaccurate to consider the media the only or most dominant etiological factor. If it were, many more men would be experiencing muscle dysmorphia. Overly focusing on the media also does a disservice to patients, as clinicians may neglect or de-emphasize important psychological or psychiatric factors. Future research is warranted to further elucidate the factors that aid in the development of muscle dysmorphia.

Muscle Dysmorphia and Normal Weight Lifting

A common misconception about muscle dysmorphia is that the concept pathologizes the sport or recreation of weight lifting (H. G. Pope et al., 2000). It is true that men with muscle dysmorphia may gravitate to bodybuilding, much like women with weight-restrictive tendencies may take up ballet or gymnastics. Various studies have focused on bodybuilding and weight lifting populations to ascertain the level of pathology in these groups. Olivardia et al. (2000) found that men with muscle dysmorphia differed significantly from a weight lifting comparison group on many indices, including obsessive thinking, mirror checking, steroid use, and prevalence of comorbid disorders. Therefore, one can be an avid weight lifter without being muscle dysmorphic. Perhaps the degree of investment constitutes the boundary between healthy and unhealthy.

Hurst, Hale, Smith, and Collins (2000) found that more experienced bodybuilders differed from less experienced ones in that the former reported more social anxiety and were more likely to exhibit signs of exercise dependence. Whitsel-Anderson (2002) divided her sample of weight lifters into four groups to ascertain whether one group was more likely to endorse muscle dysmorphia and eating disorder symptomatology. Competitive, competitive–athletic, athletic, and recreational weight lifters displayed the most to the fewest symptoms, respectively, in all areas of data analysis. The competitive and competitive–athletic groups reported the highest number of participants diagnosed with muscle dysmorphia and achieved the highest levels of eating disorder symptomatology. The recreational participants had no diagnosable cases of either disorder. Overall, 12 (23%) participants met criteria for muscle dysmorphia.

Lantz, Rhea, and Cornelius (2002) found similar results when they compared elite-level competitive bodybuilders (n = 100) and power lifters (n = 68). Power lifters differed from competitive bodybuilders in that their focus of competition was exclusively on strength. The aesthetic of a power lifter's body is not important. In fact, many famous power lifters sport large guts. Both groups completed the Muscle Dysmorphia Inventory (MDI; Rhea, Lantz, & Cornelius, 2004) at the time of or immediately before competition. Elite-level competitive bodybuilders were significantly more likely to report body size and symmetry concerns, physique protection, dietary behavior, and pharmacological use than were power lifters. These results suggest that elite-level bodybuilders are significantly more likely to have characteristics associated with muscle dysmorphia than are elite-level power lifters.

Olivardia (2001) discussed four criteria that can aid in determining whether weight lifting behavior is healthy or unhealthy. First is the presence of body image distortions. If an individual's behavior is motivated by a distorted body image perception, the behavior has a high likelihood of becoming excessive and fraught with desperation. Second, if much or all of a person's self-esteem is predicated on muscularity, it could lead to more muscle dysmorphia symptoms, simply because the need to regulate the emotions and sense of self have no other outlet than body image. Third, if the weight lifting is interfering with daily functioning or getting in the way of relationships or other important areas of life, the practice would be seen as unhealthy. The fourth criterion is whether the person is endangering his health by using anabolic steroids or other substances known to have a host of adverse effects or if his routine is excessive to the point where he is experiencing torn ligaments, broken bones, or severe soreness. Healthy exercise and weight lifting are not supposed to include frequent trips to the hospital or long stays in bed as a result of excessive stress on the muscles.

ASSESSMENT AND TREATMENT OF MUSCLE DYSMORPHIA

Because muscle dysmorphia research is still in its infancy, assessment methods specific to the condition are lacking (for a complete discussion, see chap. 5, this volume). For instance, the Drive for Muscularity Scale (McCreary, Sasse, Saucier, & Dorsch; see also chap. 4, this volume) and the Body Image Grid (BIG) Scale (Hildebrandt, Langenbucher, & Schlundt, 2004) are both methodologically sound measures for assessing behaviors, perceptions, and attitudes related to the pursuit of muscularity in general. It is unclear, however, whether a specific score is suggestive of muscle dysmorphia or not; further research is needed in this area.

Early studies attempting to assess muscle dysmorphia specifically (H. G. Pope et al., 1997; Olivardia et al., 2000) used the Structured Clinical Interview for the *DSM–IV* Axis I Disorders (First et al., 1995) module for body dysmorphic disorder (BDD) and the BDD version of the Yale–Brown Obsessive–Compulsive Disorder Scale (BDD–Y–BOCS; Phillips, Hollander, et al., 1997) and simply adapted it to muscularity concerns. Both of these instruments are semistructured interviews that require a level of expertise from the interviewer and rater.

Two measures have been created to specifically assess for muscle dysmorphia symptoms. The Muscle Appearance Satisfaction Scale (MASS), a brief, 19-item self-report measure, demonstrated good internal consistency, test–retest reliability, and construct validity (Mayville, Williamson, White, Netemeyer, & Drab, 2002). The more recent Muscle Dysmorphia Inventory, a 27-item self-report measure, had good reliability estimates (Cronbach's α .72–.94) and good construct and convergent validity. The authors of the MASS and MDI asserted that their measures can be useful for research and clinical work relating to muscle dysmorphia (Mayville et al., 2002; Rhea et al., 2004).

The treatment of muscle dysmorphia has yet to be systematically studied. For now, clinicians can borrow from interventions that have been empirically studied on related disorders such as obsessive–compulsive disorder, other forms of body dysmorphic disorder, and eating disorders. It is important to note that men with muscle dysmorphia rarely present for treatment (H. G. Pope et al., 2000). When they do, it is usually for a related issue such as depression or social anxiety. Shame, associated with feelings of emasculation and vanity, is a prominent emotion among men with muscle dysmorphia. Building a strong alliance is crucial at the beginning of treatment, because the therapist may be the first or only person to whom a patient has disclosed the muscle dysmorphia. In addition, men with muscle dysmorphia may fear treatment because it presents a catch-22 dilemma: if they don't seek treatment, they are tormented by preoccupations about being too small and may take dangerous drugs to become muscular; if they do seek treatment, the treatment would include decreasing time at the gym and ceasing steroid use, which will inevitably result in some decrease of muscle mass—their biggest fear. The insight that treatment may diminish their obsession often does not enter into the equation. Finally, men with muscle dysmorphia often spend their time exclusively at the gym or at home, another barrier to active engagement in treatment. It is not unusual for muscle dysmorphia patients to be late or not show for therapy sessions because of time spent working out.

Many men entering therapy for muscle dysmorphia have unrealistic ideas about the therapy. Marcus (age 34) felt that the therapy was going to help him accept how pathetic he looked, whereas David (age 22) expected the treatment to result in him feeling 100% confident about his body 100% of the time. Therapists must discuss these preconceived notions about what therapy can and cannot do with clients at the initiation of therapy.

Therapists should begin treatment with psychoeducation about realistic body image ideals, proper nutrition, the dangers of steroids, and a critical analysis of media images. Gaining some knowledge about the onset and development of muscle dysmorphia symptoms can be helpful. Although it is not empirically studied, psychodynamic psychotherapy can be helpful in supporting patients and validating his experience by providing a safe environment to explore any peer experiences or important events that may have contributed to the muscle dysmorphia. A discussion of the development of the patient's masculine identity is often warranted. Several transference reactions can occur in the therapy. A male therapist may feel that a patient is scrutinizing him or comparing himself with the therapist, and such a patient may ask his therapist to describe his own exercise regimen. Depending on the client's sexual orientation, he may ask the therapist to speak on behalf of all potential members of his sex: For example, "Would you and your friends be attracted to a build like mine?"

The bulk of treatment research in this arena has had a cognitive–behavioral orientation. Cognitive–behavioral treatment (CBT) focuses on the patient's thoughts and actions and appears effective for BDD (Veale, 2002; Wilhelm, Otto, Lohr, & Deckersback, 1999). Thus, it seems plausible that these interventions may also be effective for muscle dysmorphia. Cognitive strategies include identifying distorted thinking patterns and actively challenging them and finding accurate evidence for and against each thought. For example, Johnny (age 38) saw his body image in black-or-white terms. He was instructed to develop a hierarchy of 1 to 10 in which 1 represented feeling totally scrawny and out of shape and 10 represented feeling in top shape. He was instructed to quantify his out-of-shape feelings more accurately instead of always saying he was too small if he didn't work out. Eventually, he realized that there was a gray area in his body image, which helped him feel better if he missed a workout. He would report feeling a 6 if he missed the gym for a day, instead of feeling a 1. With practice, this realization influenced his behavior positively. Although he still felt self-conscious, he was able to leave his house and make plans with others, whereas before he had been housebound.

Behavioral strategies focus on limiting repetitive behaviors such as weight lifting, mirror checking, and reassurance seeking, and increasing social exposure such as taking one's shirt off in public or attending a social event after skipping a workout at the gym (Phillips, 2005; Veale, 2002). This treatment might begin with the therapist helping the patient list all of the problematic behaviors and rank them from most difficult to least difficult to tackle. The client must develop coping skills to deal with these behaviors, and relaxation training is often beneficial. Understanding the triggers for any compulsive behavior is key; interventions can focus on the trigger with the goal of preventing the compulsion altogether. Will (age 19) realized that boredom was a major trigger for him to mirror check. The therapy then focused on developing things he could do to prevent boredom, which in turn prevented the mirror checking. Stopping steroid use should also be a major goal; a substance abuse model of treatment may be appropriate.

An important component of CBT is helping patients understand the effect their thoughts have on their behavior, which then affects their environment and the people in it, which in turn affect them, creating a self-fulfilling prophecy. For example, Jim (age 26) was very self-conscious and shy and anxious in social settings. He would sweat profusely and avoid eye contact with others because he thought that others were scrutinizing his appearance (i.e., he engaged in mind reading). Instead of thinking that others did not approach or respond to him as a response to his own behavior, he automatically felt that their lack of interest directly confirmed his worst fear—that his body was offensive in some way. Part of the therapy involved helping Jim practice behaving in ways that were congruent with social openness. The therapist instructed him to focus on improving his posture, making eye contact, and initiating conversations. Even though he was still anxious, he noticed that others responded differently to him when he acted more confident. Once he realized that people were open to socializing with him, he finally began to challenge his thought that others shunned him because of his appearance. He realized that his thoughts about his body were what got him into trouble, not his body.

Case series, open-label studies, and controlled treatment trials indicate that the serotonin reuptake inhibitors (e.g., fluoxetine, citalopram, fluvoxamine, sertraline, paroxetine, and clomipramine) are effective for a majority of patients with BDD. It appears that higher doses and longer treatment trials than are usually required for depression are often needed to treat BDD. Studies indicate that it takes an average of approximately 8 weeks, and as long as 16 weeks, for a response to emerge (Phillips, 2000; Phillips, O'Sullivan, & Pope, 1997).

CONCLUSION

Muscle dysmorphia, a disorder marked by a pathological preoccupation with one's musculature, is relatively new as a clinical phenomenon. It appears that many factors contribute to the development of muscle dysmorphia, but it is unclear at this time which factors are most predictive. More research is needed to further describe the symptoms of muscle dysmorphia, elucidate risk factors, and develop efficacious treatment and prevention programs.

REFERENCES

Andersen, A. (1999). Eating disorders in gay males. *Psychiatric Annals, 29,* 206–212.

Andersen, A., Cohn, L., & Holbrook, T. (2000). *Making weight.* Carlsbad, CA: Gurze Books.

Cafri, G., & Thompson, J. K. (2004). Measuring male body image: A review of the current methodology. *Psychology of Men and Masculinity, 5,* 18–29.

Cafri, G., van den Berg, P., & Thompson, J. K. (2006). Pursuit of muscularity in adolescent boys: Relations among biopsychosocial variables and clinical outcomes. *Journal of Clinical Child and Adolescent Psychology, 35,* 283–291.

Choi, P. Y. L., Pope, H. G. Jr., & Olivardia, R. (2002). Muscle dysmorphia: A new syndrome in weight lifters. *British Journal of Sports Medicine, 36,* 375–377.

Chung, B. (2001). Muscle dysmorphia: A critical review of the proposed criteria. *Perspectives in Biological Medicine, 44,* 565–574.

DiGregorio, D. T. (2005). *Cognitive errors, depression, and body dysmorphia in male weightlifters.* Unpublished doctoral dissertation, Philadelphia College of Osteopathic Medicine, Philadelphia.

First, M. B., Spitzer, R. L., Gibbon, M., & Williams, J. B. W. (1995). *Structured Clinical Interview for DSM–IV Axis I Disorders.* New York: New York State Psychiatric Institute, Biometrics Research.

Gruber, A. J., & Pope, H. G., Jr. (1999). Compulsive weight lifting and anabolic drug abuse among women rape victims. *Comprehensive Psychiatry, 40,* 273–277.

Hildebrandt, T., Langenbucher, J., & Schlundt, D. G. (2004). Muscularity concerns among men: Development of attitudinal and perceptual measures. *Body Image, 1,* 169–181.

Hurst, R., Hale, B., Smith, D., & Collins, D. (2000). Exercise dependence, social physique anxiety, and social support in experienced and inexperienced bodybuilders and weightlifters. *British Journal of Sports Medicine, 34,* 431–435.

Lantz, C. D., Rhea, D. J., & Cornelius, A. E. (2002). Muscle dysmorphia in elite-level power lifters and bodybuilders: A test of differences within a conceptual model. *Journal of Strength and Conditioning Research, 16,* 649–655.

Leit, R. A., Gray, J. J., & Pope, H. G., Jr. (2002). The media's representation of the ideal male body: A cause for muscle dysmorphia? *International Journal of Eating Disorders, 31,* 334–338.

Leit, R. A., Pope, H. G., Jr., & Gray, J. J. (2001). Cultural expectations of muscularity in men: The evolution of *Playgirl* centerfolds. *International Journal of Eating Disorders, 29,* 90–93.

Mayville, S. B., Williamson, D. A., White, M. A., Netemeyer, R. G., & Drab, D. L. (2002). Development of the Muscle Appearance Satisfaction Scale: A self report measure for the assessment of muscle dysmorphia symptoms. *Assessment, 9,* 351–360.

McCreary, D., Sasse, D. K., Saucier, D. M., & Dorsch, K. D. (2004). Measuring the drive for muscularity: Factorial validity of the drive for muscularity scale in men and women. *Psychology of Men and Masculinity, 5,* 49–58.

McElroy, S. L., Phillips, K. A., & Keck, P. E., Jr. (1994). Obsessive–compulsive spectrum disorders. *Journal of Clinical Psychiatry, 55*(Suppl.), 33–51.

Mishkind, M. E., Rodin, J., Silberstein, L. R., & Striegel-Moore, R. H. (1986). The embodiment of masculinity: Cultural, psychological and behavioral dimensions. *American Behavioral Scientist, 29,* 545–562.

Morrison, T. G., Morrison, M. A., & Hopkins, C. (2003). Striving for bodily perfection? An exploration of the drive for muscularity in Canadian men. *Psychology of Men and Masculinity, 4,* 111–120.

Olivardia, R. (2001). Mirror, mirror on the wall, who's the largest of them all? *Harvard Review of Psychiatry, 9,* 254–259.

Olivardia, R., Pope, H. G., Jr., & Hudson, J. I. (2000). Muscle dysmorphia in male weightlifters: A case–control study. *American Journal of Psychiatry, 157,* 1291–1296.

Phillips, K. A. (2000). Pharmacologic treatment of body dysmorphic disorder: A review of empirical data and a proposed treatment algorithm. *Psychiatry Clinics of North America, 7,* 59–82.

Phillips, K. A. (2005). *The broken mirror* (2nd ed.). New York: Oxford Press.

Phillips, K. A., Hollander, E., Rasmussen, S. A., Aronowitz, B. R., DeCaria, C., & Goodman, W. K. (1997). A severity rating scale for body dysmorphic disorder: Development, reliability, and validity of a modified version of the Yale–Brown Obsessive Compulsive Scale. *Psychopharmacology Bulletin, 33,* 17–22.

Phillips, K. A., O'Sullivan, R. L., & Pope, H. G., Jr. (1997). Muscle dysmorphia. *Journal of Clinical Psychiatry, 58,* 361.

Pope, C. G., Pope, H. G., Jr., Menard, W., Fay, C., Olivardia, R., & Phillips, K. A. (2005). Clinical features of muscle dysmorphia among males with body dysmorphic disorder. *Body Image, 2,* 395–400.

Pope, H. G., Jr., & Brower, K. J. (1999). Anabolic–androgenic steroid abuse. In B. J. Sadock & V. A. Sadock (Eds.), *Comprehensive textbook of psychiatry* (Vol. 7, pp. 1085–1096). Baltimore: Williams & Wilkins.

Pope, H. G., Jr., Gruber, A. J., Choi, P., Olivardia, R., & Phillips, K. A. (1997). Muscle dysmorphia: An underrecognized form of body dysmorphic disorder. *Psychosomatics, 38*, 548–557.

Pope, H. G., Jr., Katz, D. L., & Hudson, J. I. (1993). Anorexia nervosa and "reverse anorexia" among 108 male bodybuilders. *Comprehensive Psychiatry, 34*, 406–409.

Pope, H. G., Jr., Olivardia, R., Borowiecki, J., & Cohane, G. (2001). The growing commercial value of the male body: A longitudinal survey of advertising in women's magazines. *Psychotherapy and Psychosomatics, 70*, 189–192.

Pope, H. G., Jr., Olivardia, R., Gruber, A. J., & Borowiecki, J. (1999). Evolving ideals of male body image as seen through action toys. *International Journal of Eating Disorders, 26*, 65–72.

Pope, H. G., Jr., Phillips, K. A., & Olivardia, R. (2000). *The Adonis complex: The secret crisis of male body obsession.* New York: Free Press.

Rhea, D. J., Lantz, C. D., & Cornelius, A. E. (2004). Development of the muscle dysmorphia inventory (MDI). *Journal of Sports Medicine and Physical Fitness, 44*, 428–435.

Ung, E. K., Fones, C. S., & Ang, A. W. (2000). Muscle dysmorphia in a young Chinese male. *Annals, Academy of Medicine, Singapore, 29*, 135–137.

Veale, D. (2002). Cognitive behaviour therapy for body dysmorphic disorder. In D. J. Castle & K. A. Phillips (Eds.), *Disorders of body image* (pp. 121–138). Hampshire, England: Wrightson Biomedical Publishing.

Whitsel-Anderson, S. (2002). Body dissatisfaction in males. *Dissertation Abstracts International, 62* (09), 4243B.

Wilhelm, S., Otto, M. W., Lohr, B., & Deckersback, T. (1999). Cognitive behavior group therapy for body dysmorphic disorder: A case series. *Behaviour Research and Therapy, 37*, 71–75.

7

MUSCLE ENHANCEMENT SUBSTANCES AND STRATEGIES

MICHAEL S. BAHRKE

Bodybuilders and weight lifters use a myriad of drugs, substances, and methods to enhance their muscle mass, strength, endurance, and appearance. Included in the armamentarium are anabolic–androgenic steroids (AASs), testosterone precursors or prohormones, beta-2 agonists, human growth hormone (hGH) and insulinlike growth factor (IGF-1), insulin, human chorionic gonadotropin (hCG), antiestrogenic drugs, stimulants, diuretics, analgesics, and dietary supplements. However, with the advent of gene doping, all of these drugs and substances could become passé, because bodybuilders and weight lifters may soon be able to inject genes to enhance their appearance and performance. Unfortunately, none of these drugs, substances, and methods is without adverse health effects, and the abuse of several of them may result in death.

Although it is difficult to obtain an accurate and reliable listing of the substances and methods individuals use and abuse to achieve a more muscular appearance, the 2007 Prohibited List of the World Anti-Doping Agency (WADA, 2006b) provides a reasonably accurate indication (see Table 7.1). Included among the anabolic agents used to increase muscle mass are synthetic versions (e.g., nandrolone) of naturally occurring hormones (e.g., tes-

TABLE 7.1
Typical Substances Athletes Use to Enhance Performance
and Appearance

Category	Substance
Anabolic agents	Testosterone
	Nandrolone
	Stanozolol
	Methandienone
	Clenbuterol
Glucocorticosteroids	Betamethasone
	Prednisolone
	Dexamethasone
Cannabinoids	Cannabis
Stimulants	Ephedrine
	Cocaine
	Amphetamine
Beta-2 agonists	Salbutamol
	Terbutaline
	Formoterol
Diuretics and masking agents	Furosemide
	Hydrochlorothiazide
	Acetazolamide
	Epitestosterone
	Finasteride
Hormones	Erythropoietin (EPO)
	Human growth hormone (hGH)
	Insulin
Agents with antiestrogenic activity	Tamoxifen

Note. From World Anti-Doping Code: The 2007 Prohibited List (pp. 1–11), by World Anti-Doping Agency, 2006, Montreal, Quebec, Canada: Author. Copyright 2006 by World Anti-Doping Agency. Adapted with permission.

tosterone) as well as other agents with purported anabolic activity. Erythropoietin, human growth hormone, insulin-like growth factor, mechano growth factors, gonadotropins (e.g., luteinizing hormone and human chorionic gonadotropin), insulin, and corticotrophins are also among the hormones and related substances used for muscle enhancement. Beta-2 agonists, such as clenbuterol, are also used, as are agents with antiestrogenic activity, including aromatase inhibitors (e.g., testolactone) and selective estrogen receptor modulators like tamoxifen. Diuretics (e.g., furosemide) and other masking agents such as epitestosterone, probenecid, alpha-reductase inhibitors (e.g., finasteride), and plasma expanders (e.g., albumin, dextran, hydroxyethyl starch) are among the substances used to enhance muscular definition through fluid loss and to avoid detection when using performance-enhancing substances.

In addition to substances to enhance muscle mass, bodybuilders and weight lifters frequently use other methods to improve their appearance and performance, including the enhancement of oxygen transfer via autologous, homologous, or heterologous blood doping and oxygen uptake, chemical and physical manipulation through tampering, infusions, catheterization, urine substitution, and gene doping. They may use stimulants (e.g., amphetamine, bromantan, caffeine, cocaine, ephedrine, mesocarb, methamphetamine, modafinil, phentermine, and strychnine), narcotics (e.g., fentanyl, methadone, and morphine), cannabinoids (e.g., hashish and marijuana), or glucocorticosteroids directly and indirectly as appearance-enhancing substances. Lastly, to relax and recover following intense physical training sessions, bodybuilders and weight lifters often use social and recreational drugs such as alcohol and marijuana.

Most of these substances and methods are used in various combinations to enhance muscle mass, muscle strength and endurance, and appearance, resulting in a more muscular and less feminine physique. This chapter discusses selected anabolic agents, stimulants, blood doping methods, diuretics, analgesics, recreational substances, legal dietary supplements, and current and future technologies used to enhance muscularity and their associated adverse health effects.

ANABOLIC–ANDROGENIC STEROIDS, OTHER ANABOLIC AGENTS, AND RELATED SUBSTANCES

Anabolic–Androgenic Steroids

A close look at adverse analytical findings by the International Olympic Committee (IOC) and WADA laboratories during 2005 reveals that anabolic–androgenic steroids were the most frequently detected substances (WADA, 2006a). In addition to AASs, testosterone, and testosterone precursors like androstenedione (andro), anabolic agents include several other, very different anabolic drugs such as beta-2 agonists, hGH, and IGF-1.

Anabolic–androgenic steroids are synthetic derivatives of testosterone, the natural male hormone responsible for the masculinizing (androgenic) and tissue-building (anabolic) effects during male adolescence and adulthood (Kruskemper, 1968). Athletes use AASs to increase muscle mass and strength and to reduce recovery time between training sessions. AASs are also used to enhance physical appearance.

Several new "designer steroids" have appeared on the bodybuilding and weight lifting scene, including tetrahydrogestrinone (THG), a new designer steroid thought to be a variant of an older anabolic steroid (norbolethone), developed in 1966 by Wyeth but never marketed to the public (Catlin, Ahrens, & Kucherova, 2002; "THG May Be Variant," 2004). Another designer steroid is desoxymethyltestosterone (Wilson, 2005), also known as madol (17alpha-methyl-5alpha-androst-2-en-17beta-ol; Sekera et al., 2005). Two designer steroid precursors have also been reported, 1-testosterone (1 delta-dihydrotestosterone) and 4-hydroxytestosterone (Shipley, 2002).

The short-term health effects of AASs have been increasingly studied, and several authors have reviewed the physiological and health effects of these drugs (Freidl, 2000; Wright, 1980). Although AAS use has been associated (mainly through case reports) with several adverse and even fatal effects, the incidence of serious effects reported has been extremely low (Freidl, 2000). However, for decades experts have consistently stated that the long-term health effects of AAS use are unknown (Thiblin & Petersson, 2004; Yesalis, Wright, & Bahrke, 1989).

Although the role of AASs in the etiology of various diseases in both animals and humans is still uncertain, AAS use in clinical trials and in laboratory studies is associated with numerous risk factors for cardiovascular disease, liver tumors, and infertility and in the physiology of various organs and body systems, suggesting the potential for subsequent health problems (American College of Sports Medicine, 1984; Bahrke & Yesalis, 2002; Freidl, 2000; Kruskemper, 1968; Wright, 1980). The best-documented effects are those on the liver, serum lipids, and reproductive system. Other areas of concern include the psyche and behavior, cardiomyopathy, coronary artery disease, cerebrovascular accidents, prostatic changes, and lowered immune function (Bahrke, 2000; Cafri et al., 2005; Freidl, 2000).

Beta-2 Agonists

Beta-2 agonists, such as clenbuterol, are classified as stimulants and are used to treat asthma in Europe and elsewhere (Lynch, 2002). Although beta-2 agonists are not AASs, they have been found to possess anabolic and catabolic properties, that is, to increase muscle tissue and reduce fat tissue in animals (Lynch, 2002). In fact, WADA classifies clenbuterol as an anabolic agent. The most frequently reported adverse effects associated with the use of beta-2 agonists include nausea, headaches, and insomnia (Lynch, 2002). Excessive intake of clenbuterol (the most popular beta-2 agonist) leads to symptoms such as muscle tremor, palpitations, muscle cramps, headache, and peripheral vasodilatation (Lynch, 2002). The most serious adverse effects of excessive beta-2 agonist intake are those associated with the heart (Lynch, 2002). Tachycardia is one of the first indications that beta-2 agonists are having an effect. Sudden death caused by cardiac failure has been reported in bodybuilders suspected of using clenbuterol in conjunction with diuretics (Embleton & Thorne, 1998).

Human Growth Hormone

Human growth hormone is secreted by the anterior pituitary gland (Kraemer, Nindl, & Rubin, 2002). It stimulates bone growth and affects the metabolism of protein, carbohydrates, and fat. Synthetic (recombinant human growth hormone) forms are available and are used by bodybuilders and weight lifters to increase muscle mass, decrease body fat, and speed recovery following training. However, one of the adverse effects of too much hGH is acromegaly, a condition that is associated with increases in total body water, calcium, sodium, potassium, and phosphorous retention (Kraemer, Nindl, et al., 2002). Retention of these elements can result in physical discomfort, including facial and aural soft tissue swelling; profuse sweating; deepening of the voice; and skeletal and articular changes such as gigantism, mandibular growth, widening joint space, and premature death, among other symptoms (Kraemer, Nindl, et al., 2002). Detection of hGH abuse is difficult, because this substance occurs naturally in the human body, testing is expensive, and sufficient supplies of antibodies are not always available ("Tour de France Behind on Doping Test," 2005). Bodybuilders and weight lifters use hGH because it does not show up on existing doping tests. Although the WADA claimed it had developed an effective test that was administered to 300 athletes during the 2004 Athens Olympic Games, no positive tests for hGH were reported (World Anti-Doping Agency, n.d.).

Gamma-Hydroxybutyric Acid

Gamma-hydroxybutyric acid (GHB) originally gained prominence because of its purported ability to stimulate the release of hGH and in this way to promote muscle buildup and enhance physical appearance and performance (Sanguineti & Frank, 2002). However, the highly publicized bodybuilding effect of GHB has proved fictitious, and the potentially deadly hypnotic effect of GHB has resulted in its current classification as a Schedule I controlled substance (Sanguineti & Frank, 2002). Schedule I controlled substances must meet the following criteria: (a) the drug or other substance has a high potential for abuse, (b) the drug or other substance has no currently accepted medical use in treatment in the United States, (c) there is a lack of accepted safety for use of the drug or other substance under medical supervision. Examples of Schedule I controlled substances include heroin, marijuana, and peyote, among others.

Insulin

Abuse of insulin may also be popular among athletes (Auge & Auge, 1999; Duchaine, 1989; Reaney, 2003; Reitman, 2003). Although insulin is secreted by cells within the pancreas, weight lifters and bodybuilders inject synthetic insulin to inhibit protein breakdown and boost glucose uptake and glucose storage as glycogen (which provides energy during exercise) in the liver, thereby shortening recovery times between training sessions. Bodybuilders who use insulin to bulk up their muscles and enhance their performance may experience a coma from low blood sugar, brain damage, and death. Although the use of insulin to enhance appearance and performance is banned by most major sporting organizations, it has been very popular among weight lifters since the 1980s, because it vanishes very quickly from the bloodstream and is therefore difficult to detect with standard doping tests. It is believed that as many as one in four athletes abusing anabolic steroids also abuses insulin (Reaney, 2003), and another report estimated that up to 10% of bodybuilders might be using insulin (Reitman, 2003). When taken together, anabolic steroids and insulin have the potential combined effect of significantly increasing muscle bulk.

Testosterone Precursors and Prohormones

Testosterone is the primary male sex hormone and is responsible for the androgenic and anabolic effects observed during male adolescence and adulthood (Kruskemper, 1968). Related substances include AASs as well as prohormones such as androstenedione (andro) and dehydroepiandrosterone (DHEA), which are steroids in the biosynthesis pathway (Kraemer, Rubin, French, & McGuigan, 2002). Testosterone precursors such as androstenedione (Andro*GEN, Andro Stack, Androstat, Animal Stak) became popular because athletes like Mark McGwire, in his successful quest to break professional baseball's single-season home run record, used them.

Research suggests that long-term use of steroid precursors and prohormones such as andro is related to heightened risk of liver, kidney, and heart disease as well as other potential adverse effects, including hair loss (Kraemer, Rubin, et al., 2002). Eighteen steroid precursors, including methyl-1-testosterone and THG, were declared controlled substances and added to the list of AASs banned without a prescription, with sales of the prohormones banned after January 20, 2005 (Anabolic Steroid Control Act, 2004). The passage of this act has led many experts (e.g., the American Medical Association, the Endocrine Society and Hormone Foundation, and the American Academy of Pediatrics) to believe that legislation has finally caught up with these relatively weaker anabolic agents.

Human Chorionic Gonadotropin

Human chorionic gonadotropin, which is secreted by the placenta and found in the urine of pregnant women, is not an anabolic steroid, but athletes use it to stimulate endogenous testosterone production following long-term AAS use. In addition, bodybuilders and weight lifters claim that the use of hCG enhances fat burning and loss, stimulates the testes, and increases the libido (Kammerer, 2002). Data have appeared to indicate that hCG administration may enhance endogenous testosterone production and/or normalize the production of testosterone after it has been suppressed (Kammerer, 2002). Unfortunately, potential adverse health effects of hCG use are difficult to predict (Kammerer, 2002).

Antiestrogenic Drugs

Misuse of drugs that were developed to cure patients with breast cancer is thought to be widespread among bodybuilders and weight lifters (Lord, 2004). Although tamoxifen has been used for many years, high on the list of currently abused cancer drugs are Aromasin (exemestane) and Femara (letrozole), new breast cancer drugs that prolong the breakdown of hormones and so arrest wasting in patients with degenerative diseases (Brindley, 2003). These drugs block the aromatization of testosterone. Unfortunately, the risks of taking them include accelerated aging, risk of tumors, exhaustion of bone marrow, heart attacks, and thickening of the blood, as well as an increased risk of stroke (Brindley, 2003). Abraxane, a new delivery system of microscopic particles bound to albumin, a blood protein, also shows potential for abuse (Pollack, 2003).

STIMULANTS

Bodybuilders and weight lifters often use stimulants such as caffeine, ephedrine, cathine, amphetamine, strychnine, sydnocarb and mesocarb, bromantan, and modafinil (developed for narcolepsy) to intensify psychological sensations of alertness, arousal, concentration, and self-confidence. However, stimulants also increase muscle contractility and blood flow to the muscle, decrease the sense of fatigue, and depress appetite. They may also permit athletes to perform beyond their normal limits. Adverse effects include headache, sleeplessness, and elevated anxiety. High doses of stimulants, such as amphetamines, may result in mental confusion, hallucinations, skin disorders, and ulcers, and heavy use may be associated with brain damage (Karch, 2002). According to the IOC and WADA, the most frequently detected stimulants are amphetamines and ephedrine (WADA, 2006a).

Amphetamines

Amphetamines such as dextroamphetamine and methamphetamine are powerful central nervous system stimulants that act primarily by enhancing the brain activity of norepinephrine and dopamine. In addition, amphetamine limits appetite, increases plasma-free fatty acid levels and body temperature, and has sympathetic effects on the cardiovascular and respiratory functions (Karch, 2002). Bodybuilders and weight lifters use amphetamines to improve mood states, improve confidence, increase alertness and concentration, and increase endurance. Regular amphetamine use may lead to dependency, irritability, fearfulness and apprehension, hallucination, and psychosis (Karch, 2002). Heavy users of amphetamines may be prone to sudden, violent, and irrational acts; distortions of perception; and paranoid delusions (Karch, 2002).

Ephedrine

Ephedrine, another central nervous system stimulant and beta-receptor agonist, has been included in such products as Animal Cuts, Hydroxycut, and Ripped Fuel. Bodybuilders and weight lifters use ephedrine, whose action is similar to amphetamines, to enhance muscle contractility, increase the blood output of the heart, enlarge the bronchial pathways to the lungs, and increase blood sugar levels. Because ephedrine increases thermogenesis and resting energy expenditure, ephedrine alone and in combination with caffeine and/or aspirin is often used to suppress appetite and promote weight loss (Dullo, 1993; Rawson & Clarkson, 2002).

Between 1993 and 1997, more than 800 adverse events and 34 deaths attributed to ephedrine ingestions (according to more recent claims, more than 120 deaths have been associated with ephedra use) were reported to the U.S. Food and Drug Administration (1997). Ephedrine was banned in April 2004 by the U.S. Congress, but a more recent legal decision has partially reversed the ban (Thiessen, 2005).

Caffeine

Bodybuilders and weight lifters use caffeine in their daily lives and in preparation for and during training and competition. Caffeine stimulates the central nervous system and increases psychological arousal (Motl, O'Connor, & Dishman, 2003; Plaskett & Cafarelli, 2001). It also stimulates the release of epinephrine and, in addition to stimulating the central nervous system, may enhance physiological processes such as cardiovascular function and fuel utilization, important during intense training sessions. Caffeine also facilitates the release of calcium from storage sites in the muscle cell, enabling calcium to stimulate muscle contraction more effectively. This effect could increase muscular strength and power for acute, high-intensity exercise. All of these effects may result from the actions of caffeine, epinephrine, or metabolic byproducts of caffeine. Caffeine can be unsafe for users, including athletes, with hypertension (James, 1997). Overconsumption may cause flushing of the face, nervousness, trembling, anxiety, and heart palpitations. Although caffeine was previously a banned substance above a specified limit, currently the IOC does not consider caffeine a prohibited substance. However, caffeine is one of several substances included in the 2007 IOC Monitoring Program (WADA, 2006b; see http://www.wada-ama.org/en/index/ch2), so if future caffeine abuse is significant, it could be returned to the prohibited substances list.

Cocaine

Cocaine, a powerful central stimulant, promotes strong euphoric effects in the pleasure centers of the brain. It is also a strong peripheral sympathetic stimulant that promotes an elevation in the adrenergic hormones. As a result of its central and peripheral effects, it has been touted as a potential ergogenic aid. Although research on the effects of cocaine on exercise provides little evidence of its ergogenic potential, because it of its powerful euphoric effect and increased mental alertness, it may override perceptions of fatigue and prolong endurance during exercise. In addition, the peripheral sympathetic effect may metabolize fuel substrates for the maintenance of energy production and prolong exercise (Conlee, 2002).

BLOOD-DOPING METHODS

Although athletes use blood doping primarily to enhance endurance performance, it is not unusual for athletes seeking increased muscular strength and power and increased muscularity to blood dope as well. Blood doping is the intravenous infusion of blood to produce an increase in the blood's oxygen carrying capacity. Blood doping can be accomplished via autologous, homologous, or heterologous blood transfusions. Heterologous infusion of whole blood or packed red blood cells (RBCs) always includes risks of transfusion complications such as allergic reactions and infections (Ekblom, 2002a). No practical method currently exists for the detection of autologous infusion of whole or packed RBCs.

Erythropoietin (DynEPO, Aranesp, Procrit, and Darbepoetin), used to artificially increase oxygen-carrying RBCs and enhance endurance, is another blood doping substance (Ekblom, 2002b). Injections of recombinant human erythropoietin increase hemoglobin, hematocrit, maximal oxygen consumption, and physical performance in both continuous and intermittent exercise. A negative adverse effect is increased systolic blood pressure during exercise.

Actovegin, a derivative of calf blood serum that has several medical uses including the treatment of open wounds, is also used to increase the oxygen-carrying capacity of the blood. Perfluorochemicals are used to dissolve gases, including oxygen, in the blood. Angiogenix, a nicotine-based drug, has been shown to grow new blood vessels (Jones, 2002), and more recently, calmodulin has been reported to enhance smooth muscle contraction (Isotani et al., 2004). Detecting agents such as these is difficult and expensive. Altitude tents and nitrogen houses are also used to increase RBC production and the oxygen-carrying capacity of the blood.

DIURETICS FOR FLUID LOSS AND AS MASKING AGENTS

Diuretics such as acetazolamide, furosemide, and thiazides are used medically to treat hypertension, and athletes, especially bodybuilders, use them to increase fluid loss and enhance muscular and vascular definition just before competitions (Armstrong, 2002). Athletes also use diuretics during drug testing as masking agents for other performance-enhancing substances. Other masking agents include epitestosterone (used to manipulate the testosterone–epitestosterone ratio), probenecid, alpha-reductase inhibitors (e.g., finasteride), and plasma expanders (albumin, dextran, and hydroxyethyl starch), and devices including fake bladders and the "Whizzinator" (Wood, 2005), are also used to foil drug tests. The Whizzinator is an easy-to-conceal, easy-to-use, urinating device with a very realistic prosthetic penis.

Bodybuilders also use diuretics to achieve greater muscle definition—in their jargon, to appear "cut." The general adverse effects resulting from diuretic use include fatigue, drowsiness, muscle cramps, soreness, and sensations of numbness, tingling, and prickling. However, diuretic use can be fatal when taken to an extreme. In 1992, bodybuilder Mohammed Benaziza died suddenly of cardiac arrest just days after placing fourth in the Mr. Olympia contest in Finland. The medical report cited heart failure due to use of diuretics as the cause of death. Benaziza had been using furosemide to prepare for the competition (Vest, 1993). Indeed, diuretics have been described as among the most dangerous drugs in the sport of bodybuilding because of their widespread abuse.

ANALGESICS

Bodybuilders and weight lifters frequently use analgesics, such as the nonsteroidal anti-inflammatories (NSAIDs) aspirin and ibuprofen, corticosteroids, and potent narcotics and their derivatives, to treat the pain and inflammation caused by the breakdown of the musculoskeletal system that results from strenuous physical workouts (Almekinders, 2002). NSAIDs are often used to treat acute muscle pain and soreness.

Corticosteroids (e.g., Aristocort, Aristospan) are drugs with a basic sterol structure similar to that of cortisol, which is produced in the adrenal glands. The anti-inflammatory effect of corticosteroids is one of the main reasons bodybuilders and weight lifters use them. The overall anti-inflammatory effects of corticosteroids can be dramatic and are generally more pronounced than those of NSAIDs. Although associated with beneficial effects such as decreased pain and swelling, corticosteroid use also involves an increased risk of certain adverse reactions, including the development of diabetes mellitus and disturbance of bone metabolism with chronic use (Almekinders, 2002). Potent narcotics such as Nubain and their derivatives are often used for moderate to severe pain. The use of narcotic analgesics may permit bodybuilders and weight lifters to train beyond their normal pain limits (Connors & Sudkamp, 2002).

SOCIAL AND RECREATIONAL DRUGS AND SUBSTANCES

Athletes often use social and other recreational drugs and substances such as alcohol and marijuana to relax following intense physical training sessions.

Alcohol

Although alcohol lacks ergogenic qualities for practically all sport applications, bodybuilders and weight lifters may use alcohol to reduce elevated anxiety and promote relaxation following and between heavy resistance training sessions (Stainback & Cohen, 2002).

Marijuana

Marijuana consists of the dried and crushed leaves and flowering tops of the *Cannabis sativa* plant. Although there is no evidence in the literature that bodybuilders and weight lifters use cannabis to enhance their appearance and performance for competitive events, anecdotal reports suggest that these athletes may use cannabis to relax following an intense workout and as an appetite stimulant (Heishman, 2002).

LEGAL DIETARY SUPPLEMENTS AND ADVERSE HEALTH RISKS

In 1994, Congress passed the Dietary Supplement Health and Education Act (DSHEA), which opened the door to the widespread marketing of dietary supplements in the United States. The DSHEA defined a *dietary supplement* as a food product that contains at least one of the following ingredients: vitamin, mineral, herb or botanical, amino acid, metabolite, constituent, or extract. Unfortunately, one of the effects of passage of the DSHEA was a blurring of the line between what is a drug and what is a supplement.

The DSHEA permits a product to be marketed without any scientific research to support even the most general claims made on its behalf, and the act permits labeling information to be intentionally vague. For example, the label on one brand of creatine bears a statement including the phrase "capable of promoting and sustaining muscle mass and repair while helping to prevent the breakdown of muscle tissue." On the opposite side of the label is a footnote reading, "This statement has not been evaluated by the FDA."

The DSHEA allows manufacturers of dietary supplements to distribute their products without a prescription and, more important, outside the domain of good manufacturing practice standards as they are applied to drugs. Because these products are considered dietary supplements and not drugs, they are not required to undergo safety and efficacy reviews, as all over-the-counter and prescription drugs must. Thus, athletes are risking serious adverse health effects (Delbeke, Van Eenoo, Van Thuyne, & Desmet, 2003; Reents, 2002).

Bodybuilders and weight lifters use literally thousands of supplements in their attempts to enhance appearance and performance, including such diverse substances as creatine (an amino acid derivative), DHEA (a weak anabolic steroid), ginseng (a botanical), and nitric oxide (a neuromessenger). Within the limits of this chapter, it is impossible to discuss in detail more than just a few dietary supplements. Consequently, discussion is limited to these four representative examples.

Creatine

Creatine is one of the most popular dietary supplements in the world (Branch & Williams, 2002). Examples of commercial products include Animal Max, ATP Advantage, and Create. Creatine (methylguanidine acetic acid) is an amino acid derivative that is both endogenously synthesized and consumed as part of a carnivorous diet. Creatine is an important cellular energy source for rapid resynthesis of adenosine triphosphate.

Creatine supplementation has been reported to improve skeletal muscle function and increase body mass. Short-term supplementation (20–30 grams per day for 5–7 days) has been reported to increase total muscle creatine concentration by about 20% (Branch & Williams, 2002). This increase is maintained with a low-dose maintenance supplementation of 2 to 5 grams per day (Branch & Williams, 2002). Body mass increases of about 2% have been consistently reported following creatine supplementation (Branch & Williams, 2002). Because creatine is a constituent of animal products, creatine use is not banned by sport governing bodies.

Part of the appeal of creatine is the perception that it is a "safe" compound compared with other alternatives such as AASs, IGF-1, and hGH, which are "unsafe," expensive, and illegal. The fact that a compound such as creatine occurs naturally, however, does not mean that creatine supplementation with that compound is safe. There are anecdotal reports of cramping, dehydration, and muscle strains associated with creatine use. In addition, concerns about renal dysfunction have been cited (Branch & Williams, 2002). Although early investigations have not shown renal problems during and following creatine supplementation, clinicians are concerned about the unknown effects of excessive and long-term chronic use. More research on the long-term health effects of creatine supplementation is needed.

Ginseng

Ginseng has been used in the Orient for several thousand years as an adaptogenic as well as restorative agent. It has been used to treat nervous disorders, anemia, dyspnea, forgetfulness and confusion, decreased libido, and chronic fatigue, among other disorders. However, ginseng exemplifies many of the problems typical in the use of botanicals to enhance performance.

Although studies with animals have usually shown that ginseng may improve performance, research on the effects of ginseng on performance in humans has been contradictory. One reason may be that research involving the efficacy of ginseng as an ergogenic aid in humans is often characterized by various methodological problems such as a lack of uniformity of type, form, and dosage of ginseng administered. At this time, there is no compelling research evidence regarding the efficacy of ginseng use for the purpose of improving physical performance in humans (Bahrke & Morgan, 1994, 2000).

Dehydroepiandrosterone

Dehydroepiandrosterone is a weak androgen secreted by the adrenal glands (with small amounts produced by the ovaries) and is a precursor of testosterone and estrogen (Bahrke & Yesalis, 2004). Although the prevalence and incidence of DHEA use are unknown, it is a commonly used dietary supplement. Bodybuilders and weight lifters use it in an attempt to elevate testosterone levels and ultimately to increase muscle mass and strength. In addition, it is advertised as an antiobesity and antiaging supplement also capable of improving libido, vitality, and immunity levels. However, research to support these claims is limited. Transdermal patches have been developed to enhance the availability of DHEA. Between 50 milligrams and 100 milligrams per day is the most commonly recommended dosage of DHEA. However, dosages of up to 1,600 milligrams per day have been administered to men without producing increases in serum testosterone levels. More important for bodybuilders and weight lifters, additional studies suggest that DHEA ingestion neither enhances serum testosterone concentrations nor causes adaptations associated with resistance training in young men (Bahrke & Yesalis, 2004). In women, larger doses have been shown to increase serum testosterone levels and cause adverse masculinizing effects such as hirsutism and acne (Bahrke & Yesalis, 2004). Beyond the virilizing effects, short-term use of DHEA by women can result in reduced high-density lipoprotein cholesterol, impaired insulin sensitivity, and glucose tolerance (Bahrke & Yesalis, 2004). Adverse effects have not been thoroughly investigated in young and middle-aged men. The long-term effects of DHEA use are unknown, especially in bodybuilders and weight lifters using large doses in conjunction with other performance-enhancing substances.

Nitric Oxide

Nitric oxide is a colorless free radical gas commonly found in the tissues of all mammals (Cribb, 2002). Biologically, nitric oxide has been shown to be an important neuromessenger in a number of vertebrate signal transduction processes. Nitric oxide is used in medical treatment; for example, nitroglycerin ameliorates the pain of angina by supplying nitric oxide to the blood vessels that supply the heart. The popular drug Viagra (sildenafil citrate) controls erection by regulating nitric oxide in the penile cartilage chamber. Supplement manufacturers promote nitric oxide as having the ability to dramatically increase muscle size, strength, endurance, power output, and load capacity.

Although nitric oxide acts as a cell-to-cell communicator for certain metabolic functions, muscle growth is not one of them. There is no research that indicates increasing nitric oxide levels plays a part in increasing protein synthesis, contractile strength, or any other biochemical pathway that may lead to increases in muscle mass. There also appears to be no evidence whatsoever showing that increasing nitric oxide levels enhances endurance, power output, or load capacity.

FUTURE TECHNOLOGIES THAT MAY THREATEN HEALTH

Some experts believe that the current use of AASs and other appearance- and performance-enhancing substances and methods to increase muscle mass could soon become passé, because bodybuilders and weight lifters might be able to inject genes to enhance appearance and performance. In the upcoming few decades, genetic engineering could profoundly alter the course of competitive sport by allowing scientists to create the "perfect" athlete, although the risks involved in doing so may be high. In fact, selected genetic engineering has already been achieved in animals. Researchers have shown in "Schwarzenegger mice" that a gene injected directly into a target muscle can increase muscle performance by 27% (Barton-Davis, Shoturma, Musaro, Rosenthal, & Sweeney, 1998). More recently, researchers have identified a protein transcription factor, peroxisome proliferator-activated receptor gamma coactivator-1 (PCG-1), that, when expressed at physiologic levels in mice, converts fast-twitch, strength muscles into high-endurance, slow-twitch muscles (Lin et al., 2002). Some have speculated that drugs that influence these factors may be used to increase muscle activity in humans, although much work still remains to elucidate the mechanism.

Genetic engineering and modification also include the development of myostatin blockers and gene therapy to increase levels of IGF-1. Pharmaceutical and biotechnology companies are working hard on a variety of myostatin inhibitors. Examples of the powerful effects of myostatin blockers can be seen in the Belgian Blue cattle breed, often referred to as "double muscled" because their impressive musculature is made even more impressive by an absence of myostatin, interfering with fat deposition and giving the animals an extremely lean and sculpted look. In addition, doctors have discovered a German infant from Berlin with a similar genetic mutation that boosts muscle growth (Johnson, 2004). The boy's mutant DNA segment was found to block production of myostatin, and scientists believe that the discovery could lead to drugs that block limitation to muscle growth. Bodybuilders and weight lifters certainly will want to obtain such drugs to use like steroids for bulking up.

CONCLUSION

Athletes, including bodybuilders and weight lifters, are not the only individuals who use an array of drugs, substances, and methods to enhance their muscle mass, strength, endurance, and appearance. Nonathletes seeking to become more muscular primarily for "the look" use these substances and strategies as well. However, the use of performance- and appearance-enhancing substances and methods in sport is cheating. It destroys the integrity of sport, coerces other athletes to dope, and carries with it numerous deleterious health effects that are significant to both athletes and nonathletes. Although drug testing is somewhat successful in reducing drug use in sports, validated and reliable tests for several effective doping agents are lacking. Many muscle enhancement substances are also illegal, and criminal prosecution to reduce their use within and outside sport may be the only effective deterrent.

Because dietary supplements fall under food manufacturing standards, the production of supplements is less tightly controlled than the production of pharmaceutical-grade drugs. Quality control during production is questionable for many supplements, and reports of problems concerning potency and contamination are becoming more prevalent in the scientific and clinical literature. Consequently, athletes who use supplements may risk both disqualification and serious adverse health effects.

REFERENCES

Almekinders, L. C. (2002). Nonsteroidal anti-inflammatory drugs and corticosteroids. In M. S. Bahrke & C. E. Yesalis (Eds.), *Performance-enhancing substances in sport and exercise* (pp. 125–135). Champaign, IL: Human Kinetics.

American College of Sports Medicine. (1984). Position stand on the use of anabolic–androgenic steroids in sports. *Sports Medicine Bulletin, 19,* 13–18.

Anabolic Steroid Control Act of 2004, 108th Cong. (2004).

Armstrong, L. E. (2002). Diuretics. In M. S. Bahrke & C. E. Yesalis (Eds.), *Performance-enhancing substances in sport and exercise* (pp. 109–116). Champaign, IL: Human Kinetics.

Auge, W. K., & Auge, S. M. (1999). Naturalistic observation of athletic drug-use pattern and behavior in professional caliber bodybuilders. *Substance Use and Misuse, 34,* 217–249.

Bahrke, M. S. (2000). Psychological effects of endogenous testosterone and anabolic–androgenic steroids. In C. E. Yesalis (Ed.), *Anabolic steroids in sport and exercise* (2nd ed., pp. 247–278). Champaign, IL: Human Kinetics.

Bahrke, M. S., & Morgan, W. P. (1994). Evaluation of the ergogenic properties of ginseng. *Sports Medicine, 18,* 229–248.

Bahrke, M. S., & Morgan, W. P. (2000). Evaluation of the ergogenic properties of ginseng: A review. *Sports Medicine, 29,* 113–133.

Bahrke, M. S., & Yesalis, C. E. (2002). Anabolic–androgenic steroids. In M. S. Bahrke & C. E. Yesalis (Eds.), *Performance-enhancing substances in sport and exercise* (pp. 33–46). Champaign, IL: Human Kinetics.

Bahrke, M. S., & Yesalis, C. E. (2004). Abuse of anabolic androgenic steroids and related substances in sport and exercise. *Current Opinion in Pharmacology, 4,* 614–620.

Barton-Davis, E. R., Shoturma, D. I., Musaro, A., Rosenthal, N., & Sweeney, H. L. (1998). Viral mediated expression of insulin-like growth factor 1 blocks the aging-related loss of skeletal muscle function. *Proceedings of the National Academy of Sciences USA, 95,* 15603–15607.

Branch, J. D., & Williams, M. H. (2002). Creatine as an ergogenic supplement. In M. S. Bahrke & C. E. Yesalis (Eds.), *Performance-enhancing substances in sport and exercise* (pp. 175–195). Champaign, IL: Human Kinetics.

Brindley, M. (2003, August 15). *Cancer drug abuse found in gyms. Western Mail.* Retrieved August 15, 2003, from http://icwales.icnetwork.co.uk/printable_version.cfm?objectid=13294174&siteid=50082

Cafri, G., Thompson, J. K., Ricciardelli, L. A., McCabe, M. P., Smolak, L., & Yesalis, C. (2005). Pursuit of the muscular ideal: Physical and psychological consequences and putative risk factors. *Clinical Psychology Review, 25,* 215–239.

Catlin, D. H., Ahrens, B. D., & Kucherova, Y. (2002). Detection of norbolethone, an anabolic steroid never marketed, in athletes' urine. *Rapid Communication Mass Spectrometry, 16,* 1273–1275.

Conlee, R. K. (2002). Cocaine. In M. S. Bahrke & C. E. Yesalis (Eds.), *Performance-enhancing substances in sport and exercise* (pp. 279–288). Champaign, IL: Human Kinetics.

Connors, D. F., & Sudkamp, J. (2002). Narcotic analgesics and athletic performance. In M. S. Bahrke & C. E. Yesalis (Eds.), *Performance-enhancing substances in sport and exercise* (pp. 117–124). Champaign, IL: Human Kinetics.

Cribb, P. (2002, October 17). *Nitric oxide supplements—big claims—zero science: NO2 ways about it.* Retrieved January 11, 2005, from http://www.ast-ss.com/articles/article.asp?AID=117

Delbeke, F. T., Van Eenoo, P., Van Thuyne, W., & Desmet, N. (2003). Prohormones and sport. *Steroid and Biochemistry, 83*, 245–251.

Dietary Supplement Health and Education Act of 1994, Pub. L. No. 103-417, 103rd Cong., (1994). Retrieved December 5, 2006, from http://www.fda.gov/opacom/laws/dshea.html

Duchaine, D. (1989). *Underground steroid handbook II*. Venice, CA: Technical Books.

Dullo, A. G. (1993). Ephedrine, xanthines and prostaglandin-inhibitors: Actions and interactions in the stimulation of thermogenesis. *International Journal of Obesity Related Metabolic Disorders, 17*, 35–40.

Ekblom, B. T. (2002a). Blood doping. In M. S. Bahrke & C. E. Yesalis (Eds.), *Performance-enhancing substances in sport and exercise* (pp. 93–99). Champaign, IL: Human Kinetics.

Ekblom, B. T. (2002b). Erythropoietin. In M. S. Bahrke & C. E. Yesalis (Eds.), *Performance-enhancing substances in sport and exercise* (pp. 101–108). Champaign, IL: Human Kinetics.

Embleton, P., & Thorne, G. (1998). *MuscleMag International's Anabolic Primer*. Scarborough, Ontario, Canada: Robert Kennedy.

Freidl, K. E. (2000). Effect of anabolic steroids on physical health. In C. E. Yesalis (Ed.), *Anabolic steroids in sport and exercise* (2nd ed., pp. 175–225). Champaign, IL: Human Kinetics.

Heishman, S. J. (2002). Cannabis: Clinical pharmacology and performance effects in humans. In M. S. Bahrke & C. E. Yesalis (Eds.), *Performance-enhancing substances in sport and exercise* (pp. 247–256). Champaign, IL: Human Kinetics.

Isotani, E., Zhi, G., Lau, K. S., Huang, J., Mizuno, Y., Persechini, A., et al. (2004). Real-time evaluation of myosin light chain kinase activation in smooth muscle tissues from a transgenic calmodulin-biosensor mouse. *Proceedings of the National Academy of Sciences USA, 101*, 6279–6284.

James, J. (1997). Is habitual caffeine use a preventable cardiovascular risk factor? *Lancet, 349*, 279–281.

Johnson, L. A. (2004, June 23). Doctors discover a toddler muscle man. *DailyCamera.com.* Available from http://www.dailycamera.com/bdc/nation_world_news/article/0,713,BDC_2420_2984793,00.html

Jones, D. (2002, August 13). *Heart drug could help muscle growth*. Retrieved December 5, 2006, from http://www.elitefitness.com/forum/showthread.php?t=165562

Kammerer, R. C. (2002). Human chorionic gonadotropin. In M. S. Bahrke & C. E. Yesalis (Eds.), *Performance-enhancing substances in sport and exercise* (pp. 89–92). Champaign, IL: Human Kinetics.

Karch, S. B. (2002). Amphetamines. In M. S. Bahrke & C. E. Yesalis (Eds.), *Performance-enhancing substances in sport and exercise* (pp. 257–265). Champaign, IL: Human Kinetics.

Kraemer, W. J., Nindl, B. C., & Rubin, M. R. (2002). Growth hormone: Physiological effects of exogenous administration. In M. S. Bahrke & C. E. Yesalis (Eds.),

Performance-enhancing substances in sport and exercise (pp. 65–78). Champaign, IL: Human Kinetics.

Kraemer, W. J., Rubin, M. R., French, D. N., & McGuigan, M. R. (2002). Physiological effects of testosterone precursors. In M. S. Bahrke & C. E. Yesalis (Eds.), *Performance-enhancing substances in sport and exercise* (pp. 79–88). Champaign, IL: Human Kinetics.

Kruskemper, H. L. (1968). *Anabolic steroids*. New York: Academic Press.

Lin, J., Wu, H., Tarr, P. T., Zhang, C. Y., Wu, Z., Boss, O., et al. (2002). Transcriptional co-activator PGC-1alpha drives the formation of slow-twitch muscle fibres. *Nature, 418,* 797–801.

Lord, C. (2004, August 9). Abuse of breast cancer drugs by athletes is "widespread." *Times Online.* Retrieved December 5, 2006, from http://www.timesonline.co.uk/printFriendly/0,,1-6428-1208024,00.html

Lynch, G. S. (2002). Beta-2 agonists. In M. S. Bahrke & C. E. Yesalis (Eds.), *Performance-enhancing substances in sport and exercise* (pp. 47–64). Champaign, IL: Human Kinetics.

Motl, R. W., O'Connor, P. J., & Dishman, R. K. (2003). Effect of caffeine on perceptions of leg muscle pain during moderate intensity cycling exercise. *Journal of Pain, 4,* 316–321.

Plaskett, C. J., & Cafarelli, E. (2001). Caffeine increases endurance and attenuates force sensation during submaximal isometric contractions. *Journal of Applied Physiology, 91,* 1535–1544.

Pollack, A. (2003, December 6). New drug said to improve delivery of cancer medication [Electronic version]. *The New York Times.* Retrieved December 8, 2003, from http://query.nytimes.com/gst/fullpage.html?sec=health&res=9404E1DB123DF935A35751C1A9659C8B63

Rawson, E. S., & Clarkson, P. M. (2002). Ephedrine as an ergogenic aid. In M. S. Bahrke & C. E. Yesalis (Eds.), *Performance-enhancing substances in sport and exercise* (pp. 289–298). Champaign, IL: Human Kinetics.

Reaney, P. (2003, August 4). *Body builders warned of danger of abusing insulin.* Retrieved August 4, 2003, from http://www.extremefitness.com/forum/showthread.php?t=1596

Reents, S. (2002). Determining the efficacy of performance-enhancing substances. In M. S. Bahrke & C. E. Yesalis (Eds.), *Performance-enhancing substances in sport and exercise* (pp. 21–32). Champaign, IL: Human Kinetics.

Reitman, V. (2003, September 12). Insulin is the new steroid [Electronic version]. *Toronto Star.* Available from http://www.thestar.com

Sanguineti, V. R., & Frank, M. R. (2002). Gamma-hydroxybutyric acid. In M. S. Bahrke & C. E. Yesalis (Eds.), *Performance-enhancing substances in sport and exercise* (pp. 299–304). Champaign, IL: Human Kinetics.

Sekera, M. H., Ahrens, B. D., Chang, Y. C., Starcevic, B., Georakopoulos, C., & Catlin, D. H. (2005). Another designer steroid: Discovery, synthesis, and detection of "madol" in urine. *Rapid Communication Mass Spectrometry, 19,* 781–784.

Shipley, A. (2002, December 6). New steroids sold over counter. [Electronic version]. *Washington Post*. Available from http://www.washingtonpost.com

Stainback, R. D., & Cohen, R. J. (2002). Alcohol use in sport and exercise. In M. S. Bahrke & C. E. Yesalis (Eds.), *Performance-enhancing substances in sport and exercise* (pp. 227–245). Champaign, IL: Human Kinetics.

THG may be variant of 1966 drug. (2004, July 28). *SportsIllustrated.com*. Retrieved July 28, 2004, from http://sportsillustrated.cnn.com/2004/more/07/28/bc.sport.doping.thg/index.html

Thiblin, I., & Petersson, A. (2004). Pharmacoepidemiology of anabolic androgenic steroids: A review. *Fundamental and Clinical Pharmacology, 19*, 27–44.

Thiessen, M. (2005, April 14). *Utah judge strikes down FDA ban on ephedra*. Retrieved June 15, 2005, from http://saltlakecity.about.com/gi/dynamic/offsite.htm?site=http://www.signonsandiego.com/news/nation/20050414%2D1411%2Dephedrasuit.html

Tour de France behind on doping test. (2005, June 23). *SportsIllustrated.com*. Retrieved June 27, 2005, from http://sportsillustrated.cnn.com/2005/more/06/23/bc.cyc.tourdefrance.dop.ap/index.html

U.S. Food and Drug Administration. (1997). *Dietary supplements containing ephedrine alkaloids*. Retrieved November 7, 2006, from http://vm.cfsan.fda.gov/~lrd/fr97064a.html

Vest, D. W. (1993). Wrestling looks to bodybuilding. *Wrestling USA, 29*(5), 91–92.

Wilson, S. (2005, February 1). *Scientists uncover new designer steroid*. Retrieved December 6, 2006, from https://listserv.temple.edu/cgi-bin/wa?A2=ind0502&L=net-gold&T=0&H=1&P=5087

Wood, S. (2005, May 12). Back's "Whizzinator" prompts NFL inquiry. *USA Today*, p. 1C.

World Anti-Doping Agency. (2006a). *2005 testing statistics*. Montreal, Quebec, Canada: Author.

World Anti-Doping Agency. (2006b). *World Anti-Doping Code: The 2007 prohibited list*. Montreal, Quebec, Canada: Author.

World Anti-Doping Agency. (n.d.). *Q & A: Human Growth Hormone Testing*. Retrieved January 23, 2007, from http://www.wada-ama.org/en/dynamic.chz?pageCategory.id=627

Wright, J. E. (1980). Steroids and athletics. *Exercise and Sport Science Reviews, 8*, 149–202.

Yesalis, C. E., Wright, J. E., & Bahrke, M. S. (1989). Epidemiological and policy issues in the measurement of the long term health effects of anabolic–androgenic steroids. *Sports Medicine, 8*, 129–138.

8

THE PREVENTION OF ANABOLIC STEROID USE AMONG ADOLESCENTS

LINN GOLDBERG AND DIANE L. ELLIOT

More than 7 million U.S. high school students participate in their schools' sport programs (National Federation of State High School Associations, n.d.). Being involved in athletics, however, does not protect these adolescents from substance abuse or other unhealthy behaviors (Aaron et al., 1995; Carr, Kennedy, & Dimick, 1990; DuRant, Escobedo, & Heath, 1995; Pate, Trost, Levin, & Dowda, 2000; Schwenk, 2000), and they may be at increased risk for use of performance-enhancing substances, including anabolic steroids. Abuse of anabolic-androgenic steroids by youths is a national concern (Clean Sports Act of 2005). Athletes take these agents to boost athletic performance, increase strength and muscle mass, and improve appearance (Dickinson et al., 2005; DuRant et al., 1995; Yesalis, Kennedy, Kopstein, & Bahrke, 1993). Their use can have serious adverse effects (Ajayi, Mathur, & Halushka, 1995; Baldo-Enzi, Giada, & Zuliani, 1990; Cabasso, 1994; Council on Scientific Affairs, 1990; Haupt & Rovere, 1984; Pope & Katz, 1998; Scott & Scott, 1989). This chapter focuses on the types of anabolic steroids used by adolescents, potential adverse side effects, prevalence of use, factors associated with use, and prevention efforts designed to reduce

161

use of steroids and other drugs and health-harming actions among young athletes.

WHAT ARE ANABOLIC–ANDROGENIC STEROIDS?

Anabolic–androgenic steroids include drugs or hormonal substances that are pharmacologically and chemically related to the major male hormone, testosterone. Because they are anabolic, these hormones build tissue (e.g., by increasing muscle protein and bone density; Dickinson et al., 2005). In addition, all anabolic steroids are androgenic; their use can impart certain male characteristics, including a lowered voice because of vocal cord thickening and larynx enlargement, facial hair growth, and other masculinizing effects. Certain drugs are controlled, or Schedule C, drugs and are categorized on the basis of their abuse potential. All anabolic steroids are Schedule C-III controlled substances in the United States. Schedule C-III drugs have less potential for abuse or addiction than drugs in Schedule C-I (e.g., heroin, LSD), which have no accepted medical use, or Schedule C-II drugs, or those with a high abuse risk but also safe and accepted medical uses in the United States. Anabolic steroids are separate from other classes of steroid hormones, such as those produced by the ovaries (estrogens and progesterone) and those produced by the adrenal gland; the latter include corticosteroids (cortisone), which are used to treat inflammatory conditions, and the salt-retaining hormone aldosterone, which affects the body's balance of water, sodium, and potassium. None of these other steroid hormones have muscle-building or performance-enhancing properties; just the opposite, corticosteroids are catabolic, resulting in tissue wasting.

When taken in sufficient doses, anabolic steroids, along with adequate protein intake and exercise, can increase muscle mass and strength, even at levels only slightly greater than those of normal men (Hartgens & Kuipers, 2004; Isidori et al., 2005; Wang et al., 1996; Young, Baker, Liu, & Seeman, 1993; see also chap. 7, this volume). In a review by Hartgens and Kuipers (2004), short-term steroid use by men produced strength gains of 5% to 20% and muscle mass increases of 4.5 to 11.0 pounds. There are several potential mechanisms by which anabolic steroids exert their effects. They may directly or indirectly increase muscle protein synthesis (Fryburn, 1994; Mauras et al., 1998; Wolfe, Ferrando, Sheffield-Moore, & Urban, 2000), and they also may inhibit effect on the cortisol receptors, preventing muscle breakdown (Danhaive & Rousseau, 1986).

Modifying testosterone's structure can allow different routes of drug delivery, enhance its muscle-building effects, change the duration of its action, alter the side effect profile, and make it more difficult to detect during drug surveillance. Testosterone can be taken by pill or injection, used transdermally (e.g., cream, drug-impregnated patch), or absorbed through the mouth's lining when placed between the cheek and gums. Some steroids are oil based, like Deca-Durabolin (nandrolone) and, when injected, stay in the body for a prolonged period; others are water based, like injectable Winstrol (stanozolol), and remain in the body for a more limited time. Veterinary anabolic steroids often contain the same components as human anabolic steroids but may not have the same quality.

There are appropriate medical indications for anabolic steroid use, including male hypogonadism (lack of sufficient testosterone production), either congenital or acquired, and the treatment of hereditary angioedema. In addition, testosterone has been used as palliative treatment of carcinoma of the breast, to enhance muscle mass in AIDS wasting syndrome, and as a male contraceptive (DiMonaco et al., 1995; Orr & Fiatarone, 2004; Walton & Anderson, 2005).

Designer Steroids

Tetrahydrogestrinone (THG) is referred to as a "designer steroid" (U.S. Food and Drug Administration, 2003). This anabolic steroid was developed by BALCO (Bay Area Laboratory Co-Operative). The company has become infamous because of investigations and accusations that the lab and its directors provided anabolic steroids and other banned performance-enhancing drugs to a number of elite athletes. What makes THG a designer steroid is that it was not manufactured by an established pharmaceutical company, but rather synthesized by BALCO, a private laboratory, specifically to have anabolic effects but avoid detection. It was never intended for therapeutic use and was sold to high-profile athletes ("Balco Investigation Timeline," 2006). Although the most notable designer steroid is THG, it is not the only agent; another, desoxymethyltestosterone (see chap. 7, this volume), was found in Canada before being detected in the urine of athletes. Many designer steroids are not known because they are not detected by typical laboratory methodology.

Anabolic Steroid Precursors

Anabolic steroid precursors are molecules on their way to becoming the final active male sex hormone testosterone (Delbeke, Van Eenoo, Van Thuyne, & Desmet, 2002). The steroid precursor androstenedione (also known as "andro") was made famous when Mark McGwire admitted using this hormone while breaking Roger Maris's home record (Brown, Basil, & Bocarnea, 2003). Andro is a precursor to both testosterone and the female estrogenic hormones estrone and estradiol, and after ingestion, it can be metabolized using either pathway (King et al., 1999). Which final substance predominates (estrogen or testosterone) depends on the individual's sex and the amount of androstenedione consumed.

After passage of the Anabolic Steroid Control Act of 2004, all steroid precursors were banned from sale over the counter in the United States, except dehydroepiandrosterone (DHEA), which is one step before synthesis of androstenedione. It appears that DHEA was protected by Senator Orrin Hatch. As reported in the University of California Berkeley Wellness Letter (2005),

> Congress deliberately exempted it—not because it is so different from the supplements just taken off the shelves, and certainly not with an eye to the health of the American public, but because its manufacturers wield plenty of political clout . . . . Indeed, its chief protector in Congress, Senator Orrin Hatch of Utah, has cited its benefits as an "anti-aging" pill. "It has given health and vigor to millions," the Senator wrote to the New York Times, repeating the claims of the National Nutritional Foods Association. This industry group employs . . . the Senator's son, as a lobbyist. The supplements industry is heavily concentrated in Utah.

Although there is weak conversion of DHEA into testosterone, there is also conversion into estradiol, which could be a risk factor for breast or endometrial cancer in postmenopausal women (Buvat, 2003; Genazzani et al., 2004). To date, no consistent beneficial effect has been found for men in the placebo-controlled trials for DHEA, and most studies are too short in duration or have inadequate control participants to be able to recommend treatment (Bovenberg, van Umm, & Hermus, 2005; Legrain & Gerard, 2003).

Nonsteroid Muscle-Building and Performance-Enhancing Drugs

Numerous substances besides anabolic steroids have been used to increase muscle mass and improve physiques and physical performance. Two popular substances are human growth hormone (hGH) and clenbuterol hydrochloride (Prather, Brown, North, & Wilson, 1995; Rickert, Pawlak-Morello, Sheppard, & Jay, 1992). Clenbuterol is a beta-adrenergic agonist (stimulant) that has been approved by the U.S. Food and Drug Administration (FDA) for use in horses (but not humans) affected with asthma. Other beta-adrenergic drugs used to treat asthma, including salbutamol and terbutaline, may have muscle-building and stimulant effects, and their use by athletes is banned unless the athlete has documented asthma and is prescribed those medications by a physician. National studies assessing youth prevalence of drug use do not include these substances.

NON-MUSCLE-MASS-BUILDING
PERFORMANCE-ENHANCING DRUGS

Some drugs improve performance by means other than increasing muscle mass. Erythropoietin and darbepoetin, for example, are used by endurance athletes to increase red blood cell mass and thus the oxygen-carrying capacity of the blood (Ambrose, 2004). When red cell mass is increased, more oxygen is available to exercising muscle, which can boost aerobic capacity and thus performance during distance events such as distance running, cycling, and cross-country skiing. Use of these substances during the Tour de France and the 2002 Salt Lake City Winter Olympics led to disqualifications and loss of medals (Dickinson et al., 2005). Other drugs used to gain an advantage in sport include drugs with antiestrogen activity, including raloxifene, tamoxifen, and clomiphene, and stimulants such as methylphenidate (Ritalin), ephedra compounds, amphetamines, and methamphetamines (Motram, 2003). As with the nonsteroid muscle-building agents, no national studies have assessed use by adolescents.

ADVERSE EFFECTS OF ANABOLIC STEROIDS

No randomized controlled studies of anabolic-androgenic steroid use have been conducted. Most medical articles commenting on the adverse effects of steroid use do not report the doses or the coincident use of other drugs (Hartgens & Kuipers, 2004). Although there have been lay reports that the harmful effects of high-dose steroids are unfounded, numerous case studies have reported untoward events including cholestatic jaundice; peliosis hepatis (blood-filled liver cysts; Cabasso, 1994); hepatic adenomas and malignancy with C17-alkylated steroids (Ishak & Zimmerman, 1987); cardiovascular effects including dyslipidemias, hypertension, stroke, and myocardial infarction; blood clots and pulmonary embolism (Dickinson et al., 2005; Huie, 1994; Mewis, Spyridopoulos, Kuhlkamp, & Seipel, 1996); tendon rupture (Liow & Tavares, 1995); and mood changes and possible psychotic episodes (Pope & Katz, 1998). In addition to mood disorders, adverse psychological effects may include paranoia, near homicide, and homicide (Pope et al., 1990). Overall, anabolic steroids appear to increase both aggression and hostility, and the psychological consequences (e.g., depression, hypomania, psychosis) may be related to the dose and type of steroid used (Hartgens & Kuipers, 2004).

As the level of sex hormones increases during early adolescence, they stimulate linear growth, which is then followed by permanent bone growth plate closure as testosterone reaches normal adult levels. Accordingly, anabolic steroid use by adolescents may result in premature cessation of bone growth and height stunting (Dickinson et al., 2005). Use of steroids by men may cause testicular atrophy and female-type breast enlargement, and because one quarter of users share needles, transmission of HIV and other infections is a risk. Among female users, effects can include reduced body fat and breast size, facial hair growth, clitoral lengthening, loss of scalp hair, and menstrual irregularities. In addition, anabolic steroids are in the FDA pregnancy Category X, because use is known to cause birth defects in the growing fetus.

PREVALENCE OF PERFORMANCE-ENHANCING SUBSTANCE USE

Substance use and abuse among adolescents is a significant problem in the United States (Johnston, O'Malley, Bachman, & Schulenberg, 2004; *Morbidity and Mortality Weekly Report*, 2006), and performance-enhancing drugs, especially anabolic steroids, are a growing concern. According to Monitoring the Future, a national survey sponsored by the National Institute of Drug Abuse and the Center for Disease Control's Youth Risk Behavior Survey (YRBS; Johnston et al., 2004; *Morbidity and Mortality Weekly Report*, 2006), self-reported anabolic steroid use has significantly increased over the past few years. These national self-report questionnaires have followed steroid use for more than a decade. The 2003 YRBS found that 6.1% of high school students used anabolic steroid pills or shots without a prescription. State and local surveys have identified a prevalence of lifetime illegal steroid use ranging from 2.3% to 7.4% (National Center for Chronic Disease Prevention and Health Promotion [NCCDPHP], 2003). Use was higher in boys than in girls (NCCDPHP, 2003). During 2005, the Centers for Disease Control (*Morbidity and Mortality Weekly Report*, 2006) revealed that 1 of every 25 (4%) high school students admitted to using anabolic steroids without a prescription. Thus, between 550,000 and 850,000 high school students reported current or former anabolic steroid use. Although the level of use reported in these surveys was for any anabolic steroid, those who would be more likely to develop harmful side effects would more likely be high-frequency, higher-dose users. However, those who experiment with any drug as a teen are much more likely to use drugs in the future (National Institute on Drug Abuse, 2003).

The stepwise increase in use has been dramatic. In 2004, the Monitoring the Future survey reported past-year use among 12th-grade students to be at the highest recorded level (Johnston et al., 2004). In 1993, one of every 45 high school students admitted to using anabolic steroids. By 1999, one in 27 high school students admitted to using these hormones. During 2003, self-reported use increased to one of every 16 high school students. During 2005, self-reported use remained at 1 of every 25 high school students (*Morbidity and Mortality Weekly Report*, 2006)

YOUNG ATHLETES' SUBSTANCE USE: A WEB OF INFLUENCES

Multiple factors influence adolescents' substance use. Although many believe that school sports protect students from alcohol and drug use, teens involved in athletics use drugs and alcohol at levels comparable to those of their classmates (Kulig, Brener, & McManus, 2003; Naylor, Gardner, & Zaichkowsky, 2001; Pate et al., 2000). Young male athletes are more likely to drink alcohol, engage in binge drinking, and exhibit other deviant behaviors than nonathlete male peers (Aaron et al., 1995; Carr et al., 1990; Schwenk, 2000). Some commentators have suggested that in certain cases, competitive sports may foster antisocial behavior, especially in schools more concerned with having winning teams than with forming well-educated and -adjusted athletes (Miracle & Rees, 1994).

Adolescents use steroids for many reasons. A study from the Kaiser Foundation found that about 70% of youths desired to be like high-profile athletes, and more than half (52%) believed that these athletes used performance-enhancing drugs (National Center on Addiction and Substance Abuse, 2000). DuRant et al. (1995) found that adolescent users were more likely to be men, inject drugs, use a variety of illicit drugs, drink alcohol, and be engaged in weight training.

Although studies of young women's steroid use are limited, current findings suggest that users are more likely to have disordered eating and other compulsive behaviors, concerns about their body image, and adverse psychological effects as a result of their steroid use (Gruber & Pope, 2000). In a study of more than 2,000 middle and high school girls, Elliot, Moe, Duncan, and Goldberg (1999) found that young women who reported higher intentions to use anabolic steroids in the future were younger and also had a higher prevalence of depression, lower self-esteem, and a greater "win at all costs" attitude.

Adolescent substance use, including use of anabolic steroids, is influenced by a number of factors related to the individual, his or her peer group, the school, the family, and other aspects of the social environment (National Institute on Drug Abuse, 2003). Individual factors relate to genetic susceptibility and modifiable influences such as knowledge, skills, and beliefs. Peers are highly influential. Bonding with deviant peers is a stimulus for use because of peer pressure (Eggert, Thompson, Herting, Nicholas, & Dicker, 1994). Families can have a significant impact on substance use through parental attitudes, expectations for success, and supervision. Schools influence substance abuse by enforcing related policies, and the community can affect use through the availability of drugs, depictions of drug use in the media, and use of drugs by role models. Protective factors include caring adults, healthy role models, problem-solving skills, and the provision of healthy alternatives to substance use and abuse.

The factors involved in substance abuse, in general, differ for adolescent boys and girls (Grunberg, 1998; Leshner, 1998, 1999). Data from all levels of research, including the laboratory, field, and clinical research, show gender differences in nearly all areas of substance abuse. For example, the pressures for young women to attain a thin physique may be accentuated by the requirements of their sport, which may encourage the use of body-shaping substances (e.g., tobacco, amphetamines, diet pills, laxatives, diuretics, and anabolic steroids; Becker, Burwell, Gilman, Herzog, & Hamburg, 2002; Byrne & McLean, 2001). Adolescent female athletes' drug use has been linked to disordered eating practices and depression, and the female athlete triad of disordered eating practices, amenorrhea, and osteoporosis is a well-described disorder of young women involved in sports (Byrne & McLean, 2001). However, use by young men may be more related to sensation seeking and impulsive behavior (National Institute on Drug Abuse, 1996). In general, male adolescents use more drugs than female adolescents, with greater episodic heavy drinking and more use of injectable drugs (Leshner, 1999; NCCDPHP, 2003). In addition, young men have more associated negative behavioral consequences of use, including more drinking and driving, more unprotected sex, more needle sharing, more associated legal problems, and greater suicide risk (Leshner, 1999; Pollack, 1999). Although young women are much better at hiding their use, they experience more physical adverse effects and are more easily addicted to drugs (Rosenbaum, 1998).

EFFORTS TO CURB USE

With better understanding of the factors influencing drug use, professionals can develop more effective and targeted interventions rather than a one-size-fits-all approach. Although numerous studies have assessed the prevalence and correlates of anabolic steroid use, only a few have examined the means to prevent their use, and there are as yet no science-based interventions for the treatment of steroid users.

Student Athlete Drug Testing

The legality of student drug testing was examined by the U.S. Supreme Court (*Board of Education v. Earls*, 2002; *Vernonia School District v. Acton*, 1995) and found not to violate the rights of students involved in school sports or other extracurricular school activities. Such testing is thus legal, but neither its deterrent efficacy nor its effects on the substance-related attitudes of youth athletes have been clearly established.

Approximately 10% of U.S. high schools have some type of drug testing policy and perform random drug tests (National Federation of State High School Associations, 2003; Yamaguchi, Johnston, & O'Malley, 2003). Among these schools, less than one third test for anabolic steroids. The low percentage of schools testing for steroids may be due to the expense; a standard drug screen costs about $10, but the charge for anabolic steroid screening can exceed $100.

The effects of random drug surveillance are controversial and not clearly established. One cross-sectional study (Yamaguchi et al., 2003) found nearly identical rates of drug use in schools that used testing and those that did not. However, the investigators did not assess pretesting drug use, document the type and frequency of testing, or exclude students who were not subject to the schools' drug testing policy.

Other studies have shown potential deterrent effects of drug testing. Less substance use was found among college-age athletes subjected to mandatory surveillance (Albrecht, Anderson, & McKeag, 1992; Coombs et al., 1990). The National Collegiate Athletic Association (NCAA) found a reduction of about 50% in self-reported use of anabolic steroids among Division I football players coincident with initiating drug screening. Over the same period, Division II football programs, which had yet to initiate drug testing, had an increase in anabolic steroid use ("Steroid Use Drops," 1993). Comparing 1,500 athletes from programs with random testing to athletes without testing, Coombs et al. (1990) found less reported use of marijuana, barbiturates, and LSD among those subject to drug surveillance.

A prospective, controlled, but nonrandomized study compared two small rural high schools (Goldberg et al., 2003). At one school, student athletes were subject to random drug testing for the entire school year, and at the comparison school, student athletes knew they would not be drug tested. Prior to drug testing, 6.5% of control student athletes reported illicit substance use during the past 30 days, compared with 7.4% of athletes in the school to have drug testing. At the conclusion of the year, past-30-day use of illicit drugs among testing school student athletes was 5.3%, compared with 19.4% of student athletes self-reporting illicit drug use during the same period at the end of the school year. The index of use of "athletic-enhancing substances" (including steroids) among the drug-tested athletes prior to testing was 9.8% use during the past 30 days, compared with 15% among student athletes at the school without drug testing. After a school year of testing, past-30-day ergogenic substances were self-reported as 5.3% at the drug-testing school, compared with 22.6% self-reported use at the school without testing. Although past-month substance use was lowered, some drug use risk factors increased among student athletes subjected to testing; they felt less bonded to the school, had lower belief in the benefits of drug testing, and had lower belief in the harms of drug use. These findings suggest that more research into drug testing is necessary before widespread adoption. These data also suggest that because drug testing in student athletes may elevate risk factors for future drug use, that when drug testing ceases, student athletes may have an elevated risk to use drugs (Hawkins, Catalano, Kosterman, Abbott, & Hill, 1999), and that drug testing, per se, is not a permanent solution. Although drug testing may prove to be an effective deterrent at some point, we recommend that an education and student assistance program accompany this type of intervention to aid in secondary prevention (Office of National Drug Control Policy, 2004).

Anabolic Steroid Prevention: Initial Trials

Several prospective randomized controlled trials have evaluated different educational means to deter anabolic steroid use (Elliot et al., 2004; Goldberg, Bents, Bosworth, Trevisan, & Elliot, 1991; Goldberg, Bosworth, Bents, & Trevisan, 1990; Goldberg et al., 1996, 2000). A knowledge-only intervention that presented the risks and benefits of anabolic-androgenic steroid use improved knowledge but did not reduce intentions to use anabolic steroids (Goldberg et al., 1990). A program using "scare tactics" lectures that focused only on the adverse consequences of anabolic steroids neither increased knowledge nor improved high school athletes' attitudes toward future steroid use (Goldberg et al., 1991). In fact, paradoxically, students who received the scare tactics intervention increased their desire to use steroids. Overall, the traditional methods of lectures, pamphlet distribution, or lectures on the adverse effects of steroids have no evidence of prevention efficacy.

Gender-Based Education: Athletes Training and Learning to Avoid Steroids and Athletes Targeting Healthy Exercise and Nutrition Alternatives

The use of a gender-specific approach to drug prevention was supported by observations from the Center for Substance Abuse Prevention demonstration projects, which found that gender effects can be prominent and should be addressed in designing a prevention program (DHHS, 1999). Two large school-based, sport-team-centered, gender-specific educational programs have been tested in randomized controlled trials (Elliot et al., 2004; Goldberg et al., 1996, 2000). ATLAS (Athletes Training and Learning to Avoid Steroids), an intervention for male adolescent athletes, was studied with more than 3,200 student athletes, and ATHENA (Athletes Targeting Healthy Exercise and Nutrition Alternatives), an intervention for female adolescent athletes, involved more than 900 participants.

ATLAS and ATHENA are sport team–centered programs designed to dissuade harmful behaviors using peer pressure and reasonable and readily demonstrable alternatives (sport nutrition and strength training) to performance-enhancing drug use. The intervention model was adapted from Bandura's (1977) social cognitive theory and the theory of reasoned action (Fishbein & Ajzen, 1975). The model suggests that students adopt healthy behaviors or avoid unhealthy activities, in part, because the program creates a team ethos (social network) and a strong commitment to a cohesive, influential group. Positively changing attitudes can lead to a reduction in intentions to use drugs and performance-enhancing supplements and can translate into beneficial behavior change. In addition, both ATLAS and ATHENA discuss alternatives to performance-enhancing substances, including sport nutrition and strength training workout programs, which enhance athletic abilities.

Unlike a typical classroom, the sport team provides a natural, nonstigmatizing setting with a ready-made, bonded, gender-specific peer group. Sport teams have the potential to be influential because peers work together and share common goals. In addition, the coaches of young athletes can provide an additional positive adult influence. These effects can be enhanced by continuity of the team during school with personal contact with coaching staff, role modeling by older athletes, and reinforcement during the many hours of team activities.

Both ATLAS and ATHENA are designed to occur during the sport season as a series of 45-minute team meetings that are woven into a team's usual practice activities. At those meetings, the athletes are divided into consistent learning groups of six to eight students, each with a permanent designated student squad leader. The coach facilitates the meetings, and coaches and squad leaders use scripted lesson plans to enhance fidelity and make implementation easy. There are up to six brief, targeted, interactive activities that focus on drugs use in sports, sport supplement use, strength training, sport nutrition, and decision making. Although the primary drug addressed is steroids, other drugs are targeted, including amphetamines and human growth hormone, as well as those that can harm athletic performance, such as marijuana and alcohol. Nutrition issues germane to young athletes are emphasized and include daily calorie requirements, protein needs, meal planning, substitution of high-fat foods with lower-fat products, and ways to make healthier choices in fast food restaurants. There are elements common to the two programs, with similar topics tailored to each gender and risk and protective topics that are applicable to young male and female athletes (Table 8.1).

During ATLAS weekly goal setting for sport nutrition, student–athletes choose from several alternatives, including eating a daily target amount of protein, eating breakfast more often, and making healthy snack choices. Different types of strength training regimens are discussed and the different results from each training program demonstrated. Coaches receive a binder with background information, a scripted lesson plan to train squad (peer) leaders, the 10-session curriculum guide, and overheads. Squad leaders receive the curriculum guide, and athletes use a workbook to complete the sessions. All participants use the ATLAS Sports Menu and the Training Guide to supplement the curriculum.

ATHENA athlete sessions also include sport nutrition, strength training, and drug and supplement use. Sessions focus on steroids and other body-shaping substances, including diet pills, laxatives, diuretics, and tobacco prod-

TABLE 8.1
Characteristics, Differences, and Results of the ATLAS
and ATHENA Programs

Common features	Interventions during the sport season Integrated into team activities Scripted and interactive content Predominantly student taught in small groups (about 5 students) Coach facilitated 45-minute sessions	
Topics	Use and consequences of substance use Body image Drug refusal skills Media awareness Sports nutrition as an alternative Strength training as an alternative	
Differences between the programs	ATLAS Protein and calories Impulsivity Decision making Media and muscle magazines Ten 45-minute sessions	ATHENA Protein and calcium Mood (e.g., depression prevention) Self-esteem Media and images of women Eight 45-minute sessions
Program results	Decreases in substance use and associated behaviors	
	50% reduction in new use of anabolic steroids Significant reduction in new use of athletic-enhancing drugs (anabolic steroids, human growth hormone, amphetamines) 50% reduction in new use of alcohol and illicit substances 24% reduction in drinking and driving 50% reduction in new use of sport supplements Reductions in behaviors related to risk factors Greater substance use resistance skills Reduced substance abuse risk factors (increased perceived danger and personal vulnerability to harm of steroids, heightened perception of coach intolerance to drug use, enhanced resistance skills, less belief in media advertisements)	Reduced new and ongoing use of diet pills Less new use of athletic-enhancing substances (anabolic steroids, amphetamines, and sport supplements)
	Reductions in behaviors related to protective factors	
	Improved substance abuse protective factors (e.g., better nutrition behaviors, improved perception of athletic competence) Improved strength training self-efficacy Greater use of the school's weight room	Less riding with an alcohol-consuming driver Greater seatbelt use Less new sexual activity Improved eating behaviors

ucts. Because ATHENA targets risk and protective factors for young women athletes, activities include cognitive restructuring (Clarke et al., 2001) as a depression prevention component; athletes add and record fun activities and how they affect their mood. Unlike ATLAS, ATHENA does not focus on calories. Healthy nutrition stresses protein and calcium requirements and how to choose high-quality foods for meals and snacks. Because of the influence of the media on behavior, advertisement deconstruction is a prominent feature.

ATLAS Results

ATLAS outcomes were determined in a randomized controlled trial involving three consecutive cohorts of high school football teams from 16 control high schools and 15 intervention high schools (Goldberg et al., 1996, 2000). Confidential questionnaires were collected before the program, at the season's end, and approximately 1 year after the intervention for both intervention and control schools. ATLAS was designed to aid in decision making, allow athletes to engage in discussions and practice refusal skills, and learn sport nutrition and different types of strength training techniques, the latter as alternatives to the use of anabolic steroid and other performance-enhancing drugs. In addition, the program focused on how alcohol and other illicit drugs could harm athletic performance (Elliot & Goldberg, 1996). The format included interactive educational games, role playing, creation of mock public service announcements, and weekly goal setting to practice and personalize the curriculum.

The results of the research indicate that compared with control student athletes, ATLAS-trained students had 50% lower use of athletic-enhancing supplements, 50% lower use of new illicit drugs (marijuana, narcotics, amphetamines), and a 24% reduction in cumulative drinking and driving occurrences. Although new steroid use was significantly reduced at the end of the sport season, because of the relatively low-base user rate, it did not achieve statistical significance ($p = .072$ at 1 year). However, when use of other athletic-enhancing drugs was added to provide an index of athletic-enhancing drug use (a combination of hGH, anabolic steroids, and amphetamines), significant reductions in new use ($p = .05$) were found (Goldberg et al., 2000).

ATHENA Results

ATHENA targets the risk factors for disordered eating behaviors and body-shaping and other substance use in female adolescents, including lower self-esteem, propensity toward depression, media depictions of women, and perceptions of peer norms (Elliot et al., 1999, 2006). Similar to ATLAS, ATHENA uses a scripted curriculum and cooperative learning in the atmosphere of the established sport team. Short-term benefits reported by students engaged in ATHENA as compared with a control group were a significant lowering of the following drug use risk factors (Elliot et al., 2004):

- increased knowledge of disordered eating practices and need for dietary protein,
- less perceived pressure to lose weight,
- less belief in media messages promoting thinness,
- greater perceptions that friends were against substance use,
- improved personal skills for resisting drug use offers, and
- enhanced ability to control their mood.

In addition, significant self-reported behavioral changes were found. In a longer-term follow-up of student athletes 1 year after high school graduation, those who had received the ATHENA intervention used marijuana, alcohol, and diet pills significantly less than the control graduates.

CONCLUSION

The use of anabolic steroids and other muscle-building supplements is a significant problem among youths. These substances have risks that may be more severe for the developing adolescent than for the mature adult. Both programs were evaluated using randomized controlled trials, so a social desirability response bias was present for both control groups and intervention groups and was unlikely to be a factor in the improvement of behaviors among ATLAS and ATHENA participants, who exhibited improvements in knowledge, attitudes, and intentions.

Currently, ATLAS and ATHENA represent the only drug use prevention and health promotion programs shown to reduce self-reported use of anabolic steroids. The sport setting is unique in its ability to combine bonded teammates, an influential coach, a natural prosocial gender-specific setting, and relevant healthy alternatives to harmful behaviors. Other types of educational models, including awareness programs and elite athlete testing (Clean Sports Act of 2005) touted to prevent steroid use among youths, have not been scientifically evaluated. Although sports may heighten young adults' risk for certain harmful behaviors, team-centered curricula provide the potential to couple athletic participation with positive skills and attitudes that can support a future of healthy behaviors.

REFERENCES

Aaron, D. J., Dearwater, S. R., Anderson, R., Olsen, T., Kriska, A. M., & LaPorte, R. E. (1995). Physical activity and the initiation of high-risk health behaviors in adolescents. *Medicine and Science in Sports and Exercise, 27*, 1639–1642.

Ajayi, A. A., Mathur, R., & Halushka, P. V. (1995). Testosterone increases human platelet thromboxane AZ receptor density and aggregation responses. *Circulation, 91*, 2694–2698.

Albrecht, R. R., Anderson, W. A., & McKeag, D. B. (1992). Drug testing of college athletes: The issues. *Sports Medicine, 14*, 349–352.

Ambrose, P. J. (2004). Drug use in sports: A veritable arena for pharmacists. *Journal of the American Pharmacy Association, 44*, 501–514.

Anabolic Steroid Control Act of 2004, 108th Cong. (2004).

Balco investigation timeline. (2006, June 22). *USA Today.* Retrieved January 25, 2007, from http://www.usatoday.com/sports/balco-timeline.htm

Bandura, A. (1977). *Social learning theory.* Englewood Cliffs, NJ: Prentice Hall.

Baldo-Enzi, G., Giada, F., & Zuliani, G. (1990). Lipid and apoprotein modification in body builders during and after self-administration of anabolic steroids. *Metabolism, 39*, 203–208.

Becker, A. E., Burwell, R. A., Gilman, S. E., Herzog, D. B., & Hamburg, P. (2002). Eating behaviours and attitudes following prolonged exposure to television among ethnic Fijian adolescent girls. *British Journal of Psychiatry, 180*, 509–514.

Board of Education of Independent School District No. 92 of Pottawatomie City v. Earls, 536 U. S. 822 (2002). Retrieved December 11, 2006, from http://supct.law.cornell.edu/supct/pdf/01-332P.ZS

Bovenberg, S. A., van Uum, S. H., & Hermus, A. R. (2005). Dehydroepiandrosterone administration in humans: Evidence based? *Netherlands Journal of Medicine, 63*, 300–304.

Brown, W. J., Basil, M. D., & Bocarnea, M. C. (2003). The influence of famous athletes on health beliefs and practices: Mark McGwire, child abuse prevention, and androstenedione. *Journal of Health Communication, 8*, 41–57.

Buvat, J. (2003). Androgen therapy with dehydroepiandrosterone. *World Journal of Urology, 21*, 346–355.

Byrne, S., & McLean, N. (2001). Eating disorders in athletes: A review of the literature. *Journal of Science and Medicine in Sport, 4*, 145–159.

Cabasso, A. (1994). Peliosis hepatis in a young bodybuilder. *Medicine and Science in Sports and Exercise, 26*, 2–4.

Carr, C. N., Kennedy, S. R., & Dimick, K. M. (1990, Fall). Alcohol use among high school athletes: A comparison of alcohol use and intoxication in male and female high school athletes and non-athletes. *Journal of Alcohol and Drug Education, 36*, 39–43.

Clarke, G. N., Hornbrook, M., Lynch, F., Polen, M., Gale, J., Beardslee, W., et al. (2001). A randomized trial of a group cognitive intervention for preventing depression in adolescent offspring of depressed parents. *Archives of General Psychiatry, 58*, 1127–1134.

Clean Sports Act of 2005, S. 1114, 109th Cong. (2005). Retrieved November 3, 2006, from http://www.theorator.com/bills109/s1114.html

Coombs, R. H., & Ryan, F. J. (1990). Drug testing effectiveness in identifying and preventing drug use. *American Journal of Drug and Alcohol Abuse, 16*, 173–184.

Council on Scientific Affairs. (1990). Medical and non-medical uses of anabolic–androgenic steroids. *The Journal of the American Medical Association, 246*, 2923–2927.

Danhaive, P. A., & Rousseau, G. G. (1986). Binding of glucocorticoid antagonists to androgen and glucocorticoid hormone receptors in rat skeletal muscle. *Journal of Steroid Biochemistry, 24*, 481–487.

Delbeke, F. T., Van Eenoo, P., Van Thuyne, W., & Desmet, N. (2002). Prohormones and sport. *Journal of Steroid Biochemistry and Molecular Biology, 83*(1–5), 245–251.

Department of Health and Human Services, Center for Substance Abuse Prevention. (1999). *Understanding substance abuse prevention toward the 21st century: A primer on effective programs*. (DHHS Publication No. SMA99-3301). Washington, DC: Author.

Dickinson, B., Goldberg, L., Elliot, D., Spratt, D., Rogol, A. D., & Fish, L. H. (2005). Hormone abuse in adolescents and adults. *Endocrinologist, 15*, 115–125.

DiMonaco, M., Leonardi, L., Gatto, V., Gallo, M., Brignardellop, E., & Boccuzzi, G. (1995). Dihydrotestosterone affects the growth of hormone-unresponsive breast cancer cells: An indirect action. *Anticancer Research, 15*(6B), 2581–2584.

DuRant, R. H., Escobedo, L. G., & Heath, G. W. (1995). Anabolic-steroid use, strength training and multiple drug use among adolescents in the United States. *Pediatrics, 96*(1, Part 1), 23–28.

Eggert, L. L., Thompson, E. A., Herting, J. R., Nicholas, L. F., & Dicker, B. G. (1994). Preventing adolescent drug abuse and high school dropout through an intensive school-based social network development program. *American Journal of Health Promotion, 8*, 202–215.

Elliot, D. L., & Goldberg, L. (1996). Intervention and prevention of steroid use in adolescents. *American Journal of Sports Medicine, 24*(Suppl.), 46–47.

Elliot, D. L., Goldberg, L., Moe, E. L., DeFrancesco, C. A., Durham, M. B., & Hix-Small, H. (2004). Preventing substance use and disordered eating: Initial outcomes of the ATHENA (Athletes Targeting Healthy Exercise and Nutrition Alternatives) program. *Archives of Pediatric and Adolescent Medicine, 158*, 1043–1051.

Elliot, D. L., Moe, E. L., Duncan, T., & Goldberg, L. (1999). Who are the young women at risk for anabolic steroid use? *Medicine and Science in Sports and Exercise, 31*(Suppl.), 123.

Elliot, D. L., Moe, E. L., Goldberg, L., DeFrancesco, C. A., Durham, M. B., & Hix-Small, H. (2006). Definition and outcome of a curriculum to prevent disordered eating and body-shaping drug use. *Journal of School Health, 76*, 67–73.

Fishbein, M., & Ajzen, I. (1975). *Belief, attitude, intention and behavior: An introduction to theory and research*. Reading, MA: Addison-Wesley.

Fryburn, D. A. (1994). Insulin-like growth factor I exerts growth hormone- and insulin-like actions on human muscle protein metabolism. *American Journal of Physiology, 267*(2, Part 1), E331–336.

Genazzani, A. R., Inglese, S., Lombardi, I., Pieri, M., Bernardi, F., Genazzani, A. D., et al. (2004). Long term low-dose dehydroepiandrosterone replacement therapy in aging males with partial androgen deficiency. *Aging Male, 7*, 133–143.

Goldberg, L., Bents, R., Bosworth, E., Trevisan, L., & Elliot, D. L. (1991). Anabolic steroid education and adolescents: Do scare tactics work? *Pediatrics, 87,* 283–286.

Goldberg, L., Bosworth, E., Bents, R., & Trevisan, L. (1990). Use, knowledge and attitudes of anabolic steroids among high school football players. *Journal of Adolescent Health Care, 11,* 1–5.

Goldberg, L., Elliot, D. L., Clarke, G., MacKinnon, D. P., Moe, E., Zoref, L., et al. (1996). Effects of a multi-dimensional anabolic steroid prevention intervention: The A.T.L.A.S. (Adolescents Training and Learning to Avoid Steroids) program. *The Journal of the American Medical Association, 276,* 1555–1562.

Goldberg, L., Elliot, D., MacKinnon, D. P., Moe, E. L., Kuehl, K. S., Nohre, L., et al. (2003). Drug testing athletes to prevent substance abuse: Background and pilot study results of the SATURN (Student Athlete Testing Using Random Notification) study. *Journal of Adolescent Health, 32,* 16–25.

Goldberg, L., MacKinnon, D., Elliot, D. L., Moe, E. L., Clarke, G., Cheong, J., et al. (2000). The Adolescents Training and Learning to Avoid Steroids Program: Preventing drug use and promoting health behaviors. *Archives of Pediatric and Adolescent Medicine, 154,* 332–338.

Gruber, A. J., & Pope, H. G., Jr. (2000). Psychiatric and medical effects of anabolic-androgenic steroid use in women. *Psychotherapy and Psychosomatics, 69,* 19–26.

Grunberg, N. E. (1998, April). Smoking, eating, stress, and drug use: Sex differences. In C. L. Wetherington & A. B. Roman (Eds.), *Drug addiction research and the health of women* (executive summary of pp. 1–151). Retrieved December 11, 2006, from http://www.nida.nih.gov/PDF/DARHW-exec.pdf

Hartgens, F., & Kuipers, H. (2004). Effects of androgenic-anabolic steroids in athletes. *Sports Medicine, 34,* 513–554.

Haupt, H. A., & Rovere, G. D. (1984). Anabolic steroids: A review of the literature. *American Journal of Sports Medicine, 12,* 464–484.

Hawkins, J. D., Catalano, R. F., Kosterman, R., Abbott, R., & Hill, K. G. (1999). Preventing adolescent health-risk behaviors by strengthening protection during childhood. *Archives of Pediatric and Adolescent Medicine, 153,* 226–234.

Huie, M. J. (1994). An acute myocardial infarction occurring in an anabolic steroid user. *Medicine and Science in Sports and Exercise, 26,* 408–413.

Ishak, K. G., & Zimmerman, H. J. (1987). Hepatotoxic effects of the anabolic/androgenic steroids. *Seminars in Liver Disease, 7,* 230–236.

Isidori, A. M., Giannetta, E., Greco, E. A., Gianfrilli, D., Bonifacio, V., Isidori, A., et al. (2005). Effects of testosterone on body composition, bone metabolism and serum lipid profile in middle-aged men: A meta-analysis. *Clinical Endocrinology, 63,* 280–293.

Johnston, L. D., O'Malley, P. M., Bachman, J. G., & Schulenberg, J. E. (2004). *Monitoring the future: National survey results on drug use, 1975–2004: Vol. 1. Secondary school students* (NIH Publication No. 05-5727). Bethesda, MD: National Institute on Drug Abuse.

King, D. S., Sharp, R. L., Vukovich, M. D., Brown, G. A., Reifenrath, T. A., Uhl, N. L., et al. (1999). Effect of oral androstenedione on serum testosterone and adaptations to resistance training in young men: A randomized controlled trial. *The Journal of the American Medical Association, 281,* 2020–2028.

Kulig, K., Brener, N. D., & McManus, T. (2003). Sexual activity and substance use among adolescents by category of physical activity plus team sports participation. *Archives of Pediatrics and Adolescent Medicine, 157,* 905–912.

Legrain, S., & Girard, L. (2003). Pharmacology and therapeutic effects of dehydroepiandrosterone in older subjects. *Drugs and Aging, 20,* 949–967.

Leshner, A. (1998). In C. L. Wetherington & A. B. Roman (Eds.), *Drug addiction research and the health of women* (executive summary). Bethesda, MD: U.S. Department of Health and Human Services, National Institutes of Health, National Institute on Drug Abuse.

Leshner, A. (1999). *Sixth triennial report to Congress: 25 years of discovery to advance the health of the public.* Bethesda MD: National Institutes of Health, National Institute on Drug Abuse

Liow, R. Y., & Tavares, S. (1995). Bilateral rupture of the quadriceps tendon associated with anabolic steroids. *British Journal of Sports Medicine, 29*(2), 77–79.

Mauras, N., Hayes, V., Welch, S., Rini, A., Helgeson, K., Dokler, M., et al. (1998). Testosterone deficiency in young men: Marked alterations in whole body protein kinetics, strength and adiposity. *Journal of Clinical Endocrinology and Metabolism, 83,* 1886–1892.

Mewis, C., Spyridopoulos, I., Kuhlkamp, V., & Seipel, L. (1996). Manifestations of severe coronary heart disease after anabolic drug abuse. *Clinical Cardiology, 19,* 153–155.

Miracle, A. W., & Rees, C. R. (1994). *Lessons of the locker room: The myth of school sports.* Amherst, NY: Prometheus Books.

Morbidity and Mortality Weekly Report. (2006, June 9). *Survelliance summaries: Youth Risk Behavior Surveillance—United States, 2005.* Retrieved November 3, 2006, from http://www.cdc.gov/mmwr/PDF/SS/SS5505.pdf

Motram, D. R. (Ed.). (2003). *Drugs in sport* (3rd ed.). London: Routledge.

National Center for Chronic Disease Prevention and Health Promotion. (2003). *Healthy youth! Youth Risk Behavior Surveillance System: National data files and documentation 1991–2005.* Retrieved from http://www.cdc.gov/HealthyYouth/yrbs/data/index.htm

National Center on Addiction and Substance Abuse, Columbia University. (2000, September). *Winning at any cost: Doping in Olympic sports: A report by the CASA National Commission on Sports and Substance Abuse.* New York: Author.

National Federation of State High School Associations. (2003, September 2). *13 percent of high schools have drug-testing policy.* Retrieved November 3, 2006 from http://www.nfhs.org/web/2003/11/sports_medicine_high_school_drugtesting_programs_august_2003.aspx

National Federation of State High School Associations. (n.d.). *2005–06 high school athletics participation survey.* Retrieved November 7, 2006, from http://

www.nfhs.org/core/contentmanager/uploads/2005_06nfhsparticipationsurvey.pdf

National Institute on Drug Abuse. (1996, May). *Women and gender differences research: Director's report to council.* Retrieved November 3, 2006 from http://www.nida.nih.gov/WHGD/WHGDDirRep5.html

National Institute on Drug Abuse. (2003, October). *Preventing drug use among children and adolescents: A research-based guide for parents, educators, and community leaders* (2nd ed.). Retrieved December 7, 2006, from http://www.drugabuse.gov/pdf/prevention/RedBook.pdf

Naylor, A. H., Gardner, D., & Zaichkowsky, L. (2001). Drug use patterns among high school athletes and nonathletes. *Adolescence, 36,* 627–639.

Office of National Drug Control Policy. (2004). *What you need to know about starting a student drug-testing program.* Retrieved November 3, 2006, from http://www.whitehousedrugpolicy.gov/publications/student_drug_testing/

Orr, R., & Fiatarone, S. M. (2004). The anabolic androgenic steroid oxandrolone in the treatment of wasting and catabolic disorders: Review of efficacy and safety. *Drugs, 64,* 725–750.

Pate, R. R., Trost, S. G., Levin, S., & Dowda, M. (2000). Sports participation and health-related behaviors among U.S. youth. *Archives of Pediatric and Adolescent Medicine, 154,* 904–911.

Pollack, W. S. (1999). *Real boys: Rescuing our sons from the myths of boyhood.* New York: Henry Holt.

Pope, H. G., & Katz, D. L. (1990). Homicide and near-homicide by anabolic steroid users. *Journal of Clinical Psychiatry, 51,* 28–31.

Pope, H. G., & Katz, D. L. (1998). Affective and psychotic symptoms associated with anabolic steroid use. *American Journal of Psychiatry, 145,* 487–490.

Prather, I. D., Brown, D. E., North, P., & Wilson, J. R. (1995) Clenbuterol: A substitute for anabolic steroids? *Medicine and Science in Sports and Exercise, 27,* 1118–1121.

Rickert, V. I., Pawlak-Morello, C., Sheppard, V., & Jay, M. S. (1992). Human growth hormone: A new substance of abuse among adolescents? *Clinical Pediatrics, 31,* 723–726.

Rosenbaum, M. (1998). Harm reduction. In C. L. Wetherington & A. B. Roman (Eds.), *Drug addiction research and the health of women* (executive summary). Bethesda, MD: U.S. Department of Health and Human Services, National Institutes of Health, National Institute on Drug Abuse.

Schwenk, T. L. (2000, June). Alcohol use in adolescents: The scope of the problem and strategies for intervention [Electronic version]. *The Physician and Sports Medicine, 28,* Retrieved December 7, 2006, from http://www.physsportsmed.com/issues/2000/06_00/schwenk.htm

Scott, M. J., & Scott, M. J., Jr. (1989). HIV infection associated with injections of anabolic steroids. *The Journal of the American Medical Association, 262,* 207–208.

Steroid use drops among student athletes. (1993, September 1). *NCAA News,* p. 1.

University of California Berkeley Wellness Letter. (2005, August). *Over-the-counter steroid sold as anti-aging pill: Is a younger, better physique a pill-pop away?* Berkeley, CA: Author.

U.S. Food and Drug Administration, U.S. Department of Health and Human Services. (2003, October 28). *FDA statement on THG*. Retrieved November 3, 2006, from http://www.fda.gov/bbs/topics/NEWS/2003/NEW00967.html

Vernonia School District v. Acton, 515 U.S. 646 (1995).

Walton, M., & Anderson, R. A. (2005). Hormonal contraception in men. *Current Drugs Targets—Immune, Endocrine, and Metabolic Disorders, 5,* 249–257.

Wang, C., Eyre, D. R., Clark, R., Kleinberg, D., Newman, C., Iranmanish, J., et al. (1996). Sublingual testosterone replacement improves muscle mass and strength, decreases bone resorption, and increases bone formation markers in hypogonadal men—a clinical research center study. *Journal of Clinical Endocrinology and Metabolism, 81,* 3654–3662.

Wolfe, R., Ferrando, A., Sheffield-Moore, M., & Urban, R. (2000). Testosterone and muscle protein metabolism. *Mayo Clinic Proceedings, 75*(Suppl.), 55–60.

Yamaguchi, R., Johnston, L. D., & O'Malley, P. M. (2003). Relationship between student illicit drug use and school drug-testing policies. *Journal of School Health, 73,* 159–164.

Yesalis, C. E., Kennedy, N. K., Kopstein, A. N., & Bahrke, M. S. (1993). Anabolic–androgenic steroid use in the United States. *The Journal of the American Medical Association, 270,* 1217–1221.

Young, N. R., Baker, H. W., Liu, G., & Seeman, E. (1993). Body composition and muscle strength in healthy men receiving testosterone enathate for contraception. *Journal of Clinical Endocrinology and Metabolism, 77,* 1028–1032.

IV

SPECIAL TOPICS

9

COSMETIC PROCEDURES TO ENHANCE BODY SHAPE AND MUSCULARITY

DAVID B. SARWER, CANICE E. CRERAND, AND LAUREN M. GIBBONS

This chapter discusses the use of cosmetic surgery to improve body shape and, either directly or indirectly, to enhance a muscular appearance. We begin with a discussion of the procedures specifically designed to enhance body shape and contour. We then provide an overview of what are believed to be the most common forms of psychopathology among persons looking to improve their body shape through cosmetic surgery: body dysmorphic disorder (including muscle dysmorphia) and eating disorders. The chapter concludes with a brief outline of the factors that may be contributing to the growing popularity of cosmetic surgery.

COSMETIC PROCEDURES

According to the American Society of Plastic Surgeons (ASPS, 2005), more than 9.2 million cosmetic surgical or minimally invasive procedures

This chapter was supported, in part, by funding from the National Institute of Diabetes and Digestive and Kidney Diseases (Grants K23 DK60023-04 and R03 DK067885-02) to the first author.

TABLE 9.1
Cosmetic Surgical and Minimally Invasive Procedures Performed in 2004

Surgical procedure	Total procedures	Number performed on men	% performed on men
Breast augmentation	264,041	0	0%
Breast implant removals[a]	35,208	0	0%
Breast lift (mastopexy)	75,805	0	0%
Breast reduction in men (gynecomastia)	13,963	13,963	100%
Buttock lift	3,496	210	6%
Cheek implants	9,318	3,914	42%
Chin augmentation	15,822	8,860	56%
Dermabrasion	54,018	7,563	14%
Ear surgery (otoplasty)	25,915	11,403	44%
Eyelid surgery (blepharoplasty)	233,334	32,667	14%
Facelift	114,279	10,285	9%
Forehead lift	54,993	7,699	14%
Hair transplantation	48,925	43,054	88%
Lip augmentation (other than injectables)	26,730	802	3%
Lipoplasty (liposuction)	324,891	32,489	10%
Lower body lift	8,926	1,250	14%
Nose reshaping (rhinoplasty)	305,475	109,971	36%
Thigh lift[b]	8,123	406	5%
Tummy tuck (abdominoplasty)	107,019	4,281	4%
Upper arm lift[b]	9,955	398	4%
Total surgical procedures	1,740,236	289,215	17%
Minimally invasive procedures			
Botox injection	2,992,607	329,187	11%
Cellulite treatment	44,569	5,794	13%
Chemical peel	1,090,523	109,052	10%
Laser hair removal	573,970	154,972	27%
Laser skin resurfacing	164,451	14,801	9%
Laser treatment of leg veins	103,460	14,484	14%
Microdermabrasion	858,867	214,717	25%
Sclerotherapy	544,898	5,449	1%
Soft tissue fillers			
Calcium hydroxylapatite (Radiance)	56,631	5,097	9%
Collagen	521,769	31,306	6%
Fat	56,377	4,510	8%
Hyaluronic acid (Hylaform, Restylane)	461,397	13,842	3%
Polylactic acid (Sculptra)	872	44	5%
Total minimally invasive procedures	7,470,391	903,255	12%
Total cosmetic procedures	9,210,627	1,192,470	13%

Note. Statistical data from the American Society of Plastic Surgeons (ASPS). Final figures are projected to reflect nationwide statistics and represent procedures performed by ASPS member plastic surgeons certified by the American Board of Plastic Surgery as well as other physicians certified by boards recognized by the American Board of Medical Specialties.
[a]70% of breast implant removals in 2004 were replaced. [b]76% of total 2004 thigh and upper arm lifts were after massive weight loss. [c]The number reported for 2004 Botox injections is the number of anatomic sites injected.

were performed in 2004 (see Table 9.1). The increase in the popularity of cosmetic surgery over the past decade has been dramatic, although it is impossible to calculate the specific size of the increase, because some of the most popular procedures, such as Botox (botulinum toxin type A) injections, did not exist 10 years ago. Nevertheless, examination of the numbers of persons who have undergone other procedures illustrates the burgeoning popularity of cosmetic surgery. For example, the number of liposuction and breast augmentation procedures, the two most popular body contouring procedures, has increased more than sixfold over the past decade.

The number of men who seek cosmetic surgery also has grown. In 1994, 43,983 men underwent a cosmetic procedure. In 2004, this number increased to more than 1.1 million. Over the decade, the percentage of all procedures performed on men remained relatively stable at approximately 10%. In 2004, the most common surgical procedures among men were rhinoplasty, hair transplantation, and liposuction. Botox injections, microdermabrasion, laser hair removal, and chemical peels were the most common minimally invasive procedures.

There are several surgical procedures specifically designed to improve body shape and contour. The most common of these procedures are breast augmentation, liposuction, and abdominoplasty. (Readers interested in a discussion of the psychological aspects of these procedures are referred to Sarwer, Didie, & Gibbons, 2006.) Body contouring implants are used less frequently. In addition, an unknown number of men and women undergo genital enhancement surgery each year.

Liposuction

In 2004, 32,489 men and 292,402 women underwent liposuction to alter their body shape, making it the most popular surgical procedure (ASPS, 2005). The most appropriate liposuction patients from a physical perspective have a normal or slightly elevated body mass index (BMI) with localized areas of fat that have been resistant to diet and exercise. The areas of the body treated with liposuction vary by gender. Women typically request liposuction for the lateral thighs ("saddlebags") and hips, whereas men request the procedure for fat deposits on either side of the back just below the waist ("love handles"). Despite the popularity of the procedure, little is known about the psychological characteristics of the typical patient.

There appear to be many misconceptions about liposuction among the general public. Although designed for body contouring purposes, many individuals erroneously believe that liposuction is a permanent solution to weight problems. Surprisingly, the typical weight loss experienced following liposuction has not been well documented. Fourteen overweight women reported a mean weight loss of 5.1 kilograms by 6 weeks postoperatively, with an additional 1.3 kilograms weight loss by 4 months (Giese, Bulan, Commons, Spear, & Yanovski, 2001).

Some patients mistakenly believe that fat deposits will never return to the treated areas. Between 40% and 50% of liposuction patients reported weight gain after surgery, and up to 29% claimed that fat returned to the site of the surgery (Dillerud & Haheim, 1993; Rohrich et al., 2004). Many patients similarly believe that successful liposuction will result in "washboard abs" and smooth thighs. Unfortunately, if fat cells are not removed in a consistent fashion, residual pockets of fat or cellulite may remain. Nevertheless, the majority of patients report satisfaction with the procedure and maintain an improved and more proportional shape, even if they do gain weight postoperatively (Dillerud & Haheim, 1993; Rohrich et al., 2004).

Individuals with excessive weight or shape concerns and those with formal eating disorders require particular attention before undergoing liposuction. Women and men with anorexia nervosa or bulimia nervosa, as discussed in detail later in this chapter, may mistakenly consider the procedure to be an appropriate means of controlling their shape and weight. A case report of two women with bulimia nervosa who underwent liposuction noted that they had an unrealistic expectation that the procedure would result in an improvement of their eating disorder symptoms (Willard, McDermott, & Woodhouse, 1996). Both women reported a worsening of their bulimic and depressive symptoms following liposuction, and one reported a weight gain of 25 pounds in 3 months. Unfortunately, little else is known about the relationship between eating disorders and liposuction.

Abdominoplasty

Abdominoplasty is one of the most rapidly growing cosmetic surgical procedures. The number of procedures performed annually increased by 70% between 2000 and 2004 (ASPS, 2005). One factor that may be contributing to the popularity is that increasing numbers of individuals with extreme obesity are now undergoing bariatric surgery (stomach stapling) for weight loss. Bariatric procedures typically result in a weight loss of approximately one third of an individual's preoperative body weight (Sarwer, Wadden, & Fabricatore, 2005). Unfortunately, many patients are left with excess folds of skin and fat on the abdomen, arms, and thighs following the massive weight loss. This redundant skin may contribute to increased body image dissatisfaction and, as a result, may lead patients to seek plastic surgery. Approximately 56,000 individuals underwent abdominoplasty and other body contouring procedures following the massive weight loss associated with bariatric surgery in 2004 (ASPS, 2005).

Only one study has documented the psychosocial changes associated with abdominoplasty (Bolton, Pruzinsky, Cash, & Persing, 2003). Eight weeks after the surgery, women reported significant improvements in overall body image dissatisfaction, abdominal dissatisfaction, and avoidance of body exposure during sexual activity. Patients did not report significant improvements in self-concept or general life satisfaction. These results are consistent with other postoperative studies of cosmetic surgery patients, which have found that cosmetic procedures resulted in improvement in body image discontent but not necessarily in more general psychosocial functioning (Sarwer & Crerand, 2004).

Body Contouring Implants

Originally designed for persons with congenital or acquired deformities, pectoral, calf, or gluteal implants personally tailored for size and shape are now used for cosmetic purposes. The absolute number of individuals undergoing these procedures is unknown but is believed to be relatively small. Very little is known about the psychological motivations and characteristics of those who seek body implants or the psychological changes that may occur postoperatively. Features shaped by these implants are typically covered by clothing. As a result, the changes in appearance are not readily visible to others. Thus, it is possible that some individuals who undergo these procedures may be suffering from body dysmorphic disorder or muscle dysmorphia (discussed later in this chapter).

Genital Enhancement

An unknown number of men and women are dissatisfied with the appearance of their genitalia. Some pursue what has been called "genital enhancement" or "genital beautification" procedures. From a surgical perspective, these procedures are similar to those undertaken for individuals undergoing sexual reassignment surgery. Little is known, however, about the psychological characteristics of people who undergo these procedures for purely cosmetic reasons (Sarwer et al., 2006). Men may undergo a variety of procedures to lengthen or widen their genitals.

Although these "defects" are sometimes thought of as functional (impeding urination or adversely affecting sexual functioning), there appears to be a significant aesthetic component in most cases. Patients often report that they are motivated for surgery by embarrassment either when undressed, such as in health club locker rooms or sexual situations, or when wearing tight clothing (Perovic, Radojicic, Djordjevic, & Vukadinovic, 2003). Considering the nature of these procedures, it is possible that a significant percentage of these patients are experiencing body dysmorphic disorder or another psychiatric disorder with a delusional or psychotic component. For some, the concern about the appearance of the genitals becomes quite excessive, and some individuals perform dangerous "do-it-yourself" procedures.

PSYCHIATRIC DISORDERS AMONG BODY CONTOURING PATIENTS

The presence of psychopathology among cosmetic surgery patients has been of interest to both plastic surgeons and mental health professionals for the past 50 years (Sarwer & Crerand, 2004; Sarwer, Magee, & Crerand, 2004; Sarwer, Wadden, Pertschuk, & Whitaker, 1998b). The initial investigations, which typically relied on unstructured clinical interviews of patients, suggested that the majority experienced some form of psychopathology. More recent studies, which have frequently used empirically validated measures of symptomatology, have suggested that patients have far less psychopathology than previously thought. Methodological concerns with both sets of studies, however, raise questions about the confidence that can be placed in the findings. In the absence of more methodologically sound studies, it is likely safe to conclude that most, if not all, psychiatric disorders can be found among the growing population of cosmetic surgery and body contouring patients. However, the rate of most disorders may be no greater among cosmetic surgery patients than among the general population.

Historically, male patients have been seen as more psychopathological than female patients. In the first report on male patients, all 18 were diagnosed as psychotic, neurotic, or personality disordered (Jacobson, Edgerton, Meyer, Canter, & Slaughter, 1960). This study, however, was done over 45 years ago, when the number of male patients was significantly smaller than it is today. Subsequent studies have found few differences between male and female patients (e.g., Pertschuk, Sarwer, Wadden, & Whitaker, 1998). Yet the perception of male patients as being psychopathological has endured. These perceptions may reflect a gender stereotypic bias that "normal" men are, or should be, relatively unconcerned with their appearance. Thus, men who wish to surgically alter their appearance are viewed as inherently suspect, as only psychopathology is believed to motivate such a gender-atypical request.

Regardless of this potential gender bias, two disorders with a significant body image component: body dysmorphic disorder (including muscle dysmorphia), and eating disorders may occur with greater frequency among cosmetic surgery patients, including men who present for body contouring surgery.

Body Dysmorphic Disorder and Muscle Dysmorphia

Body dysmorphic disorder (BDD) is a preoccupation with an imagined or slight defect in appearance that results in emotional suffering and disruption in daily functioning (American Psychiatric Association, 2000). It is characterized by intrusive thoughts about the perceived defect and compulsive behaviors (e.g., excessive grooming, mirror checking) related to the feature. The skin, hair, and facial features (e.g., nose) are the most commonly reported features of concern (Phillips, Menard, Fay, & Weisberg, 2005). However, any body part may become the focus, and preoccupation with more than one body part is common (Phillips, Menard, et al., 2005).

Symptom severity and level of impairment can vary, ranging from disruption in quality of life to suicidal ideation and completed suicides (Phillips, Coles, et al., 2005). The onset of the disorder is typically during adolescence, and the course tends to be chronic (Phillips, Menard, et al., 2005).

Persons with BDD frequently pursue cosmetic treatments (Crerand et al., 2005; Phillips, Grant, Siniscalchi, & Albertini, 2001). Among 200 persons with BDD, 71% sought and 64% received cosmetic treatments (e.g., dermatological and surgical procedures; Crerand et al., 2005). Rhinoplasty was the most commonly sought and received surgical procedure. However, requests for and receipt of body procedures including liposuction, abdominoplasty, pectoral implants, and genital surgery also were reported. Not surprisingly, BDD is found rather frequently among those who seek cosmetic surgical or dermatological treatments. Studies have found that between 7% and 15% of patients who seek these treatments met criteria for BDD (e.g., Aouzerate et al., 2003; Crerand et al., 2004; Dufresne, Phillips, Vittorio, & Wilkel, 2001; Phillips & Dufresne, 2000; Sarwer et al., 1998a). Retrospective outcome studies of cosmetic treatment among persons with BDD suggest that most patients experienced either no change or a worsening in symptoms (Crerand et al., 2005; Phillips et al., 2001). As a result, BDD is believed to be a contraindication for cosmetic treatments (Crerand et al., 2005; Sarwer, 2006).

Muscle dysmorphia, a form of BDD, may be found among patients who undergo liposuction or receive body contouring implants to increase the appearance of muscularity. As Roberto Olivardia discusses in detail in chapter 6 of this volume, *muscle dysmorphia* refers to a preoccupation with being insufficiently large and muscular. To our knowledge, the rate of muscle dysmorphia among cosmetic surgery patients is unknown.

Eating Disorders

Overvalued ideas of shape and weight are hallmark features of anorexia nervosa and bulimia nervosa. Given the disproportionate amount of concern that eating disorder patients place on their appearance, these disorders may be more frequent among those who seek cosmetic surgery.

Eating disorders may be a particular concern for women who seek breast augmentation surgery, because these women are frequently of below-average body weight (Brinton, Brown, Colton, Burich, & Lubin, 2000; Didie & Sarwer, 2003; Sarwer, LaRossa, et al., 2003). The study of the relationship between eating disorders and cosmetic surgery, however, has been restricted to case reports. Women with anorexia and bulimia have been found to experience an exacerbation of their eating disorder symptoms following breast augmentation, liposuction, rhinoplasty, and chin augmentation (McIntosh, Britt, & Bulik, 1994; Willard et al., 1996; Yates, Shisslak, Allender, & Wolman, 1988). It is interesting that a case report of five breast reduction patients with bulimia suggested that four of the women experienced improvements in their eating disorder symptoms and psychological distress postoperatively (Losee, Serletti, Kreipe, & Caldwell, 1997). These improvements were maintained at 10 years following surgery (Losee et al., 2004).

INFLUENCES ON THE GROWTH OF COSMETIC SURGERY

How can one understand the dramatic increase in the popularity of body contouring and other forms of cosmetic surgery? It may well be the result of an interaction between historical and contemporary views of physical attractiveness, as well as technological developments in the field of cosmetic surgery.

Evolutionary Theories of Attractiveness

People often think of the fascination with physical beauty as a modern phenomenon. In reality, humans have used a variety of strategies to enhance their physical appearance since the onset of recorded history (Etcoff, 1999). Research by evolutionary biologists and psychologists suggests that specific facial and bodily characteristics, particularly those that portray youthfulness or symmetry, indicate reproductive potential and are therefore considered attractive. Thus, physical attractiveness has an evolutionary purpose. These characteristics not only influence people's preferences for the appearance of others, but likely affect efforts to improve their own appearance as well.

Although much of this research has focused on facial characteristics, there is evidence to suggest that body shape also is an important determinant of physical attractiveness. The waist–hip ratio (WHR) is a measure of the circumference of the waist relative to the hips. It reflects the distribution of fat between the upper and lower body relative to the amount of abdominal fat and is thought to serve as a signal of reproductive potential (Singh, 1993a).

Adult women with a WHR lower than 0.8 (a waist that is less than 80% the size of the hips) have been rated by men as more attractive, younger, healthier, and more feminine looking than those with a higher WHR (Singh, 1993b, 1995; Streeter & McBurney, 2004). Waist–hip ratio may similarly influence ratings of attractiveness for men. Healthy men have WHRs between 0.85 and 0.95 (Jones, Hunt, Brown, & Norgan, 1986). Women have typically perceived such figures as more attractive than those of men with larger or smaller WHRs (Singh, 1995). It is interesting that men with a high shoulder–hip ratio and women with a low WHR report earlier age at first sexual intercourse, more sexual partners, and more sexual experiences outside of an ongoing relationship (Hughes & Gallup, 2003).

Although speculative, these evolutionary and physiological influences may contribute to the pursuit of cosmetic surgery (Sarwer, Grossbart, & Didie,

2002; Sarwer & Magee, 2006). Two of the most popular cosmetic surgical procedures, liposuction and abdominoplasty, can alter WHR. As a result, they may improve perceptions of attractiveness, although this has yet to be empirically demonstrated.

Although both women and men desire physical attractiveness in a potential mate, there appear to be significant gender differences. Men seem to be particularly drawn to physical characteristics—like youthfulness and WHR—that signal reproductive potential. Women also are attracted to specific physical characteristics. However, because of women's greater investment in reproduction, they also must consider a mate's ability to provide resources. This differential emphasis on physical appearance may partially explain the 9:1 female-to-male ratio among cosmetic surgery patients (ASPS, 2005).

Cosmetic surgery patients also report a strong investment in their health and fitness (Pertschuk et al., 1998; Sarwer, Wadden, Pertschuk, & Whitaker, 1998a) and report higher levels of physical activity than those not interested in cosmetic surgery (Didie & Sarwer, 2003). As a result, for some persons, it may make a great deal of sense, from both a psychological and an evolutionary perspective, to invest thousands of dollars in elective cosmetic surgery (Sarwer & Magee, 2006).

Contemporary Theories of Physical Appearance

Contemporary theories of physical appearance have been influenced by body image and social–psychological research. Researchers also need to consider the influence of the mass media and entertainment industries as well as the medical and surgical communities.

Body Image Research

Although precise statistics are difficult to obtain, there is little debate that millions of Americans are unhappy with their physical appearance and, as a result, report dissatisfaction with their body image. This dissatisfaction has long been believed to motivate many appearance-enhancing behaviors. It is also believed to a play a central role in both attitudes toward cosmetic surgery and the decision to undergo surgery (Cash, 2006; Sarwer, Cash, et al., 2005; Sarwer & Crerand, 2004; Sarwer et al., 2004; Sarwer, Gibbons, & Crerand, 2005; Sarwer, Pertschuk, Wadden, & Whitaker, 1998; Sarwer, Wadden, Pertschuk, & Whitaker, 1998c). Empirical studies have suggested that cosmetic surgery patients report increased body image dissatisfaction before surgery (Didie & Sarwer, 2003; Pertschuk et al., 1998; Sarwer, Bartlett, et al., 1998; Sarwer, LaRossa, et al., 2003; Sarwer, Wadden, Pertschuk, & Whitaker, 1998b). Others have found improvements in body image postoperatively (Banbury et al., 2004; Bolton et al., 2003; Cash, Duel, & Perkins, 2002; Sarwer, Gibbons, et al., 2005; Sarwer, Wadden, & Whitaker, 2002).

Social Psychological Research

A sizable body of social psychological research has studied the role of physical appearance in daily life (Eagly, Ashmore, Makhijani, & Longo, 1991; Etcoff, 1999; Feingold, 1992). The results have been remarkably consistent: In situations across the life span, attractive individuals are believed to have more positive personality characteristics and frequently receive more favorable treatment in social interactions than less attractive peers. Perhaps this research lends support to the evolutionary theory of attractiveness discussed in the preceding section, as well as to what many cosmetic surgery candidates both suspect and hope—that if they are more physically attractive, they will be seen and treated more positively.

Mass Media and Entertainment Industries

The media and entertainment industries likely have contributed to the popularity of plastic surgery in at least two ways—their depictions of certain beauty ideals and their portrayal of plastic surgery in the media. The mass media have long been criticized for the generation and promotion of unrealistic beauty ideals to women and men, who then attempt to emulate them. Alternatively, others have argued that the media may simply be reflecting public preferences for beauty in an attempt to equate physical attractiveness with desirable interpersonal characteristics to sell products (Etcoff, 1999). In either case, the barrage of images depicting unrealistic standards of beauty likely has a detrimental effect on the viewer's body image (Levine & Harrison, 2004; Striegel-Moore & Franko, 2002; Thompson & Stice, 2001). As a result, the media may contribute to the pursuit of plastic surgery and other appearance-enhancing behaviors (Sarwer et al., 2004).

Not only has exposure to these images increased over time, but the nature of the images has changed as well. This change is most readily seen in the historical progression of portrayals of female bodies. The beauty ideals found in the mass media have shifted from the voluptuous figures of the first half of the 20th century to the strikingly lean and fit figures of contemporary society. Beauty icons such as Miss America and *Playboy* centerfolds have grown increasingly lean over the past decades, with the average body weights of both groups at levels consistent with weights of women with anorexia nervosa (Katzmarzyk & Davis, 2001; Rubenstein & Caballero, 2001).

This trend toward decreased weight among beauty icons, in combination with their increased height, is in direct contradiction to the positive correlation of weight and height found in most women. Although large breasts have always been a popular feature of beauty icons, they, like height, are correlated with overall body fat, not thinness (Grammer, Fink, Moller, & Thornhill, 2003). More recently, muscularity has been added to the list of desired physical traits. As a result, one of the present dominant images of female beauty is that of a thin, muscular, yet large-breasted woman. This body type, however, does not often occur naturally without restrictive dieting, excessive exercise, and cosmetic surgery (Sarwer et al., 2004).

The mass media idealize male appearance as well. An extremely muscular physique was popularized by bodybuilders, celebrities, and models in the late 1980s and 1990s through movies, television, and print advertisements. Much like the idealized female physique, the ideal for men is often attainable only through the use of excessive exercise and extreme dieting. When such methods are not enough to reach the ideal, many men turn to the use of illegal steroids, dietary supplements, or body contouring surgery.

Within the past few years, a new mass media influence on cosmetic surgery has appeared—"reality-based" cosmetic surgery television programs. Shows such as *Extreme Makeover*, *The Swan*, and *I Want a Famous Face* have received high Nielson ratings. The popularity of these shows, coupled with the pervasiveness of print articles about cosmetic surgery in women's and, increasingly, men's health and beauty magazines, has likely put cosmetic surgery on the minds of many more individuals than ever before. Whether this translates into a further increase in cosmetic surgery or whether these programs are simply "guilty pleasures" that are enjoyed but do not influence behavior has yet to be seen.

Medical and Surgical Communities

Technological advances in cosmetic surgery have likely fueled its increasing popularity as well. The use of minimally invasive techniques has made many procedures safer. Coupled with advances in wound healing, many surgical and nonsurgical treatments have decreased recovery times and minimized scarring, enhancing their appeal to potential patients.

Physicians from a number of specialties beyond plastic surgery now offer cosmetic surgical and minimally invasive treatments. Furthermore, cosmetic surgery lends itself nicely to direct-to-consumer marketing. In the past several years, the American Society of Plastic Surgeons has run wide-scale advertising campaigns in national magazines and on prime-time television. City-based and regional magazines are often filled with advertisements for physicians who offer cosmetic treatments. Pharmaceutical companies often use these same strategies to market their products, but the advertisements rarely have the sexy, Madison Avenue look as those for cosmetic surgery.

In summary, the growing popularity of cosmetic surgery and related treatments has likely been fueled by a variety of historical and contemporary influences. Evolutionary theory suggests that men and women are "hard wired" to respond to specific physical characteristics that denote beauty and also reproductive potential. This theory may explain why humans have attempted to enhance their appearance throughout history. In a more contemporary light, body image dissatisfaction is believed to play an important role in the decision to engage in many appearance-enhancing behaviors, including cosmetic surgery. Furthermore, social psychological research has confirmed the importance of physical appearance in daily life. The current mass media and celebrity-driven culture relentlessly expose people to physical beauty and, as a result, remind them of their own physical imperfections. The vehicles of this culture—the media—also provide people with instructions on how to address dissatisfaction with their appearance through weight loss, exercise, cosmetics, fashion, and now cosmetic surgery. These influences, coupled with the technological advances in the field of cosmetic surgery, have likely promoted the recent growth of cosmetic surgery.

CONCLUSION

The number of individuals seeking cosmetic procedures has increased dramatically over the past decade. Procedures designed to enhance body shape or contouring, such as liposuction and abdominoplasty, also have evidenced a dramatic surge in popularity. Although research regarding the psychological characteristics of most cosmetic surgery patients is limited, it is likely that some of these individuals experience significant body image dissatisfaction characteristics and conditions including BDD, muscle dysmorphia, and eating disorders.

An understanding of the motivations of persons who seek out body contouring procedures will become increasingly important with the continued growth of the social acceptability of cosmetic surgery. More men now pursue these treatments, and it is unknown if their psychological characteristics differ from those of women who undergo cosmetic surgery or from men who do not undergo these procedures. As the landscape of cosmetic surgery continues to change, future studies should further investigate the rates of psychopathology among men and women who seek cosmetic surgery. The rate of BDD appears to be between 7% and 15%, but the rates of other disorders, including muscle dysmorphia and eating disorders, have not been established. Perhaps most important, additional research is needed to explore the relationship between appearance dissatisfaction, other relevant psychological characteristics, and posttreatment outcomes.

REFERENCES

American Psychiatric Association. (2000). *Diagnostic and statistical manual of mental disorders.* (4th ed., text rev.). Washington, DC: Author.

American Society of Plastic Surgeons. (2005). *National Clearinghouse of Plastic Surgery Statistics: 2005 report of the 2004 patient statistics.* Arlington Heights, IL: Author.

Aouzerate, B., Pujol, H., Grabot, D., Faytout, M., Suire, K., Braud, C., et al. (2003). Body dysmorphic disorder in a sample of cosmetic surgery applicants. *European Psychiatry, 18,* 365–368.

Banbury, J., Yetman, R., Lucas, A., Papay, F., Graves, K., & Jins, J. E. (2004). Prospective analysis of the outcome of subpectoral breast augmentation: Sensory changes, muscle function, and body image. *Plastic and Reconstructive Surgery*, *113*, 701–707.

Bolton, M. A., Pruzinsky, T., Cash, T. F., & Persing, J. A. (2003). Measuring outcomes in plastic surgery body image and quality of life in abdominoplasty patients. *Plastic and Reconstructive Surgery*, *112*, 619–625.

Brinton, L. A., Brown, S. L., Colton, T., Burich, M. C., & Lubin, J. (2000). Characteristics of a population of women with breast implants compared with women seeking other types of plastic surgery. *Plastic and Reconstructive Surgery*, *105*, 919–927.

Cash, T. F. (2006). Body image and plastic surgery. In D. Sarwer & T. Pruzinsky (Eds.), *Psychological aspects of reconstructive and cosmetic plastic surgery: Clinical, empirical and ethical perspectives* (pp. 37–59). Philadelphia: Lippincott, Williams & Wilkins.

Cash, T. F., Duel, L. A., & Perkins, L. L. (2002). Women's psychosocial outcomes of breast augmentation with silicone gel-filled implants: A 2-year prospective study. *Plastic and Reconstructive Surgery*, *109*, 263–269.

Crerand, C. E., Phillips, K. A., Menard, W., & Fay, C. (2005). Non-psychiatric medical treatment of body dysmorphic disorder. *Psychosomatics*, *46*, 549–555.

Crerand, C. E., Sarwer, D. B., Magee, L., Gibbons, L. M., Lowe, M. R., Bartlett, S. P., et al. (2004). Rate of body dysmorphic disorder among patients seeking facial cosmetic procedures. *Psychiatric Annals*, *34*, 958–965.

Didie, E. R., & Sarwer, D. B. (2003). Factors that influence the decision to undergo cosmetic breast augmentation surgery. *Journal of Women's Health*, *12*, 241.

Dillerud, E., & Haheim, L. L. (1993). Long-tem results of blunt suction lipectomy assessed by a patient questionnaire survey. *Plastic and Reconstructive Surgery*, *92*, 35.

DuFresne, R. G., Phillips, K. A., Vittorio, C. C., & Wilkel, C. S. (2001). A screening questionnaire for body dysmorphic disorder in a cosmetic dermatologic surgery practice. *Dermatologic Surgery*, *27*, 457–462.

Eagly, A. H., Ashmore, R. D., Makhijani, M. G., & Longo, L. C. (1991). What is beautiful is good, but . . . : A meta-analytic review of research on the physical attractiveness stereotype. *Psychological Bulletin*, *110*, 109–128.

Etcoff, N. (1999). *Survival of the prettiest*. New York: Anchor Books/Doubleday.

Feingold, A. (1992). Good-looking people are not what we think. *Psychological Bulletin*, *111*, 304–341.

Giese, S. Y., Bulan, E. J., Commons, G. W., Spear, S. L., & Yanovski, J. A. (2001). Improvements in cardiovascular risk profile with large-volume liposuction: A pilot study. *Plastic and Reconstructive Surgery*, *108*, 510–521.

Grammer, K., Fink, B., Moller, A. P., & Thornhill, R. (2003). Darwinian aesthetics: Sexual selection in the biology of beauty. *Biological Reviews of the Cambridge Philosophical Society*, *78*, 385–407.

Hughes, S. M., & Gallup, G. G. (2003). Sex differences in morphological predictors of sexual behavior: Shoulder to hip and waist to hip ratios. *Evolution and Human Behavior, 24,* 173–178.

Jacobson, W. E., Edgerton, M. T., Meyer, E., Canter, A., & Slaughter, R. (1960). Psychiatric evaluation of male patients seeking cosmetic surgery. *Plastic and Reconstructive Surgery, 26,* 356–372.

Jones, P. R., Hunt, M. J., Brown, T. P., & Norgan, N. G. (1986). Waist–hip circumference ratio and its relation to age and overweight in British men. *Human Nutrition, Clinical Nutrition, 40,* 239.

Katzmarzyk, P. T., & Davis, C. (2001). Thinness and body shape of *Playboy* centerfolds from 1978–1998. *International Journal of Obesity, 25,* 590–592.

Levine, M. P., & Harrison, K. (2004). Media's role in the perpetuation and prevention of negative body image and disordered eating. In J. Thompson (Ed.), *Handbook of eating disorders and obesity* (pp. 695–717). Hoboken, NJ: Wiley.

Losee, J. E., Jian, S., Long, D. E., Kreipe, R. E., Caldwell, E. H., & Serletti, J. M. (2004). Macromastia as an etiologic factor in bulimia nervosa: 10-year follow up after treatment with reduction mammaplasty. *Annals of Plastic Surgery, 52,* 452–457.

Losee, J. E., Serletti, J. M., Kreipe, R. E., & Caldwell, E. H. (1997). Reduction mammaplasty in patients with bulimia nervosa. *Annals of Plastic Surgery, 39,* 443–446.

McIntosh, V. V., Britt, E., & Bulik, C. M. (1994). Cosmetic breast augmentation and eating disorders. *New Zealand Medical Journal, 107,* 151–152.

Perovic, S. V., Radojicic, Z. I., Djordjevic, M. L., & Vukadinovic, V. V. (2003). Enlargement and sculpturing of a small and deformed glans. *Journal of Urology, 170,* 1686–1690.

Pertschuk, M. J., Sarwer, D. B., Wadden, T. A., & Whitaker, L. A. (1998). Body image dissatisfaction in male cosmetic surgery patients. *Aesthetic Plastic Surgery, 22,* 20–24.

Phillips, K. A., Coles, M. E., Menard, W., Yen, S., Fay, C., & Weisberg, R. B. (2005). Suicidal ideation and suicide attempts in body dysmorphic disorder. *Journal of Clinical Psychiatry, 66,* 717–725.

Phillips, K. A., & Dufresne, R. G. (2000). Body dysmorphic disorder: A guide for dermatologists and cosmetic surgeons. *American Journal of Clinical Dermatology, 4,* 235–243.

Phillips, K. A., Grant, J., Siniscalchi, J., & Albertini, R. S. (2001). Surgical and nonpsychiatric medical treatment of patients with body dysmorphic disorder. *Psychosomatics, 42,* 504.

Phillips, K. A., Menard, W., Fay, C., & Weisberg, R. (2005). Demographic characteristics, phenomenology, comorbidity and family history in 200 individuals with body dysmorphic disorder. *Psychosomatics, 46,* 317–325.

Rohrich, R. J., Broughton, G., II, Horton, B., Lipschitz, A., Kenkel, J. M., & Brown, S. A. (2004). The key to long-term success in liposuction: A guide for plastic surgeons and patients. *Plastic and Reconstructive Surgery, 114,* 1945–1952.

Rubinstein, S., & Caballero, B. (2001). Is Miss America an undernourished role model? *The Journal of the American Medical Association, 283,* 1569.

Sarwer, D. B. (2006). Psychological assessment of cosmetic surgery patients. In D. B. Sarwer, T. Pruzinsky, T. F. Cash, R. M. Goldwyn, J. A. Persing, & L. A. Whitaker (Eds.), *Psychological aspects of reconstructive and cosmetic plastic surgery: Clinical, empirical, and ethical perspectives* (pp. 267–283). Philadelphia: Lippincott, Williams & Wilkins.

Sarwer, D. B., Bartlett, S. P., Bucky, L. P., LaRossa, D., Low, D. W., Pertschuk, M. J., et al. (1998). Bigger is not always better: Body image dissatisfaction in breast reduction and breast augmentation patients. *Plastic and Reconstructive Surgery, 101,* 1956–1963.

Sarwer, D. B., Cash, T. F., Magee, L., Williams, E. F., Thompson, J. K., Roehrig, M., et al. (2005). Female college students and cosmetic surgery: An investigation of experiences, attitudes, and body image. *Plastic and Reconstructive Surgery, 115,* 931–938.

Sarwer, D. B., & Crerand, C. E. (2004). Body image and cosmetic medical treatments. *Body Image, 1,* 99–111.

Sarwer, D. B., Didie, E. R., & Gibbons, L. M. (2006). Cosmetic surgery of the body. In D. B. Sarwer, T. Pruzinsky, T. F. Cash, R. M. Goldwyn, J. A. Persing, & L. A. Whitaker (Eds.), *Psychological aspects of reconstructive and cosmetic plastic surgery: Clinical, empirical, and ethical perspectives* (pp. 251–266). Philadelphia: Lippincott, Williams & Wilkins.

Sarwer, D. B., Gibbons, L. M., & Crerand, C. E. (2005). Body disorder and aesthetic surgery. In F. Nahai (Ed.), *The art of aesthetic surgery: Principles and techniques* (pp. 33–57). St. Louis, MO: Quality Medical Publishing.

Sarwer, D. B., Gibbons, L. M., Magee, L., Baker, J. L., Casas, L. A., Glat, P. M., et al. (2005). A prospective, multi-site investigation of patient satisfaction and psychosocial status following cosmetic surgery. *Aesthetic Surgery Journal, 25,* 263–269.

Sarwer, D. B., Grossbart, T. A., & Didie, E. R. (2002). Beauty and society. In M. Kaminer, J. Dover, & K. Arndt (Eds.), *Atlas of cosmetic surgery* (pp. 48–59). Philadelphia: W. B. Saunders.

Sarwer, D. B., LaRossa, D., Bartlett, S. P., Low, D. W., Bucky, L. P., & Whitaker, L. A. (2003). Body image concerns of breast augmentation patients. *Plastic and Reconstructive Surgery, 112,* 83–90.

Sarwer, D. B., & Magee, L. (2006). Physical appearance and society. In D. B. Sarwer, T. Pruzinsky, T. F. Cash, R. M. Goldwyn, J. A. Persing, & L. A. Whitaker (Eds.), *Psychological aspects of reconstructive and cosmetic plastic surgery: Clinical, empirical, and ethical perspectives* (pp. 23–33). Philadelphia: Lippincott, Williams & Wilkins.

Sarwer, D. B., Magee, L., & Crerand, C. E. (2004). Cosmetic surgery and cosmetic medical treatments. In J. Thompson (Ed.), *Handbook of eating disorders and obesity* (pp. 718–737). Hoboken, NJ: Wiley.

Sarwer, D. B., Pertschuk, M. J., Wadden, T. A., & Whitaker, L. A. (1998). Psychological investigations of cosmetic surgery patients: A look back and a look ahead. *Plastic and Reconstructive Surgery, 101,* 1136–1142.

Sarwer, D. B., Wadden, T. A., & Fabricatore, A. N. (2005). Psychosocial and behavioral aspects of bariatric surgery. *Obesity Research, 13,* 639–648.

Sarwer, D. B., Wadden, T. A., Pertschuk, M. J., & Whitaker, L. A. (1998a). Body image dissatisfaction and body dysmorphic disorder in 100 cosmetic surgery patients. *Plastic and Reconstructive Surgery, 101,* 1644.

Sarwer, D. B., Wadden, T. A., Pertschuk, M. J., & Whitaker, L. A. (1998b). The psychology of cosmetic surgery: A review and reconceptualization. *Clinical Psychology Review, 18,* 1–22.

Sarwer, D. B., Wadden, T. A., & Whitaker, L. A. (2002). An investigation of changes in body image following cosmetic surgery. *Plastic and Reconstructive Surgery, 109,* 636–639.

Singh, D. (1993a). Adaptive significance of female physical attractiveness: Role of waist-to-hip ratio. *Journal of Personality and Social Psychology, 65,* 293–307.

Singh, D. (1993b). Body shape and women's attractiveness: The critical role of waist-to-hip ratio. *Human Nature, 4,* 297–321.

Singh, D. (1995). Female judgment of male attractiveness and desirability for relationships: Role of waist-to-hip ratio and financial status. *Journal of Personality and Social Psychology, 69,* 1089.

Streeter, S. A., & McBurney, D. H. (2004). Waist–hip ratio and attractiveness: New evidence and a critique of "a critical test." *Evolution and Human Behavior, 24,* 88–98.

Striegel-Moore, R. H., & Franko, D. L. (2002). Body image issues among girls and women. In T. Cash & T. Pruzinsky (Eds.), *Body image: A handbook of theory, research, and clinical practice* (pp. 183–191). New York: Guilford Press.

Thompson, J. K., & Stice, E. (2001). Thin-ideal internalization: Mounting evidence for a new risk factor for body-image disturbance and eating pathology. *Current Directions in Psychological Science, 10,* 181–183.

Willard, S. G., McDermott, B. E., & Woodhouse, L. (1996). Lipoplasty in the bulimic patient. *Plastic and Reconstructive Surgery, 98,* 276–278.

Yates, A., Shisslak, C. M., Allender, J. R., & Wolman, W. (1988). Plastic surgery and the bulimic patient. *International Journal of Eating Disorders, 7,* 557–560.

10

PURSUIT OF MUSCULARITY AMONG ADOLESCENTS

LINA A. RICCIARDELLI AND MARITA P. McCABE

The pursuit of muscularity among adolescent boys has received increasing attention during the past 20 years. To date, four comprehensive reviews have included a large focal point on the pursuit of muscularity among adolescent boys (Cafri et al., 2005; Harvey & Robinson, 2003; Labre, 2002; Ricciardelli & McCabe, 2004). In addition, two other reviews have focused on adolescent boys' body image concerns more generally (Cohane & Pope, 2001; McCabe & Ricciardelli, 2004). In this chapter, we discuss the findings presented in these reviews and provide a synthesis of the more recent studies and developments in the field. The emphasis is primarily on studies that have examined adolescent boys' body image concerns about muscularity and the body change strategies they use to increase their muscles. We also include a brief discussion of the growing number of studies that have examined the pursuit of muscularity among adolescent girls.

THE MUSCULAR IDEAL

The desire for a muscular body build is closely tied to cultural views of masculinity and the male gender role, which prescribe that men be powerful, strong, efficacious, physically fit, and athletically successful (Lerner, Orlos, & Knapp, 1976; Mishkind, Rodin, Silberstein, & Striegel-Moore, 1986; O'Sullivan & Tiggemann, 1997). However, the construct is still poorly understood, and there is no direct research on whether these attitudes and behaviors occur on a continuum, like disordered eating, or even whether the pursuit of muscularity is best viewed as a variant of disordered eating (Ricciardelli & McCabe, 2004). Extreme examples of the pursuit of muscularity include muscle dysmorphia, professional bodybuilding, and the use of anabolic steroids. Other less extreme body change strategies include taking food supplements such as protein powders, ingesting large amounts of food, and using exercise and recreational forms of bodybuilding for the purpose of gaining weight and increasing muscle mass and muscle size (McCabe & Ricciardelli, 2001; O'Dea & Rawstorne, 2001).

PREVALENCE

Ricciardelli and McCabe (2004) provided a detailed review of the prevalence of the pursuit of muscularity among adolescent boys. Therefore, we provide only a brief summary of these findings in this chapter.

As early as 1966, Huenemann, Shapiro, Hampton, and Mitchell found that the focus on muscularity was an important aspect of adolescent boys' body image concerns. Huenemann and colleagues found that about half of the surveyed adolescent boys desired larger biceps, wrists, shoulders, and chests. More recent studies have confirmed Huenemann et al.'s findings; estimates suggest that about a third of adolescent boys desire a larger and more muscular body build, whereas another third desire a thinner body size (Furnham & Calman, 1998; Ricciardelli & McCabe, 2003). Findings that boys want to be thinner may reflect a desire for less body fat rather than a small frame (Cafri, Strauss, & Thompson, 2002). It is not always possible to separate these two dimensions, because the majority of reviewed studies with adolescent boys have used contour silhouette scales that vary only according to adiposity. Future work with adolescent boys using the Somatomorphic Matrix (see Cafri et al., 2002, for a summary), which consists of silhouettes that vary in degree of both muscularity and adiposity, will help clarify the nature of boys' body image concerns.

Many adolescent boys also have specific dissatisfaction with their muscle size, height, strength, shoulders, biceps, and chests (McCabe & Ricciardelli, 2001; Raudenbush & Meyer, 2003; Ricciardelli, McCabe, & Ridge, 2006). Although the thin and the muscular ideal body builds appear to be at opposite ends of the spectrum and are different from what girls often aspire to, an increasing number of studies show that boys engage in both strategies to increase muscles and strategies to decrease weight. They frequently adopt these strategies simultaneously or alternatively in order to achieve what Leon, Fulkerson, Perry, Keel, and Klump (1999) called "the masculine ideal of lean muscularity" (p. 194). For example, boys may use one set of strategies to achieve slimness in the lower body areas and other strategies to achieve strength and body mass in the upper body parts.

One of the most extreme methods that adolescent boys may use to achieve muscles and gain body size and weight is the use of anabolic steroids. Estimates of the number of boys who have ever used steroids range from 1% to 12% (Ricciardelli & McCabe, 2004). One study (Irving, Wall, Neumark-Sztainer, & Story, 2002) showed that 5.4% of adolescent boys had used steroids in the past year, and another showed that 2.3% of boys had used steroids in the past week (Neumark-Sztainer, Story, Falkner, Beuhring, & Resnick, 1999). Less is known about other specific supplements; however, the use of some of these seems fairly widespread. It is estimated that between 7.9% and 23.0% of adolescent boys have used creatine supplement (Ricciardelli & McCabe, 2004). In one study, the lifetime prevalence of ephedrine use was found to be 6% and that of prohormone, 4.5% (Cafri, van den Berg, & Thompson, 2006).

Other strategies to increase muscles or weight include ingesting large amounts of food and exercising. Estimates of the prevalence of these body change strategies have been found to range from 21.2% to 47.0% for adolescent boys (Ricciardelli & McCabe, 2004). The extent to which these behaviors are relatively benign and normative and the degree to which they may lead to more hazardous body change strategies has yet to be evaluated.

HEALTH RISKS

Although many body change strategies used to increase body size and muscles are relatively benign or even normative among adolescent boys (Ricciardelli & McCabe, 2003), many potential health problems associated with fluctuating periods of weight loss and weight gain may result from extreme strategies to increase muscles (e.g., steroid use, ephedrine use, and anabolic–catabolic cycling). Cafri et al. (2005) provided a detailed exposition of the health risks associated with the strategies adolescent boys use to pursue muscularity.

The main physical and psychological health risks associated with the use of anabolic steroids include atherosclerosis, mood changes, aggression, and dependence on the substance (Cafri et al., 2005). The acute effects associated with ephedrine–caffeine combinations include increased systolic blood pressure, increased heart rate, other symptoms of excitatory central nervous system stimulation, increased plasma glucose, headaches, irritability, motor restlessness, nausea, sleeplessness, tachycardia, urinary disorders, vomiting, and dependence on the substance (Cafri et al., 2005).

Alternating between anabolic and catabolic phases of eating is another strategy many bodybuilders use to gain adipose tissue in addition to muscle mass (Cafri et al., 2005). In the anabolic phase, bodybuilders eat above a maintenance level, which leads to gains in adipose tissue and muscle mass. Then, to reduce the adipose tissue, the bodybuilder goes through a catabolic phase during which he or she eats below maintenance level. The negative effects associated with this cycling include a decrease in metabolism and serum testosterone levels, changes in renal functioning, electrolyte shifts, and fluctuations in blood pH (Cafri et al., 2005).

INCREASING SOCIOCULTURAL PRESSURES

Boys' concerns with muscularity were widespread as early as 1966, and there is a consensus that these concerns may be increasing (McCabe & Ricciardelli, 2004). During the past 10 years, there has been a targeted focus by psychology researchers on men's and boys' muscular body image concerns, which have been partly attributed to the growing trend for male bodies to be featured in popular magazines and the greater number of muscular male images depicted in films (Frederick, Fessler, & Haselton, 2005; Grogan, 1999; Pope, Olivardia, Borowiecki, & Cohane, 2001; Pope, Phillips, & Olivardia, 2000). Since 1971, there has also been a significant increase in the body mass indexes of elite high school football players (Wang, Yesalis, Fitzhugh, Buckley, & Smiciklas-Wright, 1994).

Similarly, male models in magazines have become more muscular since the 1950s (Leit, Pope, & Gray, 2001; Spitzer, Henderson, & Zivian, 1999). For example, Spitzer et al. (1999) found that the body size of male *Playgirl* models increased from the 1950s to 1997, and they noted that this increase was more likely to be due to an increase in muscle and lean body mass than body fat. Likewise, Leit et al. (2001) found that the body sizes of *Playgirl* models had become more dense and muscular from 1973 to 1997. The same trend is also reflected in action figure heroes, such as G. I. Joe, who over the past 30 years have become more muscular, with physiques comparable to advanced bodybuilders and sometimes exceeding the muscularity of even the largest bodybuilders (Pope, Olivardia, Gruber, & Borowiecki, 1999). In addition, with the advent of steroids, bodybuilders have become more muscular (Pope et al., 1999), and weight training has become more prevalent and is even viewed as a normative behavior among many men (Connan, 1998).

RISK FACTORS AND CORRELATES ASSOCIATED WITH THE PURSUIT OF MUSCULARITY

Ricciardelli and McCabe (2004) conducted a detailed review of the correlates and risk factors associated with the pursuit of muscularity among adolescent boys. In the following sections we summarize the role played by biological factors such as body mass index (BMI) and pubertal growth and timing, by individual factors, and by sociocultural factors such as messages from the media and from parents and peers and the role of sport and culture.

Body Mass Index

Lower BMI has been found to be associated with steroid use (Ricciardelli & McCabe, 2004); however, lower BMI is not always associated with other body change strategies that adolescent boys use to gain weight and muscles (Ricciardelli & McCabe, 2003). This latter finding is consistent with studies that show that many adolescent boys and adult men who have average BMIs are dissatisfied with their body build (e.g., Raudenbush & Zellner, 1997; Rosenblum & Lewis, 1999). Therefore, even adolescent boys and adult men with average BMIs may perceive themselves as too small and may use weight lifting, bodybuilding, and other strategies to increase their body mass, body frame, or muscles. Nevertheless, other research suggests that underweight men continue to be one of the most at-risk groups.

Underweight adult men have been found to have an extremely negative self-image and to view themselves as being less handsome and less good natured and as having less sex appeal than other men and women (Harmatz, Gronendyke, & Thomas, 1985). A study also showed that underweight boys experienced the greatest pressure from their peers and appearance-related teasing (Crawford, Newman, & Jones, 2005).

Pubertal Development and Timing

The findings from studies that have examined the relationship between pubertal status and body change strategies to increase weight and muscles are inconsistent (Ricciardelli & McCabe, 2004). This inconsistency may in part reflect the difficulty of obtaining an accurate assessment of pubertal status in adolescent boys, as there is no particular biological marker that signifies the onset of puberty for boys. Another difficulty is that the majority of studies have relied on self-reports, which have been shown to be unreliable (Krieg, Smolak, Howard, Shisslak, & Taylor, 2005).

We found only one longitudinal study that examined the role of pubertal timing in understanding attitudes and behaviors associated with the pursuit of muscularity (McCabe & Ricciardelli, 2004). Late-maturing boys were found to be more likely to use food supplements to build up their body than early maturing boys, and this factor moderately predicted an increased use of strategies to increase muscle size. Further research is needed that more fully examines the impact of pubertal timing and its interactions with other factors. The timing of puberty is considered one of the most salient factors for determining whether or not puberty is associated with any emotional or social adjustment difficulties (Graber, Lewinsohn, Seeley, & Brooks-Gunn, 1997). From a developmental deviance perspective, experiencing pubertal development out of synchrony with one's peers may foster feelings of alienation and depression. This phenomenon has been more fully elaborated as the "off-time hypothesis," which predicts that both early- and late-maturing adolescents manifest more social, emotional, and behavioral problems than their on-time age mates (Ge, Conger, & Elder, 1996; Williams & Currie, 2000).

Individual Influences

Several individual variables have been found to be consistently associated with weight and muscle gain strategies in adolescent boys, including body image importance, negative affect, self-esteem, perfectionism, use of alcohol and other drugs, and other risk-taking behaviors (Ricciardelli & McCabe, 2004). However, because much of the work with boys is based on cross-sectional research, it is not possible to separate causes from consequences. As a result, many of the variables that have been identified as risk factors may in fact be consequences. Prospective studies are generally better than cross-sectional studies if one is interested in making inferences about risk factors, as correlations over time will be a more accurate depiction of the relationship than a correlation of constructs measured at the same time. However, even prospective studies cannot establish causality.

One prospective study by McCabe and Ricciardelli (2006) examined the role of depression in adolescent boys' development of the pursuit of muscularity. The authors found that depression predicted the use of food supplements to increase muscle size over a 16-month period.

Another variable that may prove to be important, but that was assessed in only one located published study among adolescent boys, is perfectionism (Furnham & Calman, 1998). Perfectionism was found to be weakly correlated with a new measure devised by the study's authors to assess a desire to become bigger and the wish to gain weight. It may be that boys who have high levels of perfectionism have higher standards for pursuing a muscular build. Further studies, including longitudinal research, are needed to test this hypothesis.

Sexual orientation is one variable that has consistently been found to be associated with disordered eating and body image concerns among adult men (McCabe & Ricciardelli, 2004; Ricciardelli & McCabe, 2004). There is also increasing evidence that this relationship is evident among adolescent boys (Austin, Najat Kahn, Camargo, Colditz, & Field, 2004). However, only one study, located after our earlier review (Ricciardelli & McCabe, 2004), examined the pursuit of muscularity among gay and bisexual adolescent boys, and the results were inconclusive (Austin et al., 2004). Although gay and bisexual boys reported making a greater effort to look like boys and men in the media compared with that reported by heterosexual boys, gay and bisexual boys reported less interest in having bigger muscles. However, the latter finding only approached statistical significance. Moreover, it may be difficult to clarify these findings, because gay identity is not always well defined at adolescence (Cass, 1984; Morrow, 2006; Safren & Pantalone, 2006; Savin-Williams, 2005).

Media Influences

Adolescent boys are exposed through television, movies, magazines, and other sources to an idealized male body image that is far more muscular than an average man. However, only limited research has examined whether boys internalize these messages and whether these messages have any impact on their muscle concerns and strategies used to increase muscles (for a review of the literature, see Levine & Harrison, 2004). When researchers have examined the impact of muscular images, they frequently have not adequately assessed boys' concerns with muscles. For example, in one study, Hargreaves and Tiggemann (2004) evaluated the impact of exposure to idealized muscular commercials on adolescent boys (mean age 14.3 years). This exposure was not found to be related to body dissatisfaction. However, body dissatisfaction in this study was not assessed using a well-validated scale that focused specifically on boys' body image concerns.

Apart from the inadequacy of some of the measures that have been used with adolescent boys and adult men (see Cafri & Thompson, 2004a, 2004b, for reviews of measures developed to assess the pursuit of muscularity among men), another possibility is that boys may not develop a vulnerability to muscular-ideal media images until later adolescence or early adulthood (Hargreaves & Tiggemann, 2004). Studies have more consistently shown that exposure to muscular images is associated with body image concerns among adult men (Agliata & Tantleff-Dunn, 2004; Grogan, Williams, & Connor, 1996; Hatoum & Belle, 2004; Leit, Gray, & Pope, 2002; Lorenzen, Grieve, & Thomas, 2004). The differences between adolescent boys and adult men may be due to the cumulative effects of media exposure from adolescence to adulthood. However, there may also be maturational differences; men develop greater levels of fat during adulthood. McCabe and Ricciardelli (2004) evaluated some of the developmental changes in men's body image concerns across the life span.

In another study, Murnen, Smolak, Mills, and Good (2003) found that young boys between 6 and 12 years of age were aware of sociocultural messages about the ideal body, but they were not affected as much as girls. For example, boys were found to be as aware of the muscular ideal as girls were of the thin, sexy ideal, but this awareness did not predict boys' body image concerns. Overall, these findings suggest that already during preadolescence, boys may be better equipped to ignore and not internalize sociocultural messages about ideal weight and muscles. Alternatively, body image concerns may not be particularly important to adolescent boys, and so these concerns do not shape their behaviors in relation to altering their bodies.

In contrast to some findings with both adolescent and preadolescent boys, Botta (2003) found that the reading of health and fitness magazines was related to higher levels of muscularity among adolescent boys. However, the findings were further moderated by social comparisons. For boys who did not spend a lot of time comparing their bodies to the bodies they saw in magazines, increased sports magazine reading was related to higher levels of body satisfaction. However, for boys who spent a lot of time comparing their bodies to those they saw in magazines, increased sports magazine reading was related to lower levels of body satisfaction. Another moderating variable in these findings may be body image importance, which was not evaluated in the studies we discussed previously.

In another study, McVey, Tweed, and Blackmore (2005) found that a range of sociocultural indexes were associated with young boys' (10–14 years old) muscle-gaining behaviors, including the internalization of overall media messages (both the thin ideal and awareness of male stereotypes), size acceptance (acceptance of varying body shapes and sizes), and teasing (about being too thin or too big). Similarly, Smolak, Murnen, and Thompson (2005) found that perceived media influence from television, movies, and magazines (e.g., "Looking at magazines makes me want to change the way I look"), social comparisons, perceived peer influences, and parental comments all contributed significantly to muscle-building behaviors among adolescent boys between 11 and 16 years old

Messages From Parents and Peers

Both cross-sectional and longitudinal studies have shown that perceived pressure to increase muscles from parents and peers is associated with weight and muscle gain strategies in adolescent boys (Ricciardelli & McCabe, 2004; Smolak et al., 2005). For example, McCabe and Ricciardelli (2005) found that perceived pressure to increase muscles from mothers, fathers, and male friends predicted adolescent boys' strategies to gain muscles at both 8 months and 16 months. Additional research is needed that examines the association between adolescent boys' perceived messages and the actual messages from parents and peers. Further information is also required from adolescent boys, parents, and peers concerning the exact nature of the way in which mothers, fathers, and peers relay their messages about the pursuit of muscularity. For example, potential strategies include talking, role modeling, teasing, encouragement, and other kinds of positive or negative comments.

One study by Jones and Crawford (2005) specifically investigated how weight and muscle concerns among adolescent boys were embedded within distinct social contexts and how this could be assessed through appearance-related conversations with friends. These conversations "direct attention to appearance-related issues, reinforce the value and importance of appearance, and promote the construction of appearance ideals" (Jones & Crawford, 2005, p. 631). As predicted, Jones and Crawford found that levels of muscularity concerns were found to be significantly higher among adolescent boys who reported more frequent muscle-building conversations (e.g., "I talk with my friends about ways to build muscles" and "My friends and I talk about building our muscles"). Further research is needed to more fully evaluate these findings using both longitudinal research and more in-depth interview studies.

Role of Sport

Sport plays an important socializing role for adolescent boys and has links to the physical body, so it is surprising that few studies have examined the role of sport in defining and shaping boys' feelings about the body. In one study, Ferron, Narring, Cauderay, and Michaud (1999) showed that adolescent boys who had the highest levels of sport activity reported a more positive body image and were more satisfied with both their physical appearance and their weight. Similarly, adult male college athletes who engaged in a wide range of sports reported more body satisfaction than nonathletes (Petrie, 1996).

Ricciardelli and colleagues (2006) found that the sporting context provided adolescent boys with an acceptable and nonthreatening medium for explicitly discussing and comparing their bodies with other boys. Even though the media are increasingly drawing attention to the aesthetics of men's body image (Grogan & Richards, 2002; Pope et al., 2000), many of the adolescent boys were reluctant in semistructured interviews to openly discuss their body image concerns. Several of the boys were also not willing to admit that they were improving their body for cosmetic reasons and felt safer to couch their language about their bodies within the confines of sport. However, it was clear from the interviews that many of the boys were quite fixated on their bodies and appearance and were eager to talk about their body image.

Grogan and Richards (2002) also found that there are limited contexts in which adolescent boys and older men feel justified in discussing their body image concerns. In their focus group study of preadolescent boys, adolescent boys, and adult men, Grogan and Richards found that boys and men in all age groups found discussions of muscularity acceptable primarily within the boundaries signifying masculinity—that is, when it was closely linked to fitness and athleticism. Moreover, although participants from all age groups gave primarily cosmetic reasons for wanting to attain the lean and muscular look, they resisted representing men's bodies as objects of aesthetic interest by shifting their discussions to how bodies looked in relation to function, fitness, and health.

Participation in sport, in particular in "power" sports such as field events and weight lifting, has also been identified as a risk factor for higher use of supplements such as steroids and creatine and of strategies specifically to increase weight and muscles (Ricciardelli & McCabe, 2004). One study showed that one in four young male athletes were using supplements to gain weight and muscle mass, with the highest use among lacrosse players and track and cross-country runners (Raudenbush & Meyer, 2003). More research is needed to help identify why these group of athletes may be more at risk. However, the focus also needs to shift to a study of the moderating and mediating factors that may place some young athletes at greater risk.

Social Comparisons

There is little research that has examined the specific role that social comparisons play in the development of body image concerns and the pursuit of muscularity among adolescent boys. However, in one study, several adolescent boys reported using sport as a socially acceptable forum for comparing their bodies with other adolescent boys (Ricciardelli et al., 2006). They competed both by playing the sport and by using their sport performance to make favorable social comparisons about their body size. Boys talked about being "the best on the field," "the strongest in the class," and "wanting to be bigger than their friends." This focus on competition, showing off, and making favorable social comparisons is consistent with our earlier work with adolescent boys. In one study (Ricciardelli, McCabe, & Banfield, 2000), we found that only a few boys felt negatively about their body when they compared it with others. In fact, most boys who used social comparisons reported feeling either more positive or neutral about their body. This pattern of findings is not typically seen among adolescent girls; girls are more likely to make unfavorable social comparisons in comparing their appearance with targets who are perceived to be more attractive, findings associated with lower feelings of self-worth and higher body dissatisfaction (Stormer & Thompson, 1996). Other research has shown that adolescent girls report higher levels of social comparisons than boys (Jones, 2001) and that social comparisons predict body dissatisfaction over a 12-month period in girls but not in boys (Jones, 2004).

One of the limitations of much of past work with boys is that the focus has been on body image concerns that are more pertinent among girls. In one study, increased social comparisons were found to be associated with higher levels of muscularity in adolescent boys (Botta, 2003). Similarly, another study found social comparisons to be associated with strategies to gain weight and the use of steroids to increase muscle mass among adolescent boys (Morrison, Kalin, & Morrison, 2004). Finally, Smolak et al. (2005) also found that social comparisons directly predicted muscle-building techniques and that social comparisons partially mediated the influence of media, peer, and parental influences.

Effects of Culture

One way of understanding the sociocultural influences on the development of the pursuit of muscularity is to study these attitudes and behaviors among different cultures and the differential impact of the cultures on the body image of both boys and girls. Our review of the literature (Ricciardelli, Williams, & McCabe, 2005) included research with Samoans and other Pacific Islanders, Black and other minority men in the United States, and indigenous Australian adolescents. The overall evidence suggests that adolescent boys from minority groups have more body image concerns and engage in more body change strategies than girls, including the pursuit of muscularity. These findings are also consistent with the lower levels of self-esteem found among men from many minority groups as compared with women from the same minority groups (Twenge & Crocker, 2002). The overall findings suggest that being from a nonminority group carries more positive social and health implications for men, whereas being from a minority group carries positive social and health implications for women (Ricciardelli, McCabe, Ball, & Mellor, 2004; Twenge & Crocker, 2002). These differences may in part reflect power relations and the level of integration of men and women in minority groups. Women in some minority groups tend to have higher levels of community support than men (Ricciardelli et al., 2004). However, further studies are needed to examine these hypotheses, as there are likely to be several factors that may moderate or mediate these relationships.

In contrast to the findings with minority groups of men living in Western countries like the United States and Australia, men who were not exposed to the same volume or the direct and explicit Western media messages about muscular male bodies have been shown to display little body dissatisfaction. Such studies have addressed Taiwanese men (Yang, Gray, & Pope, 2005) and men among the Ariaal, a group of pastoral nomads in northern Kenya (Campbell, Pope, & Filiault, 2005). For example, although U.S. magazines frequently portray undressed Western men, Taiwanese magazines rarely portray undressed Taiwanese men (Yang et al., 2005); Ariaal men live in a society with relatively little media exposure. Parallel work with adolescent boys among these cultures is needed.

PURSUIT OF MUSCULARITY AMONG ADOLESCENT GIRLS

There is increasing pressure for women and girls also to achieve a more muscular, toned body shape rather than simply a slim body (Saling, 2003). This influence is evident in popular magazines, in the appearance of fashion models, and in the media in general (Guillen & Barr, 1994; Markula, 1995; Morris, Cooper, & Cooper, 1989; Wiseman, Gray, Mosimann, & Ahrens, 1992). Moreover, some women have also been found to prefer a muscular body type, especially with regard to the upper body (Lenart, Goldberg, Bailey, Dallal, & Koff, 1995).

The level of steroid and other supplement use among adolescent girls is lower than that found among boys; however, the data indicate that it is by no means a problem only for boys. Estimates suggest that between 0.2% and 9.0% of adolescent girls have used steroids sometime in their life (Ricciardelli & McCabe, 2004). Other estimates indicate that approximately 2.9% of girls have used steroids in the past year (Irving et al., 2002) and that 0.5% of girls have used steroids in the past week (Neumark-Sztainer et al., 1999). It is also estimated that between 0.3% and 2.0% have used creatine (Ricciardelli & McCabe, 2004). Finally, a review of several studies suggested that between 6.3% and 9.1% of adolescent girls use other strategies to increase their muscles and/or weight, such as exercising more and eating special foods (Ricciardelli & McCabe, 2004). It is also possible that many adolescent girls are interested in improving their muscle tone and definition; however, there are no specific studies that have separated this component from broader strategies to decrease weight and/or increase muscles.

Overall, McCabe and Ricciardelli (2005, 2006) found similar predictors of adolescent girls' body change strategies to increase muscles over a 16-month period as those found with boys, including perceived pressure to gain muscles from female friends, mothers, and the media (McCabe & Ricciardelli, 2005). In addition, body dissatisfaction, body image importance, and depression predicted adolescent girls' use of food supplements, which included a large focus on increasing muscles (McCabe & Ricciardelli, 2006).

Other researchers have not found the same associations with muscle gain behaviors among girls that have been shown among boys (e.g., Botta, 2003; McCreary & Sasse, 2000; McVey et al., 2005). One of the limitations of these studies is that the relationships have been examined only cross-sectionally. Moreover, the measures used to assess muscle gain behaviors have not been developed and validated as thoroughly with adolescent girls as those designed by Ricciardelli and McCabe (2002). These inconsistent findings need to be examined further.

CONCLUSION

Research findings indicate that an increasing focus on muscularity has occurred among adolescent boys in the past 20 years. A slim, toned, muscular body is the ideal body form that is presented in the media. This ideal is also endorsed by parents and peers and appears to affect the self-image of adolescent boys. Those who fail to conform to the ideal are most likely to be at risk of developing adjustment problems and adopting risky behaviors to change their bodies. The extent to which the size and shape of one's body is important to boys in defining their sense of self is likely to be another factor to consider in future research evaluating these interrelationships.

Many research questions still need to be resolved in relation to the pursuit of muscularity among adolescent boys. The most fundamental question concerns the nature of these behaviors and the extent to which they pose health risks for adolescent boys. It is important to determine if it is the intensity of behaviors that constitutes a health risk or if specific types of behaviors are a problem. It is also likely that some boys are more focused on muscularity than other boys. In addition, longitudinal and longer-term prospective studies are essential to more fully evaluate the importance of the relative biological, individual, and sociocultural factors.

Some research suggests that the pursuit of muscularity may be becoming a problem area for adolescent girls as well as adolescent boys. However, the nature of muscularity requires further conceptualization and validation at both the theoretical and the psychometric levels. The construct may refer to one or all of the following: muscle mass, muscle tone, muscle definition, muscle development in certain parts of the body and leanness in others, and actual strength and physical power (Ricciardelli & McCabe, 2004). It is also possible that these meanings differ widely between adolescent boys and girls and across cultures. Therefore, more robust, appropriate, and psychometrically sound assessment tools need to be developed to assess these behaviors among both adolescent boys and girls and across different cultural groups.

REFERENCES

Agliata, D., & Tantleff-Dunn, S. (2004). The impact of media exposure on males' body image. *Journal of Social and Clinical Psychology, 23,* 7–22.

Austin, S. B. Z., Najat Kahn, J. A., Camargo, C. A., Colditz, G. A., & Field, A. E. (2004). Sexual orientation, weight concerns, and eating-disordered behaviors in adolescent girls and boys. *Journal of the American Academy of Child and Adolescent Psychiatry, 43,* 1115–1123.

Botta, R. A. (2003). For your health? The relationship between magazine reading and adolescents' body image and eating disturbances. *Sex Roles, 48,* 389–399.

Cafri, G., Strauss, J., & Thompson, J. K. (2002). Male body image: Satisfaction and its relationship to well-being using the Somatomorphic Matrix. *International Journal of Men's Health, 1,* 215–231.

Cafri, G., & Thompson, J. K. (2004a). Evaluating the convergence of muscle appearance attitude measures. *Assessment, 11,* 224–229.

Cafri, G., & Thompson, J. K. (2004b). Measuring male body image: A review of the current methodology. *Psychology of Men and Masculinity, 5,* 18–29.

Cafri, G., Thompson, J. K., Ricciardelli, L. A., McCabe, M. P., Smolak, L., & Yesalis, C. (2005). Pursuit of the muscular ideal: Physical and psychological consequences and putative risk factors. *Clinical Psychology Review, 25,* 215–239.

Cafri, G., van den Berg, P., & Thompson, J. K. (2006). Pursuit of muscularity in adolescent boys: Relations among biopsychosocial variables and clinical outcomes. *Journal of Clinical Child and Adolescent Psychology, 35*, 283–291.

Campbell, B. C., Pope, H. G., & Filiault, S. (2005). Body image among Ariaal men from northern Kenya. *Journal of Cross-Cultural Psychology, 36*, 371–379.

Cass, V. C. (1984). Homosexual identity formation: Testing a theoretical model. *Journal of Sex Research, 20*, 143–167.

Cohane, G. H., & Pope, H. G. (2001). Body image in boys: A review of the literature. *International Journal of Eating Disorders, 29*, 373–379.

Connan, F. (1998). Machismo nervosa: An ominous variant of bulimia nervosa? *European Eating Disorders Review, 6*, 154–159.

Crawford, J. K., Newman, J. B., & Jones, D. C. (2005, April 8–12). *Body image during adolescence: Gender and body mass variations in the social ecology of the peer acceptance culture.* Poster presented at the biennial meeting of the Society for Research in Child Development, Atlanta, GA.

Ferron, C., Narring, F., Cauderay, M., & Michaud, P. A. (1999). Sport activity in adolescence: Associations with health perceptions and experimental behaviours. *Health Education Research, 14*, 225–233.

Frederick, D. A., Fessler, D. M. T., & Haselton, M. G. (2005). Do representations of male muscularity differ in men's and women's magazines? *Body Image: An International Journal of Research, 2*, 81–86.

Furnham, A., & Calman, A. (1998). Eating disturbance, self-esteem, reasons for exercising and body weight dissatisfaction in adolescent males. *European Eating Disorders Review, 6*, 58–72.

Ge, X., Conger, R. D., & Elder, G. H. (1996). Coming of age too early: Pubertal influences on girls' vulnerability to psychological distress. *Child Development, 67*, 3386–3400.

Graber, J. A., Lewinsohn, P. M., Seeley, M. S., & Brooks-Gunn, J. (1997). Is psychopathology associated with the timing of pubertal development? *Journal of the American Academy of Child and Adolescent Psychiatry, 36*, 1768–1776.

Grogan, S. (1999). *Body image: Understanding body dissatisfaction in men, women and children.* London: Routledge.

Grogan, S., & Richards, H. (2002). Body image: Focus groups with boys and men. *Men and Masculinities, 4*, 219–232.

Grogan, S., Williams, Z., & Connor, M. (1996). The effects of viewing same-gender photographic models on body-esteem. *Psychology of Women Quarterly, 20*, 569–575.

Guillen, E. O., & Barr, S. I. (1994). Nutrition, dieting, and fitness messages in a magazine for adolescent women, 1970–1990. *Journal of Adolescent Health, 15*, 464–472.

Hargreaves, D. A., & Tiggemann, M. (2004). Idealized media images and adolescent body image: "Comparing" boys and girls. *Body Image: An International Journal, 1*, 351–361.

Harmatz, M. G., Gronendyke, J., & Thomas, T. (1985). The underweight male: The unrecognized problem group of body image research. *Journal of Obesity and Weight Regulation, 4*, 258–267.

Harvey, J. A., & Robinson, J. D. (2003). Eating disorders in men: Current considerations. *Journal of Clinical Psychology in Medical Settings, 10*, 297–306.

Hatoum, I. J., & Belle, D. (2004). Mags and abs: Media consumption and bodily concerns in men. *Sex Roles, 51*, 397–407.

Huenemann, R. L., Shapiro, L. R., Hampton, M. D., & Mitchell, B. W. (1966). A longitudinal study of gross body composition and body conformation and association with food and activity in teenage population: Views of teenage subjects on body conformation, food and activity. *American Journal of Clinical Nutrition, 18*, 323–338.

Irving, L. M., Wall, M., Neumark-Sztainer, D., & Story, M. (2002). Steroid use among adolescents: Findings from Project EAT. *Journal of Adolescent Health, 30*, 243–252.

Jones, D. C. (2001). Social comparison and body image: Attractiveness comparison to models and peers among adolescent girls and boys. *Sex Roles, 45*, 645–664.

Jones, D. C. (2004). Body image among adolescent girls and boys: A longitudinal study. *Developmental Psychology, 40*, 823–835.

Jones, D. C., & Crawford, J. K. (2005). Adolescent boys and body image: Weight and muscularity concerns as dual pathways to body dissatisfaction. *Journal of Youth and Adolescence, 34*, 629–636.

Krieg, D. B., Smolak, L., Howard, C., Shisslak, C., & Taylor, B. (2005, 8–12 April). *The reliability of self-reports of pubertal timing.* Poster presented at the biennial meeting of the Society for Research in Child Development, Atlanta, GA.

Labre, M. P. (2002). Adolescent boys and the muscular male body ideal. *Journal of Adolescent Health, 30*, 233–242.

Leit, R. A., Gray, J. J., & Pope, H. G. (2002). The media's representation of the ideal male body: A cause for muscle dysmorphia? *International Journal of Eating Disorders, 31*, 334–338.

Leit, R. A., Pope, H. G., Jr., & Gray, J. J. (2001). Cultural expectations of muscularity in men: The evolution of Playgirl centerfolds. *International Journal of Eating Disorders, 29*, 90–93.

Lenart, E. B., Goldberg, J. P., Bailey, S. M., Dallal, G. E., & Koff, E. (1995). Current and ideal physique choices in exercising and non-exercising college women from a pilot Athletic Image Scale. *Perceptual and Motor Skills, 81*, 831–848.

Leon, G. R., Fulkerson, J. A., Perry, C. L., Keel, P. K., & Klump, K. L. (1999). Three to four year prospective evaluation of personality and behavioral risk factors for later disordered eating in adolescent girls and boys. *Journal of Youth and Adolescence, 28*, 181–196.

Lerner, R., Orlos, J. B., & Knapp, J. R. C. (1976). Physical attractiveness, physical effectiveness and self-concept in late adolescents. *Adolescence, 43*, 313–326.

Levine, M. P., & Harrison, K. (2004). Media's role in the perpetuation and prevention of negative body image and disordered eating. In J. K. Thompson (Ed.), *Handbook of eating disorders and obesity* (pp. 695–717). New York: Wiley.

Lorenzen, L. A., Grieve, F. G., & Thomas, A. (2004). Exposure to muscular male models decreases men's body satisfaction. *Sex Roles, 51,* 743–748.

Markula, P. (1995). Firm but shapely, fit but sexy, strong but thin: The postmodern aerobicizing female bodies. *Sociology of Sport Journal, 12,* 424–453.

McCabe, M. P., & Ricciardelli, L. A. (2001). Body image and body change techniques among young adolescent boys. *European Eating Disorders Review, 9,* 335–347.

McCabe, M. P., & Ricciardelli L. A. (2004). Weight and shape concerns of boys and men. In J. K. Thompson (Ed.), *Handbook of eating disorders and obesity* (pp. 606–634). New York: Wiley.

McCabe, M. P., & Ricciardelli, L. A. (2005). A prospective study of pressures from parents, peers, and the media on extreme weight change behaviors among adolescent boys and girls. *Behaviour Therapy and Research, 43,* 653–668.

McCabe, M. P., & Ricciardelli, L. A. (2006). A prospective study of extreme weight change behaviors among adolescent boys and girls. *Journal of Youth and Adolescence, 35,* 425–434.

McCreary, D. R., & Sasse, D. K. (2000). An exploration of the drive for muscularity in adolescent boys and girls. *Journal of American College Health, 48,* 297–304.

McVey, G., Tweed, S., & Blackmore, E. (2005). Correlates of weight loss and muscle-gaining behavior in 10- to 14-year-old males and females. *Preventive Medicine, 40,* 1–9.

Mishkind, M. E., Rodin, J., Silberstein, L. R., & Striegel-Moore, R. H. (1986). The embodiment of masculinity. *American Behavioral Scientist, 29,* 545–562.

Morris, A., Cooper, T., & Cooper, P. J. (1989). The changing shape of female fashion models. *International Journal of Eating Disorders, 8,* 593–596.

Morrison, T. G., Kalin, R., & Morrison, M. A. (2004). Body-image evaluation and body-image investment among adolescents: A test of sociocultural and social comparison theories. *Adolescence, 39,* 571–592.

Morrow, D. F. (2006). Gay, lesbian, bisexual and transgender adolescents. In D. F. Morrow & L. Messinger (Eds.), *Sexual orientation and gender expression in social work practice: Working with gay, lesbian, bisexual and transgender people* (pp. 177–195). New York: Columbia University Press.

Murnen, S. K., Smolak, L., Mills, J. A., & Good, L. (2003). Thin, sexy women and strong muscular men: Grade-school children's responses to objectified images of women and men. *Sex Roles, 49,* 427–437.

Neumark-Sztainer, D., Story, M., Falkner, N. H., Beuhring, T., & Resnick, M. D. (1999). Sociodemographic and personal characteristics of adolescents engaged in weight loss and weight/muscle gain behaviors: Who is doing what? *Preventative Medicine, 28,* 40–50.

O'Dea, J. A., & Rawstorne, P. R. (2001). Male adolescents identify their weight gain practices, reasons for desired weight gain, and sources of weight gain information. *Journal of the American Dietetic Association, 101*, 105–107.

O'Sullivan, G. A., & Tiggemann, M. (1997). Body dissatisfaction and body image distortion in men who train with weights. *Journal of Gender, Culture, and Health, 2*, 321–329.

Petrie, T. A. (1996). Differences between male and female college lean sport athletes, nonlean sport athletes, and nonathletes on behavioral and psychological indices of eating disorders. *Journal of Applied Sport Psychology, 8*, 218–230.

Pope, H. G., Jr., Olivardia, R., Borowiecki, J. J., III, & Cohane, G. H. (2001). The growing commercial value of the male body: A longitudinal survey of advertising in women's magazines. *Psychotherapy and Psychosomatics, 70*, 189–192.

Pope, H. G., Olivardia, R., Gruber, A., & Borowiecki, J. (1999). Evolving ideals of male body image as seen through action toys. *International Journal of Eating Disorders, 26*, 65–72.

Pope, H. G., Phillips, K. A., & Olivardia, R. (2000). *The Adonis complex: The secret crisis of male body obsession*. New York: Free Press.

Raudenbush, B., & Meyer, B. (2003). Muscular dissatisfaction and supplement use among male intercollegiate athletes. *Journal of Sport and Exercise Psychology, 25*, 161–170.

Raudenbush, B., & Zellner, D. A. (1997). Nobody's satisfied: Effect of abnormal eating behaviors and perceived and actual weight status on body image satisfaction in males and females. *Journal of Social and Clinical Psychology, 16*, 95–110.

Ricciardelli, L. A., & McCabe, M. P. (2002). Psychometric evaluation of the Body Change Inventory: An assessment instrument for adolescent boys and girls. *Eating Behaviors, 3*, 45–59.

Ricciardelli, L. A., & McCabe, M. P. (2003). A longitudinal analysis of the role of biopsychosocial factors in predicting body change strategies among adolescent boys. *Sex Roles, 48*, 349–359.

Ricciardelli, L. A., & McCabe, M. P. (2004). A biopsychosocial model of disordered eating and the pursuit of muscularity in adolescent boys. *Psychological Bulletin, 130*, 179–205.

Ricciardelli, L. A., Williams, R. J., & McCabe, M. P. (2005, August 31–September 2). *The role of culture in the construction of male body and self-image*. Poster presented at the European Health Psychology Conference, Galway, Ireland.

Ricciardelli, L. A., McCabe, M. P., Ball, K., & Mellor, D. (2004). Sociocultural influences on body image concerns and body change strategies among indigenous and non-indigenous Australian adolescent girls and boys. *Sex Roles, 51*, 731–741.

Ricciardelli, L. A., McCabe, M. P., & Banfield, S. (2000). Body image and body change methods in adolescent boys: Role of parents, friends, and the media. *Journal of Psychosomatic Research, 49*, 189–197.

Ricciardelli, L. A., McCabe, M. P., & Ridge D. (2006). The construction of the adolescent male body through sport. *Journal of Health Psychology, 11*, 577–588.

Rosenblum, G. D., & Lewis, M. (1999). The relations among body image, physical attractiveness and body mass in adolescence. *Child Development, 70,* 50–64.

Safren, S. A., & Pantalone, D. W. (2006). Social anxiety and barriers to resilience among lesbian, gay and bisexual adolescents. In A. M. Omoto & H. S. Kurtzman (Eds.), *Sexual orientation and mental health: Examining identity and development in lesbian, gay and bisexual people* (pp. 55–77). Washington, DC: American Psychological Association.

Saling, M. (2003). *A longitudinal study of children's disordered eating and muscle preoccupation.* Unpublished doctor of psychology thesis, Deakin University, Melbourne, Australia.

Savin-Williams, R. C. (2005). *The new gay teenager.* Cambridge, MA: Harvard University Press.

Smolak, L., Murnen, S. K., & Thompson, J. K. (2005). Sociocultural influences and muscle building in adolescent boys. *Psychology of Men and Masculinity, 6,* 227–239.

Spitzer, B. L., Henderson, K. A., & Zivian, M. T. (1999). Gender differences in population versus media body sizes: A comparison over four decades. *Sex Roles, 40,* 545–565.

Stormer, S. M., & Thompson, J. K. (1996). Explanations of body image disturbance: A test of maturational status, negative verbal commentary, social comparison, and sociocultural hypotheses. *International Journal of Eating Disorders, 19,* 193–202.

Twenge, J. M., & Crocker, J. (2002). Race and self-esteem: Meta-analyses comparing Whites, Blacks, Hispanics, Asians, and American Indians, and comment on Gray-Little and Hafdahl (2000). *Psychological Bulletin, 128,* 371–408.

Wang, M. Q., Yesalis, C. E., Fitzhugh, E. C., Buckley, W. E., & Smiciklas-Wright, H. (1994). Desire for weight gain and potential risk of adolescent males using anabolic steroids. *Perceptual and Motor Skills, 78,* 267–274.

Williams, J. M., & Currie, C. (2000). Self-esteem and physical development in early adolescence: Pubertal timing and body image. *Journal of Early Adolescence, 20,* 139–149.

Wiseman, C. V., Gray, J. J., Mosimann, J. E., & Ahrens, A. H. (1992). Cultural expectations of thinness in women: An update. *International Journal of Eating Disorders, 11,* 85–89.

Yang, C. F. J., Gray, P., & Pope, H. G. (2005). Male body image in Taiwan versus the West: Yanggang Zhiqi meets the Adonis complex. *American Journal of Psychiatry, 162,* 263–269.

11

A MORE MUSCULAR
FEMALE BODY IDEAL

AMANDA J. GRUBER

Title IX, which arose out of the feminist movement of the 1970s, is part of the Education Amendments passed in 1972. This amendment banned sex discrimination in schools, both for academics and athletics, and provided increased athletic opportunities for girls and women (*About Title IX*, 2005). After more than 3 decades of increased participation in sports by girls and women, the perception of normal and attractive women's bodies has changed (Dworkin & Heywood, 2003). Prior to the late 19th century, when athletics became more prevalent among upper class women in Western society, many women feared that visible muscles were unfeminine and unattractive to men (Dworkin & Heywood, 2003; Talbot, 2005). Today, a large portion of women have developed some degree of muscularity from their athletic experiences as girls and young women (Dworkin & Heywood, 2003). Many of these women are considered attractive, regularly go to a gym, and raise athletic daughters who start playing sports in preschool soccer leagues. Muscles are no longer automatically considered a threat to femininity. Indeed, the female body ideal in U.S. society has been changing from thin and soft (with no muscle) toward lean and toned (with visible muscles).

During the 1970s, the health community realized that lack of exercise was associated with many chronic illnesses and promoted exercise as a valuable tool for attaining and maintaining a healthy weight and body (President's Council on Physical Fitness and Sports, n.d.). The government responded by strengthening its national fitness campaign, and health insurers responded by giving financial incentives for gym membership. As a result of the emphasis on fitness, even nonathletic women who were not directly affected by Title IX have been exposed to public health messages promoting activities that develop muscles (President's Council on Physical Fitness and Sports, n.d.).

Women go to the gym to gain the health benefits of fitness and to push their mental functioning to peak levels, but they also go for aesthetic reasons, such as achieving a toned physique to appear younger or more competent (Wilson, 2002). It seems reasonable to hypothesize that a force driving the acceptance and desirability of a more muscular female body ideal is that women themselves are becoming more muscular. Representations of the ideal feminine body in the media reflect and encourage this new muscularity, which has become pervasive in U.S. society and culture. For example, far from decrying her practices as unfeminine, the media presented Secretary of State Condoleezza Rice working out daily as an admirable model of a woman powerful in both her public role and her muscular physique (Feller, 2006). Thus, an increasing portion of the female population is more muscular and comfortable with a more muscular female body ideal.

INCREASES IN WOMEN'S FITNESS ACTIVITIES

Actress Jane Fonda became the prototype of the fit American woman with a series of fitness videos beginning in 1982. Since then, exercise has become an integral part of the lives of an increasing number of U.S. women. In 2003, 54.9% of frequent exercisers (defined as exercising more than 100 days in the past year or approximately twice a week) were women (SGMA International, 2003). In 2000, 24.1 million women walked for fitness (SGMA International, 2001). A 2002 survey reported that women had participated in a number of fitness activities more than 100 times in the past year (SGMA International, 2003). These activities included lifting free weights (6.1 million), using a treadmill (6.0 million), running or jogging (4.7 million), stationary cycling (3.3 million), resistance training (3.2 million), using stair-climbing machines (1.4 million), swimming (1.1 million), and working out in home gyms (0.5 million; SGMA International, 2003).

Opportunities for exercise are readily available to women. An increasing number are joining gyms. In 1999, women held 54% of gym memberships (SGMA International, 2000). Women's gym memberships almost doubled between 1990 (20.7 million) and 2003 (39.4 million; SGMA International,

2004). Women are not just doing cardiovascular exercises; lifting free weights increased 134%, from 8.3 million in 1990 to 19.4 million in 1999 (SGMA International, 2000). One study of muscle-gaining behaviors found that nearly 20% of girls reported lifting weights and 70% reported exercising specifically to gain muscle (McVey, Tweed, & Blackmore, 2005). These trends reflect a desire among women for increased muscle.

There has also been a demand for gyms designed specifically for women. Traditional gyms, designed for men, had equipment for lifting heavy weights a small number of repetitions, the strategy most efficient for gaining muscle mass quickly. Women prefer free weights and machines in circuits that involve lifting smaller amounts of weight a larger number of repetitions, a method that produces less muscle mass but strong, well-defined muscles. The most successful of these gyms, Curves®, offers a 30-minute resistance-training circuit aimed at women with a wide range of ages and fitness levels. Curves® was founded in 1992, and by 2004 it had more than 6,000 franchises, with clubs in every state (Curves®, 2005; Tufts Nutrition, 2004).

Women begin fitness programs for many reasons in addition to the push for fitness and health. Women exercise as part of weight loss programs, not just to be healthier but also for aesthetic reasons: to obtain a flatter tummy and firmer arms, legs, and buttocks (Wilson, 2002). Part of the increased interest in exercise is driven by baby boomers fighting their aging bodies. Without exercise, people naturally lose muscle and often gain fat, making the body appear flabbier. Given U.S. society's emphasis on youth, baby boomers have a high incentive to delay these effects of aging through exercise (Lam & Sulindro, 2000).

The more muscular female body ideal can be seen in the proliferation of magazines and articles in general women's publications that support women in their quest to achieve the new female body ideal. Both the number of publications and the percentage of articles focusing on increasing muscularity in women have increased (Thompson, Heinberg, Altabe, Tantleff-Dunn, 1999).

Self, *Women's Fitness*, *Shape*, and *Women's Health* were all founded since the mid-1970s. *Women's Health* magazine was launched in November 2005 with an initial circulation of 400,000 (womenshealthmag.com, 2006a). *Self* magazine was founded in 1979 and has a circulation of almost 1.5 million. (Condé Nast Publications, 2006) These circulation numbers, along with the availability of these magazines at supermarket checkout counters and so forth, indicate that these are not niche magazines and appeal to many women. Fitness is a main section in these magazines, so every issue contains at least one article on improving fitness. For example, *Women's Health* claims on its fitness Web site, "Look no further for the firmest glutes, flattest abs, and strongest arms" (womenshealthmag.com, 2006b).

The increase in women's gym memberships and gyms specifically for women and in the number and popularity of women's health and fitness magazines suggest that fitness is increasingly important to U.S. women. It is reasonable to hypothesize that the millions of U.S. women regularly going to gyms and reading magazine articles about fitness are seeking the ideal of a fit body that is lean and muscular (Thompson et al., 1999).

INCREASE IN ATHLETIC PARTICIPATION

Participation in athletics has become increasingly common among U.S. girls and women. Athletic activity starts early and is a normal part of girlhood and young womanhood. Girls are aware of their own muscles and observe those of their peers. A body with visible muscles is no longer unusual for a girl or woman (Dworkin & Heywood, 2003).

Preschool and Elementary School

In the early 1970s, girls did not have many opportunities to play organized sports. Today, a girl can play her first team sport in coeducational preschool soccer and T-ball leagues. The T-ball USA Association (2005) reported that of 2.2 million players ages 4 to 8 years, 35% were girls. In 2000, almost 2.7 million children played youth soccer, more than half of them girls (Soccer Association for Youth, 2005). Throughout their school years, girls have opportunities to participate in sports in school or in the community. In 2002, 54% of U.S. children between the ages of 6 and 17 played on at least one organized sports team; 41% of these children were girls (SGMA International, 2002). The percentage of girls ages 6 to 11 years who participated frequently in vigorous sports increased from 20.4% of girls (2 million) in 1987 to 32.4% of girls (3.8 million) in 1997 (SGMA International, 1998).

High School

In 1971, fewer than 295,000 girls (7% of high school athletes) participated in high school athletics; in 2004, more than 2.9 million girls (41.5% of high school athletes) participated (National Federation of State High School Associations, 2005). In 1971, 1 out of 27 girls participated in high school sports; in 2001, 1 out of 2.5 girls participated, an 800% increase (National Federation of State High School Associations, 2005).

College

In 1971–72, fewer than 30,000 women competed in intercollegiate athletics; by 2000–01, more than 150,000 (43% of intercollegiate athletes) participated, a 403% increase (National Coalition for Women and Girls in Education, 2002). Among schools participating in the National Collegiate Athletic

Association (NCAA), the average number of women's sports teams per school in 1970 was two; the average number of teams in 2004 was more than eight (Acosta & Carpenter, 2004). Between 1998 and 2004, 1,155 new women's teams were added to the NCAA roster (Acosta & Carpenter, 2004). Basketball is the most popular NCAA sport, followed by volleyball and cross-country track. Soccer is rapidly catching up: Women's NCAA soccer grew 150% during the 1990s. Over the past 5 years, however, lacrosse has been the fastest-growing NCAA sport for women (Acosta & Carpenter, 2004).

Intercollegiate women athletes represent a small fraction of women participating in sports and fitness activities during their college years. An Internet search of *intramural sports* and *colleges* and *women* showed that hundreds of colleges are advertising their intramural athletic programs to attract female students. Colleges are also competing for female students by building state-of-the-art fitness centers. In response to demand, these centers offer equipment preferred by women, such as stair-climbing machines, recumbent bikes, and light free weights (Fickes, 1999).

After College

The participation of women in sports during their school years has created a demand for continued opportunities to participate after graduation. In 1999, there were almost 2 million women playing in adult softball leagues, 7.3 million in soccer leagues, and 12.7 million in basketball leagues (SGMA International, 2000). From 1987 to 1999, the number of women playing in adult soccer leagues increased 20%; those playing in basketball leagues increased 15% (SGMA International, 2000). The lifelong participation of women in athletic activities is increasingly accepted and expected in contemporary culture, and it is a reasonable assumption that the muscularity developed in athletics predisposes women to embrace a muscular female body ideal.

MUSCULAR WOMEN IN THE MEDIA

Sports

Women's intercollegiate sports have been gaining not just in attendance, but in media attention. In 1989, the University of Connecticut's women's basketball team played in front of 287 fans; in 2002, they played in front of 24,611 fans (National Women's Law Center, 2002). ESPN signed an 11-year, $160 million contract with the NCAA that will include coverage of every women's basketball tournament game, Division II basketball, soccer, softball, swimming, volleyball, and indoor track (Women's Sports Foundation, 2005, p. 25). ESPN's coverage of the 2002 NCAA Women's National

Basketball Championship game was viewed by nearly 3.5 million households, more than any other ESPN collegiate broadcast, and was ranked among the top 10 sports broadcasts on cable television (Street & Smith's Sports Group, 2002). The 2004 NCAA Women's National Basketball Championship game had the largest TV audience of any basketball game in ESPN history up to that time (Women's Sports Foundation, 2005, p. 28).

The Women's United Soccer Association (WUSA), the first women's professional soccer league, started in 2001 (Litterer, 2005). For the 22-week 2002 season, one game a week was broadcast nationally on PAX TV, and an additional 55 games were broadcast regionally. Sponsorship of the league doubled for the next season, from seven national sponsors in 2001 to 14 in 2002 (Women's Sports Foundation, 2005, p. 25). Women's soccer is especially popular among young girls, if the number of fans viewing the games is any indication: In 2003, about two thirds of the fans were girls under 18 (Women's Sports Foundation, 2005, p. 28).

The Women's National Basketball Association (WNBA), an affiliate of the men's NBA, was started in 1997. In the 2002 season, 47 games were broadcast nationally and another 109 were broadcast locally; more than 60 million people watched WNBA games in 2002 (Women's Sports Foundation 2005, p. 16). Like the WUSA, the WNBA is also providing role models for girls, and posters of the WUSA's and WNBA's most popular athletes are available (Dworkin & Heywood, 2003).

The women's national soccer team has attracted high attendance and media attention. For the 1999 Women's World Cup, held in the United States, more than 650,000 tickets were sold; 90,000 of these were for the final match played at the Rose Bowl. The game was broadcast on ABC, and an estimated 40 million people watched it, making it the most-watched soccer match in U.S. television history (FIFAworldcup.com, 1999; Gildea, 1999). Almost half of the TV audience was adult men (Street & Smith's Sports Group, 1999). Brandi Chastain celebrated her winning penalty kick by taking off her shirt and waving it exuberantly, exposing to millions her strong, athletic body.

The number of female Olympic athletes has been increasing. In 1972, 1,058 women (14.8% of all athletes) participated in the Summer Olympic Games; in 2000, 4,069 women (38.2% of all athletes) participated (International Olympic Committee, 2005a). In 1972, women competed in 22% of the events; in 2000, they competed in 44% (International Olympic Committee, 2005b). Between the 1994 Winter Games and the 2002 Winter Games, women's participation increased 69.4%; in 2002, 886 female athletes (36.9% of all athletes) competed in 47.4% of the events (International Olympic Committee, 2005b). Although overall women's Olympic media time lags behind men's, some events receive a great deal of media attention—for example, gymnastics, diving, and swimming during the Summer Olympics and figure skating during the Winter Olympics. In the first quarter of 2002, the women's figure skating long program was the third-ranked network tele-vision broadcast behind the Super Bowl and the Super Bowl Kickoff Show (Street & Smith's Sports Group, 2002).

In summary, media coverage of women's sports provides broad exposure of female bodies with significant musculature. Exposure and acceptance of these muscular female athletes supports the adoption of a more muscular female body ideal.

Entertainment

Many contemporary actresses display well-defined muscles on screen, yet these strong women are considered feminine and attractive. Examples include Jessica Biel (*Blade, Trinity*; Lynch, 2005), Hilary Swank (who won an Oscar nomination for her role in *Million Dollar Baby*); Jennifer Garner (*Elektra*); Angelina Jolie (*Tomb Raider* films); Demi Moore (*G. I. Jane*); Lucy Lawless (*Xena: Warrior Princess* movie and TV series); Lucy Liu, Cameron Diaz, and Drew Barrymore (*Charlie's Angels*), and Meryl Streep (*The River Wild*). Lynch (2005) interviewed Bobby Strom, the fitness consultant who worked with Jessica Biel and other actresses, and he observed that these ac-tresses had athletic, healthy-looking bodies, rather than the overly lean bod-ies of many fashion models. Of course, there are downsides to every ideal, and Lynch (2005) pointed out that these new superfit, lean women with well-defined muscles may produce another ideal that is just as difficult for the average woman to achieve as the extremely thin, no-muscle ideal (Lynch, 2005). The presence of more muscular female entertainment stars may pro-duce in girls and women a desire to emulate the new female body ideal.

THE FEMALE BODY IDEAL: INCREASED MUSCULARITY

The *Psychology Today* Body Image Study was conducted in 1972, 1985, and 1997. Women's dissatisfaction with their muscle tone increased over that time period, rising from 30% in 1972 to 45% in 1985 and 57% in 1997 (Garner, 1997). These findings indicate that the female body ideal is becom-ing increasingly muscular. In addition, another study compared women's ideal level of muscularity with their actual level of muscularity and found that women wished to be more muscular than they were (Cafri & Thompson, 2004).

The increase in images of more muscular women in the media engen-ders pressure on girls and women to become more muscular; this has been demonstrated in several studies of factors influencing body dissatisfaction and body change strategies in adolescent girls. These studies support the idea that there is a new female body ideal that is not just thin but also has toned muscles (McCabe & Ricciardelli, 2001, 2005a, 2005b; McCabe, Ricciardelli, & Finemore, 2002). Moreover, the results of exploratory factor analyses indicate that there exists a unique dimension of sociocultural influence centered on the internalization of an athletic ideal (Thompson, van den Berg, Roehrig, Guarda, & Heinberg, 2004).

To date, no one has studied the gradations of muscularity in women to determine what degree of muscularity represents today's ideal. Existing studies have not captured the level of muscularity that women desire and consider attractive. Because women evaluate themselves on the basis of muscularity as well as thinness, studies are needed that evaluate both of these variables. Traditional methods of evaluating female body image, such as silhouette scales, were designed to measure perceptions of body fat and are not capable of distinguishing gradations of muscularity. One body image measurement tool, the Somatomorphic Matrix, allows the subject to choose images along two dimensions, body fat percent and muscularity (Gruber, Pope, Borowiecki, & Cohane, 2000). Little work with the Somatomorphic Matrix has involved women, but given the more muscular female body ideal, it may be a useful tool for examining the range of muscularity that is socially acceptable and for determining the point that represents the female body ideal. Because the female body ideal is an area of active sociocultural change, research is needed on all aspects of its evolution, including forces producing the changes, associated psychological and medical benefits and risks for individuals, and the impact of these changes on society.

Muscularity, like thinness, occupies a continuum. Just as women can be too thin, they can be too muscular. No studies have examined the degree of muscularity that defines the new, more muscular, female body ideal, so one must infer it from evidence in the culture. The popularity of the actresses listed in the previous section suggests that their degree of muscularity may be close to the ideal. One could argue that the *Sports Illustrated* swimsuit issue defines the female body ideal. It is significant that in recent years, four professional tennis players—Steffi Graf, Anna Kournikova, and Venus and Serena Williams—have been featured. What is common among these women is that although their muscles are not big and bulky, they are visible and well defined. One can assume that the editors of the *Sports Illustrated* swimsuit issue believe that their audience perceives these women to be feminine and attractive. A reasonable inference is that the muscularity displayed by these actresses and athlete–models represents the more muscular, female body ideal.

Elite women athletes, many of whom possess a level of muscularity a notch above the new female body ideal, have received increased media exposure as discussed in the previous section on women in the media. Both men and women enjoy watching them, indicating that their appearance is acceptable and not unattractive (Dworkin & Heywood, 2003; FIFAworldcup.com, 1999; Gildea, 1999; International Olympic Committee, 2005a, 2005b;

Litterer, 2005; National Women's Law Center, 2002; Street & Smith's Sports Group, 1999, 2002; Women's Sports Foundation, 2005). Although they have a level of muscle that is beyond that of the female body ideal, these athletes are admired, and their posters hang in the rooms of many girls (Dworkin & Heywood, 2003). For example, Mia Hamm, a Women's World Cup soccer star, has thighs that would make most men proud, but she endorses many products, has done some high-visibility commercials, and has made *People* magazine's list of the 50 most beautiful people in the world (*Microsoft Encarta Online Encyclopedia*, 2005). Her example suggests that the level of muscularity for the female body ideal may increase or at least broaden over time as people are increasingly exposed to more muscular women.

EXTREME MUSCULARITY

There is a limit beyond which muscle mass becomes unfeminine and unattractive. Krane, Choi, Baird, Aimar, and Kauer (2004) reported that some women athletes whose muscularity exceeds that of the current female body ideal experience a conflict between the desire to be an athlete and the desire to remain feminine. These athletes believed that they were perceived as less feminine by others because of their muscular physiques. In a focus group study of women college athletes specifically selected because they wanted to discuss their degree of muscularity, the subjects described the "cultural ideal body" as one that has muscle definition but not muscle bulk. They reported the source of this ideal as people pictured in magazines, actresses, and models. Training for their sports gave these women more muscle bulk than they would have liked, although they reported that seeing more women on campus with bodies like theirs made them feel more comfortable with their bodies. In fact, their comments on the conflict between being an athlete and being feminine related less to their appearance and more to their competitive and aggressive behavior while playing; they did not consider their desire to "beat the crap out of somebody" to be feminine. Indeed, the women realized that they were perceived as sexy in their revealing uniforms and that men came to watch their games because they enjoyed seeing their bodies. It seems likely that as more women, athletes and nonathletes, have muscular physiques, levels of muscularity beyond the current female body ideal will be increasingly accepted.

In a study involving interviews with seven female bodybuilders, the authors stated that these athletes described the ideal body as "athletic, toned, and healthy" and that none mentioned "large or highly muscled" (Grogan, Evans, Wright, & Hunter, 2004, p. 54). The authors concluded that being "athletic and toned are feminine-appropriate" (Grogan et al., 2004, p. 54). Even though they were bodybuilders, the women wanted to be muscular but not too muscular and to appear feminine (Grogan et al., 2004). This desire is consistent with a request by the International Federation of Bodybuilders (IFBB) that

> for aesthetics and health reasons, the IFBB Professional Division requests that female athletes in Bodybuilding, Fitness and Figure decrease the amount of muscularity by a factor of 20%. This request for a 20% decrease in the amount of muscularity applies to those female athletes whose physiques require the decrease regardless of whether they compete in Bodybuilding, Fitness or Figure. All professional judges have been advised of the proper criteria for assessing female physiques. (IFBB, 2004)

Essentially, the IFBB asserted that the masculine bodybuilding ideal of maximum muscularity does not apply to women. Thus, extreme muscularity is not the ideal even for women bodybuilders.

Why, then, do some women strive to increase their muscle mass beyond what is considered attractive and beyond what is healthy? Unlike men, who can develop a desire for a high degree of muscularity from mainstream societal influences, women typically need to be exposed to a subculture that places a high value on muscularity. In our laboratory's study of 75 female bodybuilders, we discovered a number of ways that these women had gotten interested in bodybuilding (Gruber & Pope, 2000). Most typically, nonathletes who wanted to be more fit and athletes who began weight training joined gyms and weight rooms with a man-oriented culture of muscularity, which they adopted. Other women joined gyms that they knew were "muscle gyms" specifically to become more muscular. Two of the female bodybuilders in our study had gender identity disorder and wanted to become more muscular because they wanted to look like men. Ten of the 75 bodybuilders had a history of sexual assault as a teenager or adult; 9 of these women described either starting bodybuilding or significantly increasing their bodybuilding activities to become bigger and stronger, both so they could protect themselves and to become less attractive to men (Gruber & Pope, 1999). Exposure to a muscle gym culture enabled the women to learn how to become more muscular by using diet, resistance training, and in some cases anabolic agents (Gruber & Pope, 2000).

Some of the women in the Gruber and Pope (2000) study developed muscle dysmorphia, a diagnostic entity first proposed in 1997 (Pope, Gruber, Choi, Olivardia, & Phillips, 1997). The defining features of muscle dysmorphia are the chronic preoccupation that one is not muscular enough, in spite of being much more muscular than average, and the persistence of the preoccupation despite significant impairment or distress (Pope et al., 1997). The lives of people with muscle dysmorphia revolve around their diet and workout schedule to the point that their social and/or occupational functioning is impaired (Pope et al., 1997). Sixty-five of the 75 women bodybuilders (87%) in the Gruber and Pope (2000) study had muscle dysmorphia. Women with a history of anorexia nervosa or bulimia appear to be predisposed to develop muscle dysmorphia, replacing their previous extremely thin body ideal with an extremely muscular and lean body ideal. Of the 75 female bodybuilders, we found that 31 (41%) had a history of a traditional eating disorder (Gruber & Pope, 2000).

Female bodybuilders want bodies that are muscular and also very lean so that the muscle definition can be clearly seen. For the majority of women, this body ideal is difficult to attain. Not only do they need to spend hours at the gym lifting heavy weights, but they also have to adhere to high-calorie, high-protein, low-fat diets, typically consumed in the form of preprepared meals and supplements eaten at regularly scheduled intervals up to half a dozen times per day. The regimen of extreme high-protein diet and frequent, intense workouts, and often the use of ergogenic drugs, all put these women at risk for multiple health problems.

For both men and women, lifting increasingly heavy weights builds muscle mass and breaks down muscle tissue. High amounts of protein are required to build the muscles back up, making a high-protein diet critical to success. High-protein diets, in combination with dehydration—often used to increase the visibility of muscle striations (called a "ripped look")—can result in kidney failure. There have been reports that lifting heavy weights increases the risk of injuries to muscles, tendons, and ligaments. In many women, bodybuilding results in menstrual irregularities like *amenorrhea* or *oligomenorrhea*. These chronic menstrual irregularities are associated with irreversible osteoporosis, cervical dysplasia and cancer, infertility, and miscarriages (Bahrke & Yesalis, 2004; Eklof, Thurelius, Garle, Rane, & Sjoqvist, 2003; Hartgens & Kuipers, 2004; Volk, 2004). Of the 75 bodybuilders in the Gruber and Pope (2000) study, 6 had experienced at least one bone fracture, which may be an indicator of osteoporosis.

A small number of women who have difficulty achieving their body ideal choose to use ergogenic drugs. The most commonly used drugs to achieve a muscular and lean body are anabolic–androgenic steroids (AASs) and stimulants. Other drugs used include clenbuterol (a beta-agonist with anabolic properties), human growth hormone, human chorionic gonadotropin, tamoxifen, thyroid hormones, and designer drugs (Gruber & Pope, 2000; Kaplan, 2004).

AASs build muscle, decrease recovery time after workouts and injuries, and promote loss of body fat. Women experience most of the same adverse effects of AASs as men do, including acne, increased risk of cardiovascular disease because of decreases in high-density lipoproteins and increases in low-density lipoproteins, hypertension, acute thrombosis, liver tumors, kidney tumors, fluid retention, galactorrhea, increased libido, irritability, aggressiveness, moodiness, euphoria, and poor judgment. Fatigue, depression, and muscle aches are common after stopping an AAS course (Gruber & Pope, 2000; Pope & Katz, 1994). A number of the 25 AAS users in our study reported characteristics of AAS dependence (Gruber & Pope, 2000). Despite acknowledging adverse effects, they continued to use AASs for the euphoric effect ($n = 3$) and to avoid withdrawal effects like depression ($n = 10$; Gruber & Pope, 2000). In addition, women experience gender-specific adverse effects from AAS use, including amenorrhea and its associated health risks (osteoporosis, cervical dysplasia and cancer, infertility and miscarriages), growth of facial and body hair, coarsening of the skin, deepening of the voice, and clitoral enlargement. Many of these adverse effects (i.e., osteoporosis, growth of facial and body hair, coarsening of the skin, deepening of the voice, and clitoral enlargement) are not reversible (Bahrke & Yesalis, 2004; Gruber & Pope, 2000; Hartgens & Kuipers, 2004).

AAS use is less common among women than among men. The last National Household Survey that included questions about AAS found that of 7,514 women between the ages of 15 and 44, only 18 (0.2%) reported AAS use (Substance Abuse and Mental Health Data Archive, 1994). A report presented to Congress on June 15, 2005, made a strong case that the rate of AAS use by adolescents and young women has always been and remains extremely low (Pope, 2005). In another study, questionnaires were given to 511 men and women at five gymnasiums selected for being "hard core" (frequented by bodybuilders) in the Boston area. None of the 177 women but about 5% (18 of 334) of the men reported AAS use (Kanayama, Gruber, Pope, Borowiecki, & Hudson, 2001). In another Boston-area study, female AAS users were aggressively recruited from bodybuilding shows and the most hard-core gyms, where AAS-using women would most likely be found, and over almost 2 years only 17 women who had used AASs were found (Gruber & Pope, 2000). Notably, two had gender identity disorder, and the masculinizing effects of the AASs were a contributing reason for using them. Because extreme muscularity in women is not seen as being consistent with femininity and because knowledgeable women fear the permanent masculinizing effects of AASs, AAS use among women is likely to remain uncommon (Pope, 2005).

Stimulants like ephedrine are effective for attaining and maintaining low body fat and also for increasing energy and alertness. Among the 75 female bodybuilders in our study, 36 reported chronic, long-term ephedrine use (Gruber & Pope, 1998). Seven (19%) had full-blown ephedrine dependence, with tolerance and withdrawal symptoms and significant adverse effects, including insomnia, tremor, anxiety, agitation, irritability, palpitations, and feelings of being "hyper" or "wired" (Gruber & Pope, 1998). Less common adverse effects include sudden death, stroke, and psychosis. Furthermore, ephedrine contributes to amenorrhea and its associated health risks (Cafri et al., 2005; Shekelle et al., 2003).

It is possible that as a greater number of women train to be elite athletes, more women will begin using AASs and stimulants. However, this increase remains to be seen. Many athletic events that might benefit from the increased strength and muscularity derived from AASs or the leanness from ephedrine have subjective judging (e.g., gymnastics). The judges for these events may decide (as the IFBB judges have) that too much muscularity or leanness is not aesthetically pleasing in women, and therefore they will not reward use of these ergogenic drugs.

CONCLUSION

Title IX and the fitness movement have resulted in U.S. women becoming more muscular. The pervasiveness of muscular women in media images has been driving the increased muscularity of the female body ideal, and this trend may continue. More muscular women, not just athletes, are seen in media and represent body ideals toward which women strive. Furthermore, athletes are now common role models for the increasing number of girls who participate in organized sports. Girls and women are evaluating their appearance not just in terms of desired weight or thinness but also in terms of muscle tone and definition.

There is definitely a limit beyond which women's musculature is deemed unfeminine and unattractive. The majority of U.S. women do not want to be big and muscular. The new female body ideal is lean, with visible, well-defined muscles. There are women, however, who pursue a degree of muscularity beyond the female body ideal. Many of these women have muscle dysmorphia, and through extreme diets, workouts, and sometimes ergogenic substance use, they put their bodies at risk for a multitude of serious medical problems. Clinicians should be aware that girls or women who present with amenorrhea, rapid increases in muscularity, and rapid decreases in body fat may have muscle dysmorphia and need psychological treatment by a therapist experienced in body image disorders.

There has been much research on the thin, no-muscle female body ideal but almost none on the new lean and muscular female body ideal. To accurately measure this new female body ideal, studies must be done with tools that examine how women perceive both body fat and muscularity, how they perceive themselves, what they desire for themselves, and what they believe society's ideal is. Research needs to be done to demonstrate the health benefits of the new female body ideal and to determine the factors that cause some of the many women pursuing the more muscular body ideal to develop muscle dysmorphia or to choose to take ergogenic drugs. Gaining an understanding of how women are trying to achieve more muscular bodies will enable psychologists to create strategies to prevent the unhealthy pursuit of muscularity and to promote healthy behaviors that support pursuit of the new female body ideal.

REFERENCES

About Title IX. (2005). Retrieved November 16, 2006, from http://bailiwick.lib.uiowa.edu/ge/aboutRE.html

Acosta, R. V., & Carpenter, L. J. (2004). *Women in intercollegiate sport: A longitudinal study—Twenty-seven year update, 1977–2004.* Unpublished manuscript, Brooklyn College, New York.

Bahrke, M. S., & Yesalis, C. E. (2004). Abuse of anabolic androgenic steroids and related substances in sport and exercise. *Current Opinions in Pharmacology, 4,* 614–620.

Cafri, G., & Thompson, J. K. (2004). Evaluating the convergence of muscle appearance attitude measures. *Assessment, 11,* 224–229.

Cafri, G., Thompson, J. K., Ricciardelli, L., McCabe, M., Smolak, L., & Yesalis, C. E. (2005). Pursuit of the muscular ideal: Physical and psychological consequences and putative risk factors. *Clinical Psychology Review, 25,* 215–239.

Condé Nast Publications. (2006). *Self: Circulation/Demographics.* Retrieved November 16, 2006, from http://www.condenastmediakit.com/sel/circulation.cfm

Curves®. (2005). *About Curves: The Curves® story.* Retrieved November 7, 2006 from http://curves.com/about_curves/curves_story.php

Dworkin, S. L., & Heywood, L. (2003) *Built to win: The female athlete as cultural icon.* Minneapolis: University of Minnesota Press.

Eklof, A. C., Thurelius, A. M., Garle, M., Rane, A., & Sjoqvist, F. (2003). The anti-doping hot-line: A means to capture the abuse of doping agents in the Swedish society and a new service function in clinical pharmacology. *European Journal of Clinical Pharmacology, 59,* 571–577.

Feller, B. (2006, March 2). *Condi sweats for the cameras.* Retrieved September 21, 2006, from http://www.cbsnews.com/stories/2006/03/02/politics/main1364032.shtml

Fickes, M. (1999, July). Outfitting campus fitness centers. *College Planning & Management.* Retrieved November 7, 2006, from http://www.peterli.com/archive/cpm/126.shtm

FIFAworldcup.com. (1999, June 19–July 10). *FIFA Women's World Cup—USA 1999.* Retrieved November 7, 2006, from http://fifaworldcup.yahoo.com/03/en/p/pwc/1999.html

Garner, D. M. (1997, February). Survey says: Body Image Poll results. *Psychology Today,* pp. 32–84.

Gildea, W. (1999, July 11). U.S. effort nets second World Cup title. *The Washington Post,* p. A1.

Grogan, S., Evans, R., Wright, S., & Hunter, G. (2004). Femininity and muscularity: Accounts of seven women body builders. *Journal of Gender Studies, 13,* 49–61.

Gruber, A. J., & Pope, H. G., Jr. (1998). Ephedrine abuse among 36 female weightlifters. *American Journal of Addictions, 7,* 256–261.

Gruber, A. J., & Pope, H. G., Jr. (1999). Compulsive weightlifting and anabolic drug abuse among women rape victims. *Comprehensive Psychiatry, 40,* 23–27.

Gruber, A. J., & Pope, H. G., Jr. (2000). Psychiatric and medical effects of anabolic-androgenic steroid use in women. *Psychotherapy and Psychosomatics, 69,* 19–26.

Gruber, A. J., Pope, H. G., Borowiecki, J. J., & Cohane, G. (2000). The development of the Somatomorphic Matrix: A bi-axial instrument for measuring body image in men and women. In K. Norton, T. Olds, & J. Dollman (Eds.), *Kinanthropometry VI* (pp. 217–231). Adelaide, Australia: International Society for the Advancement of Kinanthropometry.

Hartgens, F., & Kuipers, H. (2004). Effects of androgenic–anabolic steroids in athletes. *Sports Medicine, 34*, 513–554.

International Federation of Bodybuilding and Fitness. (2004, December 6). *IFBB advisory notice 2004-006*. Retrieved November 7, 2006, from http://www.ifbb.com/ifbbpro/2004news/decrease20.htm

International Olympic Committee. (2005a, December 8). *Factsheet: Women in the Olympic movement*. Retrieved November 8, 2006, from http://multimedia.olympic.org/pdf/en_report_846.pdf

International Olympic Committee. (2005b). *Atlanta–Nagano–Sydney–Salt Lake City*. Retrieved November 8, 2006, from http://multimedia.olympic.org/pdf/en_report_206.pdf

Kanayama, G., Gruber, A. J., Pope, H. G., Jr., Borowiecki, J. J., & Hudson, J. I. (2001). Over-the-counter drug use in gymnasiums: An underrecognized substance abuse problem? *Psychotherapy and Psychosomatics, 70*, 137–140.

Kaplan, P. (2004). *The dark side of bodybuilding*. Retrieved November 16, 2006, from http://www.philkaplan.com/thefitnesstruth/darksideofbodybuilding.htm

Krane, V., Choi, Y. L., Baird, M., Aimar, C. M., & Kauer, K. J. (2004). Living the paradox: Female athletes negotiate femininity and muscularity. *Sex Roles, 50*, 315–329.

Lam, M., & Sulindro, M. (2000). The baby boomer's anti-aging program. *Academy of Anti-Aging Research*. Retrieved November 16, 2006, from http://www.dayspaassociation.com/mainpages/anti_aging.htm

Litterer, D. (2005, February 9). *Women's soccer history in the USA: An overview*. Retrieved November 8, 2006, from http://www.sover.net/~spectrum/womensoverview.htm

Lynch, R. (2005, February 16). Hard body means hard work [Electronic version]. *Los Angeles Times*. Retrieved February 16, 2006, from http://www.latimes.com

McCabe, M. P., & Ricciardelli, L. A. (2001). Parent, peer, and media influences on body image and strategies to both increase and decrease body size among adolescent boys and girls. *Adolescence, 36*, 225–240.

McCabe, M. P., & Ricciardelli, L. A. (2005a). A longitudinal study of body image and strategies to lose weight and increase muscles among children. *Applied Developmental Psychology, 26*, 559–577.

McCabe, M. P., & Ricciardelli, L. A. (2005b). A prospective study of pressures from parents, peers, and the media on extreme weight change behaviors among adolescent boys and girls. *Behavior Research and Therapy, 43*, 653–668.

McCabe, M. P., Ricciardelli, L. A., & Finemore, J. (2002). The role of puberty, media and popularity with peers on strategies to increase weight, decrease weight and increase muscle tone among adolescent boys and girls. *Journal of Psychosomatic Research, 52,* 145–153.

McVey, G., Tweed, S., & Blackmore, E. (2005). Correlates of weight loss and muscle-gaining behavior in 10- to 14-year old males and females. *Preventive Medicine, 40,* 1–9.

Microsoft Encarta Online Encyclopedia. (n.d.). Mia Hamm. Retrieved November 8, 2006, from http://encarta.msn.com/encyclopedia_461510918/Hamm_Mia.html

National Coalition for Women and Girls in Education. (2002, June). *Title IX at 30: Report card on gender equity,* pp. 14–16. Retrieved November, 8, 2006, from http://www.ncwge.org/title9at30-6-11.pdf

National Federation of State High School Associations. (2005). *High school athletics participation survey.* Retrieved November 16, 2005, from http://www.nfhs.org/core/contentmanager/uploads/2005_06NFHSparticipationsurvey.pdf

National Women's Law Center. (2002, June). *The battle for gender equity in athletics: Title IX at thirty.* Retrieved November 8, 2006, from http://www.nwlc.org/pdf/Battle%20for%20Gender%20Equity%20in%20Athletics%20Report.pdf

Pope, H. G., Jr. (2005, June 15). *Widespread anabolic steroid use in American girls and women: An illusion?* Congressional hearing presentation. Retrieved November 16, 2006, from http://reform.house.gov/UploadedFiles/McLean%20Hospital%20-%20Pope%20Testimony.pdf

Pope, H. G., Jr., Gruber, A. J., Choi, P. Y., Olivardia, R., & Phillips, K. A. (1997) Muscle dysmorphia: An underrecognized form of body dysmorphic disorder. *Psychosomatics, 38,* 548–557.

Pope, H. G., Jr., & Katz, D. L. (1994). Psychiatric and medical effects of anabolic–androgenic steroid use. *Archives of General Psychiatry, 51,* 375–382.

President's Council on Physical Fitness and Sports. (n.d.). *President's council history: History of the president's council on physical fitness and sports—1953–2002 (selected highlights).* Retrieved November 8, 2006, from http://www.fitness.gov/about_history.htm

SGMA International. (1998). *Gaining ground: A progress report on women in sports.* North Palm Beach, FL: Author.

SGMA International. (2000). *Gaining ground: A progress report on women in sports.* North Palm Beach, FL: Author.

SGMA International. (2001). *Tracking the fitness movement.* North Palm Beach, FL: Author.

SGMA International. (2002). *Sports participation in America.* North Palm Beach, FL: Author.

SGMA International. (2003). *Sports participation in America.* North Palm Beach, FL: Author.

Shekelle, P. G., Hardy, M. L., Morton S. C., Maglione, M., Mojica, W. A., & Suttorp, M. J. (2003). Efficacy and safety of ephedra and ephedrine for weight loss and athletic performance: A meta-analysis. *Journal of the American Medical Association, 289,* 1537–1545.

Soccer Association for Youth. (2005). *SAY soccer.* Retrieved November 8, 2006, from http://www.saysoccer.us

Street & Smith's Sports Group. (1999, July 19–25). Ticket run smashes all expectations. *Street & Smith's SportsBusiness Journal.* Retrieved December 13, 2006, from http://www.sportsbusinessjournal.com/index.cfm?RequestTimeout=1500&fuseaction=search.perform_search&keyword=&SearchType=keyword&year=2006&fr_mo=9&fr_dy=12&fr_yr=1998&to_mo=12&to_dy=13&to_yr=2006&dateType=issue&sp_mo=7&sp_dy=19&sp_yr=1999&sort=recent&SubmitButton=Search

Street & Smith's Sports Group. (2002, April 29–May 5). First Quarter TV Report. *Street & Smith's SportsBusiness Journal.* Retrieved December 13, 2006, from http://www.sportsbusinessjournal.com/index.cfm?RequestTimeout=1500&fuseaction=search.perform_search&keyword=first+quarter+tv+report&SubmitButton=Search+Now&searchType=whole&year=2006&fr_mo=9&fr_dy=12&fr_yr=1998&to_mo=12&to_dy=13&to_yr=2006&dateType=issue&sp_mo=4&sp_dy=29&sp_yr=2002&sort=recent

Substance Abuse and Mental Health Data Archive. (n.d.). *National survey on drug use and health series.* Retrieved November 8, 2006, from http://webapp.icpsr.umich.edu/cocoon/SAMHDA-SERIES/00064.xml

T-Ball USA Association. (2005). *T-Ball USA Association.* Retrieved November 8, 2006, from http://www.teeballusa.org

Talbot, E. (2005). *Athleticism, the female body and history.* Retrieved December 13, 2006, from http://www.hyperhistory.org/index.php?option=displaypage&Itemid=711&op=page

Thompson, J. K., Heinberg, L. J., Altabe, M. N., & Tantleff-Dunn, S. (1999). *Exacting beauty: Theory, assessment, and treatment of body image disturbance.* Washington, DC: American Psychological Association.

Thompson J. K., van den Berg, P., Roehrig, M., Guarda, A. S., & Heinberg, L. J. (2004). The Sociocultural Attitudes Towards Appearance Questionnaire—3 (SATAQ-3). *International Journal of Eating Disorders, 35,* 293–304.

Tufts Nutrition. (2004, February). A gym for the non-lycra crowd? The pluses—and minuses—of Curves for women. *Health & Nutrition Letter.* Retrieved November 7, 2006, from http://healthletter.tufts.edu/issues/2004-02/curves.html

Volk, E. (2004). Female athletes and menstrual irregularities. *Think Muscle.* Retrieved November 8, 2006, from http://www.thinkmuscle.com/articles/volk/menstrual-cycle.htm

Wilson, P. M. (2002). Cross-validation of the revised motivation for physical activity measure in active women. *Research Quarterly for Exercise and Sport.* Retrieved December 13, 2006, from http://findarticles.com/p/articles/mi_go2597/is_200212/ai_n6486543

womenshealthmag.com. (2006a). *Circulation*. Retrieved November 16, 2006, from http://www.womenshealthmag.com/mediakit/circulation/subscriptionperf.html

womenshealthmag.com. (2006b). *Fitness*. Retrieved November 16, 2006, from http://www.womenshealthmag.com/channel/0,607,s1-1-0-0-0,00.html

Women's Sports Foundation. (2005, October). *Women's sports and fitness facts and statistics*. Retrieved November 8, 2006, from http://www.womenssportsfoundation.org/binary-data/WSF_ARTICLE/pdf_file/106.pdf

V

CONCLUSION

12

THE MUSCULAR IDEAL: FUTURE DIRECTIONS AND CLOSING COMMENTS

JOAN C. CHRISLER AND SAM V. COCHRAN

Feminist scholarship that initially focused attention on the effects of how Western culture constructs and promotes the ideal of a thin body for women and punishes those who fail to achieve this ideal has now begun to elucidate the "mirror" of this phenomenon—the muscular ideal, or drive for muscularity. The drive for muscularity is one manifestation of the value U.S. culture places on power and strength. It should be no surprise, then, that concerns of muscularity, although certainly identified and described in women, have been primarily studied in men.

The surge of interest in muscularity is evidence that this topic has drawn the attention of scholars from a number of disciplines, including psychology, psychiatry, physiology, nutrition, gender studies, and cultural studies. This volume collects these diverse viewpoints on muscularity. What future directions might prove beneficial to this work? We outline several suggestions for future direction and include recommendations for specific areas of inquiry that will further illuminate this important concern.

THEORETICAL ISSUES

How is the study of the muscular ideal situated in scholarly inquiry? In what theory bases is the study of muscularity embedded, and which of those bases appear to be most useful in accounting for the phenomenon of muscularity? A number of useful perspectives have been proposed, including cultural theory, feminist theory, psychologically derived perspectives, and evolutionary theory. We encourage scholars to give careful attention to how a particular research question is situated within a theoretical model, how that particular model accounts for what is known about muscularity, and how a particular research program will further inform theory building. Having identified an important topic and having begun the initial work of describing, analyzing, and exploring the topic, researchers must now look toward situating this work in a coherent and compelling theoretical framework.

Psychology has provided meaningful models for understanding muscularity that should be further elaborated. Does objectification theory predict the attitudes and behaviors of bodybuilders and compulsive exercisers in the same way it does those of dieters and disordered eaters? What psychological constructs are related to the drive for muscularity? How do these constructs predict adaptive and maladaptive expressions of the drive for muscularity or muscle dysmorphia? Certainly, the initial work that has correlated the drive for muscularity with various aspects of masculine gender role socialization is important and will provide a springboard for further investigation. Parallel work relating the drive for muscularity to aspects of women's gender role socialization and women's gender role conflict will add to this line of inquiry.

Evolutionary theory has also been a useful tool for analyzing aspects of social behavior. The application of evolutionary theory to a socially constructed phenomenon such as muscularity will likely prove controversial. Is there a useful role for this theory in understanding what appears to be a distinct gender difference in concerns with muscularity and muscle enhancement strategies? How do men and women view muscularity in the context of reproductive fitness and mate selection? What are the implications of a drive for muscularity in the context of social relations between men and women? Exploration of these and other evolutionary-based hypotheses might highlight the tension between cultural and constructionist models and the more biologically rooted models of muscularity.

MEASUREMENT AND ASSESSMENT ISSUES

As with any emerging topic of scholarly inquiry, initial investigation usually produces a variety of empirically derived measures designed to describe and quantify the subject of interest. Muscularity measures have been developed and are currently undergoing rigorous psychometric analysis. Two areas of future work appear useful. First, continued refinement of the basic psychometric properties of the relevant scales will further an understanding of muscularity from both descriptive and measurement perspectives. Second, a critical refinement of the scales, perhaps through comparative analysis, would provide researchers with better information to use when selecting instruments for future research.

Additional inquiry in the realm of measurement and assessment could be devoted to elaborating how women experience and manifest muscularity concerns. The Drive for Muscularity Scale (see the discussion in chap. 4, this volume) shows great promise for advancing an understanding of this and related questions. Furthermore, an emerging literature has begun to document men's experiences with eating disorders. A parallel inquiry into these experiences would be useful as researchers further investigate the issues raised in this volume and relate them to women's concerns (see chap. 11, this volume).

As Guy Cafri and J. Kevin Thompson note in chapter 5 of this volume, work that demonstrates the validity of the scales will provide both the necessary psychometric underpinnings of the measurement tools and allow researchers to begin to unpack the unanswered questions related to the description and definition of muscularity. Are there psychological characteristics of men and women that predict their interest in muscle enhancement, as well as in cosmetic procedures, liposuction, reconstructive procedures, and genital enhancement? What other psychological characteristics are associated with concerns about muscularity? Are there other comorbid or co-occurring psychological or psychiatric disorders that are associated with muscularity or muscle dysmorphia, and, if so, what is the best way to differentiate these?

Further research is also needed to illuminate the clinical expression of the drive for muscularity. What assessment strategies differentiate an adaptive drive for muscularity from a maladaptive one? Is the maladaptive expression of the drive for muscularity a variant of body dysmorphic disorder, as some have proposed (e.g., chap. 6, this volume)? What treatment strategies are most beneficial for those whose drive for muscularity veers off in maladaptive and self-destructive directions? Are the symptoms of muscle dysmorphia similar for women and for men? What are the implications for studying muscularity as a clinical phenomenon apart from muscle dysmorphia or body dysmorphic disorder?

TREATMENT AND PREVENTION ISSUES

As researchers begin to understand the maladaptive manifestations of the drive for muscularity, questions pertaining to best practices regarding not only assessment but treatment and prevention will be raised. Roberto Olivardia (in chap. 6, this volume) describes the clinical features of muscle dysmorphia, a clinical syndrome related to the drive for muscularity. Although the treatment of muscle dysmorphia has not been studied in any systematic manner yet, treatments for eating disorders, obsessive–compulsive disorder, and body dysmorphic disorder appear promising. Research is needed in this area.

In addition to the future study of the treatment of muscle dysmorphia and clinical manifestations of the drive for muscularity, prevention issues will need to be addressed. What questions of values are raised when researchers address the issue of preventing a drive that some may perceive to have adaptive consequences? Are there definable at-risk populations toward whom professionals could or should direct educational and prevention efforts, such as early adolescent boys or persons who present with aspects of body dysmorphic disorder? Can prevention approaches that have proved beneficial for addressing eating disorders in girls be adapted to the work of preventing muscle dysmorphia in boys?

CULTURE AND GENDER ISSUES

Important aspects of the drive for muscularity are embedded in the cultural construction of body image, gender, beauty, attractiveness, power, and control. A number of investigations have addressed these connections, and more are needed. Important work has been done to document how changes in popular culture have affected people's concerns with muscularity, including changes in male models, action figures, cartoon characters, actors, and athletes (see chap. 1, this volume). Scholars must continue to track these important cultural changes. For example, are these changes reflected in the U.S. national preoccupation with militarism and the epidemic levels of violence?

One of the most promising, and challenging, areas of future inquiry will be the study of how U.S. cultural values related to muscularity are transmitted on an individual level. What kinds of messages do boys and girls receive pertaining to muscularity? How does viewing television or other visual media lead to increased interest in muscularity and then to the enhancement of the drive for muscularity? Content and discourse analysis will uncover how these messages are received and the learning that occurs when children and adults are exposed to certain kinds of messages. Additional study of the subcultures that have developed around muscularity, such as bodybuilders (e.g., chap. 3, this volume), will illuminate how U.S. culture's valuing of muscularity takes root and is manifest in the daily lives of those who subscribe to these subcultures.

U.S. culture's fascination with the transformation of the body via cosmetic surgery, chemical enhancements, and exercise can also be further analyzed. Content analyses of media stories about cosmetic surgery and a comparison of those messages targeted toward men and those targeted toward women would be particularly illuminating. Do as many men as women believe that because it is possible to change "defective" aspects of one's body that those aspects should be changed? What are the origins of this belief in popular culture and daily discourse? How is this belief transmitted?

PHYSICAL HEALTH AND MUSCULARITY

Longitudinal studies are needed to determine the long-term effects of the use of steroids and other muscle-enhancing substances. Michael S. Bahrke (in chap. 7, this volume) describes the array of substances used and abused to enhance muscularity and performance, and the variety of the substances is staggering. Short-term effects (physical, emotional, and cognitive) of many of these substances are known, and many are serious. However, many individuals use combinations of these substances, in addition to marijuana, alcohol, caffeine, and cocaine. More data are needed on the effects of insulin manipulation and the abuse of tamoxifen. Little is known about the effects of various combinations of these substances. Moreover, long-term consequences of abuse of these substances will not be known for a number of years.

As David B. Sarwer, Canice E. Crerand, and Lauren Gibbons discuss in chapter 9 of this volume, the number of individuals undergoing cosmetic surgery has grown exponentially in just the past 10 years. Studies of the long-term physical and psychological effects of repeated cosmetic surgeries are needed. This inquiry might locate a particular subculture of persons interested in muscularity, those who repeatedly obtain cosmetic surgery to enhance their muscular appearance. What are the psychological characteristics of these persons? Might any gender differences be identified among them? Is the interest in surgical alteration of the body related to other, already established psychological variables?

DIVERSITY ISSUES

As the study of muscularity develops, researchers will need to pay increased attention to issues of diversity. As we noted, one area where this gap is evident is in the study of muscularity issues in women. Are girls using performance-enhancing substances in the same ways that boys appear to be using them? How does women's gender role socialization relate to concerns about muscularity? In addition to further explorations of the gender connection to this topic, more data are needed on muscularity issues in diverse racial, ethnic, age, and social class groups. In Lina Ricciardelli and Marita McCabe's (chap. 10, this volume) discussion of the issue of muscularity among adolescents, a number of questions are raised. Does the timing of puberty predict body dissatisfaction in boys? Will other developmental issues in both boys and girls be found to be related to concerns about muscularity? Does the natural decline of the physical body with age influence concerns with muscularity? Does sexual orientation predict a drive for muscularity in men?

A NOTE ON POPULATIONS AND METHODOLOGIES

Finally, as the study of muscularity expands, researchers must pay more attention to clinical populations. Assessment models based on work with clinical populations are needed to fill in gaps in the existing research. Moreover, as researchers include clinical populations in their research, a logical next step is the exploration of treatment protocols for muscle dysmorphia in men and women as well as the development and testing of prevention programs geared to mitigate the harmful effects of the drive for muscularity.

To augment studies that have used easily accessible samples, methodologies such as qualitative inquiry and longitudinal designs will further enhance an understanding of how muscularity develops in individuals and over time. Snapshot studies that relate various hypothesized constructs to muscularity in limited samples are important but are limited in the detail, depth, and nuance they might uncover. We encourage researchers to consider additional research designs that will expand the current understanding of the important issues raised in this volume.

CONCLUSION

As is evident throughout this volume, the muscular ideal has emerged as an important issue for psychologists and other researchers. A diverse range of scholars representing a number of disciplines has built a solid foundation, but much remains to be learned about this emerging area. We look forward to reading a future volume in which many of these questions will be answered.

AUTHOR INDEX

Numbers in italics refer to listings in the references.

Embleton, P., 144, *157*
English, B., 78, *81*
Escobedo, L. G., 161, *176*
Etcoff, N., 23, 26, *34*, 190, 192, *195*
Evans, R., 225, *230*
Ewen, E., 53, *60*
Ewen, S., 53, *60*
Eyre, D. R., *180*

Fabricatore, A. N., 186, *198*
Fair, J., 68, 79, *81*
Faith, M. S., 90, *102*
Falkner, N. H., 201, *214*
Fallon, E. A., 57, *61*
Faludi, S., 19, *34*
Farnham, A., 55, *60*
Fawkner, H. J., 54, *60*
Fay, C., 124, *138*, 188, *195*, *196*
Faytout, M., *194*
Feingold, A., 87, 88, *102*, 192, *195*
Feller, B., 218, *230*
Ferrando, A., 162, *180*
Ferron, C., 207, *212*
Fessler, D. M. T., 17, *35*, 50, *61*, 88, *102*, 202, *212*
Fiatarone, S. M., 163, *179*
Fickes, M., 221, *230*
Field, A. E., *104*, 204, *211*
"FIFAWomen's World Cup," 222, 224, *230*
Filiault, S., 31, *34*, 209, *212*
Finemore, J., 21, *36*, *231*
Fink, B., 192, *195*
Fiore, R., 73, *81*
First, M. B., 113, *118*, 131, 134, *137*
Fish, L. H., *176*
Fishbein, M., 170, *176*
Fisher, E., 16, 27, *35*
Fitzhugh, E. C., 202, *216*
Flegal, K. M., 21, *35*
Fleming, A., 55, *60*
Fones, C. S., 31, *39*, 129, *139*
Foster, F. P., 49, *60*
Foucault, M., 68, *81*
Fouts, G., 54, *60*
Frank, M. R., 145, *158*
Franko, D. L., 192, *198*
Frederick, D. A., 16, 17, 23, 27, *35*, 50, *61*, 88, 91, *102*, 202, *212*
Freidl, K. E., 144, *157*
Freitas, G., *103*
French, D. N., 146, *158*
Friedan, B., 48, *61*

Friedl, K., *59*
Frieze, I. H., 52, *61*
Fryburn, D. A., 162, *176*
Fulkerson, J. A., 200, *213*
Furnham, A., 91, *102*, 111, *118*, 200, 204, *212*
Fussell, S., 55, 56, *61*, 68, 73, 75, *81*, *82*

Gaines, J., 78, *82*
Gale, J., *175*
Gallo, M., *176*
Gallup, G. G., 190, *196*
Gardner, D., 167, *179*
Garfield, D., 24, *37*
Garfinkel, P., 90, *102*
Garle, M., 227, *230*
Garner, D. M., 16, 17, *35*, 87, 88, 90, 94, 100, *102*, 108, *118*, 223, *230*
Gatto, V., *176*
Ge, X., 204, *212*
Gehman, R., 49, *61*
Geist, W. E., 50, *61*
Genazzani, A. D., 164, *176*
Genazzani, A. R., *176*
Georakopoulos, C., *159*
Giada, F., 161, *175*
Gianfrilli, D., *177*
Giannetta, E., *177*
Giant, C. L., 16, *39*
Gibbon, M., 113, *118*, 131, 134, *137*
Gibbons, L. M., 185, 191, *195*, *197*
Giese, S. Y., 185, *195*
Gildea, W., 222, 224, *230*
Gilman, S. E., 168, *175*
Gilmore, D., 69, *82*
Gilroy, H., 49, *61*
Gimlin, D., 78, *82*
Gipson, M. T., 116, *119*
Girard, L., 164, *178*
Glat, P. M., *197*
Glenn, A. A., 17, *36*
Goffman, E., 79, *82*
Gokee, J. L., 21, *38*
Goldberg, J. P., 210, *213*
Goldberg, L., 167, 169, 170, 173, *176*, *177*
Goldberg, V., 46, *61*
Goldfried, G. S., 25, *35*
Goldstein, W., 43, *61*
Goldwyn, R. M., *11*
Good, L., 205, *214*
Goodfellow, J., *39*
Goodman, W. K., *138*

Pollack, A., 147, *158*
Pollack, W. S., 168, *179*
Pope, C. G., 124, *138*
Pope, H. G., 4, 5, *11*, 16, 17, 18, 19, 20, 24,
    25, 26, 28, 29, 30, 31, 32, 34, *36*,
    37, *38*, *39*, 42, 54, 57, 58, 59, *61*,
    62, *63*, *64*, 68, 82, 87, 88, 89, 90,
    91, 100, *102*, *103*, *105*, 107, 111,
    114, 116, 117, *118*, *119*, 123–124,
    125, 126, 127, 129, 130, 131, 132,
    134, 137, *137*, *138*, *139*, 161, 165,
    167, *177*, *179*, 199, 202, 205, 207,
    209, *212*, *213*, *215*, *216*, 224, 226,
    227, 228, *230*, *231*, *232*
Prather, I. D., 164, *179*
President's Council on Physical Fitness and
    Sports, 218, *232*
Pruzinsky, T., 3, 4, *11*, 186, *195*
Pujol, H., *194*

Quindlen, A., 45, *63*

Radojicic, Z. I., 187, *196*
Rane, A., 227, *230*
Rappaport, R., 70, *82*
Rasmussen, S. A., *138*
Raudenbush, B., 89, *105*, 200, 203, 208, *215*
Rawson, E. S., 148, *158*
Rawstorne, P. R., 89, *105*, 200, *215*
Reaney, P., 145, 146, *158*
Redondo, G., *105*
Reents, S., 152, *158*
Rees, C. R., 167, *178*
Reidy, C., 68, 77, *82*
Reifenrath, T. A., *178*
Reiter, J., 115, *119*
Reitman, V., 145, 146, *158*
Rennebohm, J., 95, *104*
Resnick, M. D., 201, *214*
Rhea, D. J., 133, 134, *138*, *139*
Ricciardelli, L., 4, *11*, 16, 21, 22, 28, 29, 32,
    34, *36*, *38*, 89, *101*, *104*, *118*, *156*,
    199, 200, 201, 202, 203, 204, 205,
    206, 207, 208, 209, 210, 211, *211*,
    214, *215*, 224, *230*, *231*
Richards, H., 95, 99, *102*, 207, *212*
Rickert, V. I., 164, *179*
Ridge, D., 200, *215*
Rini, A., *178*
Robinson, J. D., 199, *213*
Rodin, J., 16, *36*, 88, *104*, 132, *138*, 200,
    214

Roehrig, M., 5, *11*, *118*, *197*, 224, *233*
Rogol, A. D., *176*
Rohrich, R. J., 186, *196*
Rosen, C., 58, *63*
Rosen, J. C., 88, 89, *105*, 115, *119*
Rosenbaum, M., 168, *179*
Rosenblum, G. D., 203, *216*
Rosenstein, M., 55
Rosenthal, N., 154, *156*
Rotundo, E. A., 44, *63*
Rousseau, G. G., 162, *176*
Rovere, G. D., 161, *177*
Rowan, E. T., 91, *104*, 109, *119*
Rubin, M. R., 144, 146, *158*
Rubinstein, S., 192, *197*
Russell, J., 52, *61*
Rutsztein, G., 97, *105*
Ryan, F. J., *175*

Sabini, J., *39*
Sadava, S. W., 89, 98, *104*
Safren, S. A., 205, *216*
Saling, M., 209, *216*
Sallis, J. F., 89, *103*
Salzman, A., 56, 57, *63*
Sampson, A., 52, *63*
Sanders, D. M., 27, *35*
Sanguineti, V. R., 145, *158*
Sargent, R., 29, *38*, *39*
Sarwer, D. B., 4, *11*, 185, 186, 187, 188, 189,
    190, 191, 192, 193, *195*, *196*, *197*,
    198
Sasse, D. K., 5, *11*, 16, 19, *36*, 54, *62*, 88,
    90, 91, 92, 96, 98, 100, *104*, 108,
    109, *119*, 134, *138*, 210, *214*
Saucier, D. M., 5, *11*, 92, 95, *104*, 109, *119*,
    134, *138*
Savin-Williams, R. C., 205, *216*
Sayre, J., 46, *63*
Schlundt, D. G., 112, *118*, 134, *137*
Schulenberg, J. E., 166, *177*
Schuler, R., 21, *38*
Schulsinger, F., 90, *106*
Schwade, S., 55, *63*
Schwartz, J. P., 16, *39*, 96, *106*, 110, *119*
Schwenk, T. L., 161, 167, *179*
Scott, D. M., 42, *63*
Scott, M. J., 161, *179*
Scott, M. J., Jr., 161, *179*
Scott, R. P. J., *103*
Seeley, M. S., 204, *212*
Seeman, E., 162, *180*

SUBJECT INDEX

Drive for Muscularity Attitudes Questionnaire (DMAQ), 91–92, 109–110, 117

Drive for Muscularity Scale (DMS), 87–101, 108–110, 117, 134, 239; concurrent validity, 96–97; construct validity, 95–96; convergent validity, 97–99; development, 92–101; discriminant validity, 99–100; limitations, 100–101; reliability, 94–95

Drive for thinness, 88; and DMS, 99–100. *See also* thin ideal

Drug testing, 4, 155; for elite athletes, 174; for student athletes, 168–170. *See also* AASs (anabolic–androgenic steroids), use/abuse of

DSHEA (Dietary Supplement Health and Education Act, 1994), 151–152

Duggan, S. L., 96, 98, 100

Duncan, T., 167

Dynamic Tension system, 45

Eating Attitudes Test (EAT), 90, 94, 98, 100

Eating disorders, 42, 71, 123, 131, 133–134, 183, 227; and cosmetic surgery, 186, 189–190, 194

Eating Disorders Inventory (EDI), 90, 100

Elite athletes, female, 224–225, 228

Elliot, Diane L., 9, 167

Enlightenment, 79

Entertainment industry. *See* media and entertainment industries; movies; movie stars

Ephedrine, use/abuse of, 148, 201, 228

Erythropoietin (DynEPO, Aranesp, Procrit, Darbepoetin), 149, 164–165

ESPN, 77, 221–222

Estradiol, 163–164

Estrone, 163

Etcoff, N., 26

Etiological theories, of muscle dysmorphia, 131–132

Europe, 59

Evolutionary biology, 190–191

Evolutionary theory, 238; of muscularity, 17–18; of physical attractiveness, 190–193

Exercise: lack of, 218; women and, 218

Exposure, to muscular ideal, 20, 27

Factor structure, for DMS, 95–96

Father, influence of, 21

Father–son relationship, bodybuilders and, 73

Fay, C., 124

Female body ideal, change in, 208, 217–219, 223–225, 229

Femara (letrozole), 147

Femininity, and extreme muscularity, 225–229

Feminism, 48, 79

Feminist theory, 238

Feminization, fears about, 44

Ferron, C., 207

Fieldwork, on competitive bodybuilders, 69–70

Figure skating, 222–223

Fiji, 58

Fitness activities, women and, 218–220

Fitness campaign, national, 218

Fitness centers, at colleges, 221

Fitness programs, and national defense, 47

Fitness videos, 218

Flex, 77

Florenz, Gregory, 56

Fluid loss, use of diuretics for, 150

Fonda, Jane, 218

Form *vs.* function, in bodybuilding, 74–75

Foster, Frank, 49

Foucault, M., 68

Friedan, Betty, 48

Fulkerson, J. A., 200–201

Fussell, Sam, 55

Future research, topics for, 33, 100–101, 237–242

Future technologies, possible health effects of, 154–155

G. I. Joe action figure, 25, 202

Gable, Clark, 24

Gamma-hydroxybutric acid, 145

Garner, D. M., 94

Garner, Jennifer, 223

Gay adolescents, 204–205

Gay identity, adolescent, 205

Gay men, 28; and pornography, 24

Gay subculture, 48–49, 79

Gender differences: in AAS use/abuse, 167–168; in physical attraction, 191

Gender identity disorder, 228

Gender issues, 90, 92, 240–241; and DMS, 95–96, 98. *See also* women

Gender power balance, 58

Gender role socialization, 238

Gene doping, 141

Muscle Dysmorphia Symptom Questionnaire (MDSQ), 115
Muscle Dysmorphic Disorder Inventory (MDDI), 116
Muscle gyms, 226
Muscular ideal, 202, 237; adolescents and, 199–201, 205–206, 210–211; growing interest in, 3–5; research evidence for, 26–27; women and, 192–193, 223–225
Muscularity: meanings of, 27, 42; theories of, 17–22. *See also* drive for muscularity; muscular ideal
Muscularity, extreme, women and, 225–229
Muscularity Rating Scale, 111
Music videos, 69
Myostatin blockers, 154–155

Narcissism, 51–52
Narcotics, 150–151
Narring, F., 207
National Household Survey, 228
NCAA (National Collegiate Athletic Association), 169, 220–221
Nervous exhaustion, 43
New Jersey, and steroid testing, 4
New Republic, 53
New York Times, 52, 55
Nieber, H., 72
Nigeria, 31
Nitric oxide, use/abuse of, 152, 154
Nitrogen houses, 149
Norway, 30–31
NSAIDS (nonsteroidal anti-inflammatories), 150
Nubain, 150–151
Nunnally, J. C., 93–95

Obesity, prevalence of, 20–21
Objectification, of male body, 54, 58
Objectification theory, 238
Obsessive–compulsive disorder, 125, 131, 134
Obsessiveness, of bodybuilders, 71
Odysseus (Greek hero), 17
"Off-time hypothesis," 204
Older men, and implants, 54–55. *See also* baby boomers
Oligomenorrhea, 227
Olivardia, R., 4, 9, 17, 58, 114–115, 124, 131, 133, 189, 239
Olympic Games, 145; women and, 222–223

Olympic sport, bodybuilding as, 70, 77
Osteoporosis, 227
Overtraining, 127–128, 130

Palmer, Jim, 53
Parents, influence of, 21–22, 206–207
Pathological narcissism, 51
PAX TV, 222
PCG-1 (peroxisome proliferator-activated receptor gamma coactivator-1), 154
Peer experiences, 132
Peer influence, 21–22, 167, 206–207
Peer popularity, 21–22
People magazine, 225
Perceived Somatotype Scale, 111
Perfectionism, 204
Perfluorochemicals, 149
Performance drugs, 56. *See also* AASs (anabolic–androgenic steroids); AASs (anabolic–androgenic steroids), use/abuse of; *names of substances*
Perry, C. L., 200–201
Personal advertisements, 50–51
Personality traits, and DMS, 98–99
Personalization, of men with muscle dysmorphia, 127
Phillips, K. A., 4, 17, 58, 124
Physical appearance: contemporary theories of, 191–194; enhancement of, 143; men and, 125–126, 188
Physical attraction, gender differences in, 191
Physical attractiveness, 4, 20, 52, 88; evolutionary theory of, 190–193
Physical Culture, 44–45
Physical education in schools, 47
Physical strength, decreasing importance of, 19
Picot, A. K., 98
Pitt, Brad, 24
Pitts, M., 97
Playboy, 192
Playgirl, 22, 28, 54, 132, 202
Pope, C. G., 124
Pope, H. G., 4, 17, 29, 58, 107, 114, 124, 132, 226
Populations, 242
Pornography, 24
Posing, bodybuilders and, 72, 74–75
Power, imagery of, 76–77
Power lifting, 74, 76, 133. *See also* bodybuilding
Prevention issues, 239–240

ABOUT THE EDITORS

J. Kevin Thompson, PhD, is a professor of psychology at the University of South Florida in Tampa. He has worked in the area of body image and eating disorders for 25 years, with current interests in the areas of measurement, adolescent risk factors, media influences, and body image issues in diverse samples. He has been on the editorial board of the *International Journal of Eating Disorders* since 1990 and is currently an associate editor of *Body Image: An International Journal of Research*. He has authored, coauthored, edited, or coedited five books in the field, including three published by the American Psychological Association: *Body Image, Eating Disorders, and Obesity* (1996); *Exacting Beauty: Theory, Assessment, and Treatment of Body Image Disturbance* (1999); and *Body Image, Eating Disorders, and Obesity in Youth* (2001).

Guy Cafri, MA, is a doctoral student in clinical psychology at the University of South Florida in Tampa. He received a BA in psychology and philosophy from Macalester College in St. Paul, Minnesota, and an MA from the University of South Florida. He has published extensively in the area of body image, particularly as it relates to the pursuit of muscularity, and he has also studied thin-ideal internalization and the relationship between tanning motives and skin cancer risk. His interests in body image focus on assessment, psychopathology, and health risk behaviors. He also has an interest in quantitative psychology.